Lecture Notes in Artificial Intelligence

Edited by R. Goebel, J. Siekmann, and W. Wahlst_

Subseries of Lecture Notes in Computer Science

George Vouros   Alexander Artikis
Kostas Stathis   Jeremy Pitt (Eds.)

# Organized Adaption in Multi-Agent Systems

First International Workshop, OAMAS 2008
Estoril, Portugal, May 13, 2008
Revised and Invited Papers

 Springer

Series Editors

Randy Goebel, University of Alberta, Edmonton, Canada
Jörg Siekmann, University of Saarland, Saarbrücken, Germany
Wolfgang Wahlster, DFKI and University of Saarland, Saarbrücken, Germany

Volume Editors

George Vouros
University of the Aegean
Karlovassi, Samos 83200, Greece
E-mail: georgev@aegean.gr

Alexander Artikis
National Centre for Scientific Research "Demokritos"
Athens 15310, Greece
E-mail: a.artikis@iit.demokritos.gr

Kostas Stathis
Royal Holloway, University of London
Egham, Surrey TW20 0EX, UK
E-mail: kostas@cs.rhul.ac.uk

Jeremy Pitt
Imperial College
London, SW7 2BT, UK
E-mail: j.pitt@imperial.ac.uk

Library of Congress Control Number: Applied for

CR Subject Classification (1998): I.2.11, C.2.4, C.2, D.2.12, D.1.3, H.3, H.4

LNCS Sublibrary: SL 7 – Artificial Intelligence

ISSN        0302-9743

ISBN  978-3-642-02376-7 Springer Berlin Heidelberg New York

Typesetting: Camera-ready by author, data conversion by Scientific Publishing Services, Chennai, India
Printed on acid-free paper        SPIN: 12608911        06/3180        5 4 3 2 1 0

# Preface

Adaptation, for purposes of self-healing, self-protection, self-management, or self-regulation, is currently considered to be one of the most challenging properties of distributed systems that operate in dynamic, unpredictable, and potentially hostile environments. Engineering for adaptation is particularly complicated when the distributed system itself is composed of autonomous entities that, on one hand, may act collaboratively and with benevolence, and, on the other, may behave selfishly while pursuing their own interests. Still, these entities have to coordinate themselves in order to adapt appropriately to the prevailing environmental conditions, and furthermore, to deliberate upon their own and the system's configuration, and to be transparent to their users yet consistent with any human requirements. The question, therefore, of "how to organize the envisaged adaptation for such autonomous entities in a systematic way" becomes of paramount importance.

The first international workshop on "Organized Adaptation in Multi-Agent Systems" (OAMAS) was a one-day event held as part of the workshop program arranged by the international conference on Autonomous Agents and Multi-Agent Systems (AAMAS). It was hosted in Estoril during May, 2008, and was attended by more than 30 researchers.

OAMAS was the steady convergence of a number of lines of research which suggested that such a workshop would be timely and opportune. This includes the areas of autonomic computing, swarm intelligence, agent societies, self-organizing complex systems, and 'emergence' in general.

In autonomic computing, for example, the intention is to go beyond standard definitions of fault-tolerance (the capacity to endure faults until fixed by the intervention of an external operator), by modeling a computer system as a self-regulating biological system, i.e., a system with the capacity to repair faults by itself. In particular, there is a requirement, *inter alia*, for an autonomic system to configure, and re-configure itself, in the light of unexpected events, and the system must have, find, or generate for itself rules by which to optimize this (re-)configuration. An important metaphor in this field of research is the human auto-immune system, in particular the immune system's pattern recognition, memory, and learning capabilities which enable it to develop appropriate responses to a changing environment.

Swarm intelligence also exploited metaphors from biological systems, in this case how the behavior of a population of relatively simple agents, each of whom were following local rules and interacting only with their 'nearest' neighbors, could produce systems with complex global properties. Such examples abound in nature, in mammal herds, fish schools, and bird flocks, but it was important pioneering work in ant colony optimization by Marco Dorigo, using a computational equivalent of pheromone trails, that showed how natural and artificial systems could be bridged. The ant metaphor has subsequently been extended to develop systems of self-assembling robots which demonstrate collective behavior in order to accomplish tasks that are beyond a singe individual.

Agent societies are an idea introduced into the modeling and engineering of multi-agent systems (MAS), in part to deal with the issue of "intelligence at the edge" (a function of increasing autonomy, heterogeneity, and decentralization in communication networks), but also because that intelligence was increasingly social in nature. In other words, cognitive, socio-cognitive, and even legal concepts, for example, trust, reputation, and contracts, were important in forming and conditioning the links between network nodes; and furthermore the interactions between nodes were more like "speech acts" than object invocations, and had a richer semantics, particularly with respect to conventional significance. The rich body of literature in organizational, social, and legal systems theory is then also relevant in designing methodologies for engineering a new paradigm for social MAS.

However, it is a given of organizational, social, and legal systems that they change over time, and in response to environmental conditions. Equally, it is evident that increasing application complexity, and expected system longevity, requires engineered agent societies to also change. While adaptation is almost a property *since qua non* of autonomic systems and swarm intelligence, the development of agent societies had tended to be based on formal specifications, from which could be derived proofs of particular properties. The challenge now was to make those formal specifications *adaptable*, either by under-specification at design-time and completion – by the agents themselves – at run-time; or, a complete specification given at design-time and modification – again, by the agents themselves – at run-time.

We are primarily interested in the principles of social intelligence and social development that distinguish agent societies as a significant innovation in adaptive systems. We seek to go beyond emergent behavior seen, for example, in swarm intelligence, i.e., the non-introspective application of hard-wired local computations, with respect to physical rules and/or the environment, which achieve unintended or unknown global outcomes; in agent societies the object of concern is the introspective application of soft-wired local computations, with respect to physical rules, the environment, and conventional rules, in order to achieve intended and coordinated global outcomes. This conscious, deliberate, and targeted adaptation of conventional rules, i.e., rules agreed among the participants, which effectively defined their behaviors (what some philosophers of language would call *constitutive rules*), was the focus of what we called *organized adaptation*.

Two invited presentations underlined the interdisciplinary nature of research on organized adaptation by considering real-world applications of autonomic computing and the life-cycle of norms in agent societies. The first invited talk was given by Jeffrey Kephart of IBM Research, USA. Dr. Kephart described the efforts at IBM Research to apply multi-agent concepts and principles to the development of autonomic technologies that work coherently with one another, in order to reduce energy consumption in data centers without unduly sacrificing performance. The second invited talk was given by Jan Broersen, a lecturer at the University of Utrecht. In his talk, the contents of which appear in this volume as an invited submission, Dr. Broersen discussed several issues concerning the design of logical models of norm change.

Apart from Dr. Broersen's invited contribution, two regular papers focus on the theme of norm change. Bou and colleagues, in the paper entitled "Adapting Autonomic Electronic Institutions to Heterogeneous Agent Societies," present case-based reasoning techniques in order to dynamically adapt the norms of an institution, given the changes in the agents' behaviors and the institutional goals. Carr and Pitt, in the paper entitled "Adaptation of Voting Rules in Agent Societies," present a logical framework for modifying at run-time the norms of a voting protocol.

Three papers present organizational models of adaptive MAS. Kota and colleagues, in their paper entitled "Decentralized Structural Adaptation in Agent Organizations," demonstrate a decentralized approach for adapting the structure of an organization in order to achieve an 'optimal' allocation of tasks. Renz and Sudeikat, also focusing on adaptive organizations, aim to address, in their article entitled "Modeling Feedback Within MAS: A Systemic Approach to Organizational Dynamics," the need for tools expressing the dynamics of multi-agent organizations. Keogh and colleagues, in their article entitled "Coordination in Adaptive Organizations: Extending Shared Plans with Knowledge Cultivation," study the requirements of coordination in complex 'unfolding scenarios,' where there is no fixed organizational structure, with the aim of developing a simulation framework as a part of a training system in the domain of emergency management.

The last part of the proceedings includes two papers on simulations of adaptive MAS. Bonnet and Tessier in their paper entitled "An Incremental Adaptive Organization for a Satellite Constellation," present their results on a simulated satellite constellation where a collaboration method, based on an incremental coalition formation algorithm, is used for achieving the objectives of a coalition. The paper of Roesli and colleagues, entitled "Modelling Actor Evolution in Agent-Based Simulations," presents an extension to the i* agent- and goal-oriented formalism used in requirements engineering, for modelling the knowledge about how an actor may evolve—a mapping to the ConGolog simulation environment is provided.

Following the tradition of associated workshops, all regular papers were reviewed once for the workshop pre-proceedings; and revised, re-submitted, and re-reviewed, for inclusion in this final proceedings volume.

During AAMAS 2008 it became clear that the issues addressed by organized adaptation in MAS were prime issues of concern to the Coordination, Organizations, Institutions and Norms (COIN) community, and had, perhaps, been under-represented in this workshop series to date. The quality of the submitted papers, the strong representation at the OAMAS workshop, and the lively contributions to the discussions suggested that the embryonic community aggregating around the subject of organized adaptation was sufficiently well-founded to sustain an independent scientific event. However, the organizers are strongly of the opinion that the AAMAS workshops should be used to cohere the agents community, not to fragment it, and enhance the quality of scientific research, not to dilute it.

The OAMAS workshop organizers were therefore happy to entertain a discussion with the COIN Steering Committee, and since this is a now well-established workshop series with a good scientific reputation, we accepted their invitation to fuse the two organizing bodies and highlight *organized adaptation* as a key theme for any future COIN call for papers.

This, then, is the Final Proceedings of the First International Workshop on Organized Adaptation in Multi-Agent Systems. It is also the Final Proceedings of the Last International Workshop on Organized Adaptation in Multi-Agent Systems. For the authors contributing to this volume, we hope for their continued participation in the subject of organized adaptation, and look forward keenly to their constructive interaction with and within the COIN community. These authors can also reflect on the fact that their collective contributions have had a scientific impact on an established institution (the COIN workshop) which changed its membership, charter, and rules to accommodate this body of work. We believe this is an example of organized adaptation.

November 2008

George Vouros
Alexander Artikis
Kostas Stathis
Jeremy Pitt

# Organization

## OAMAS 2008 Organizers

| | |
|---|---|
| George Vouros | University of the Aegean, Greece |
| Alexander Artikis | NCSR "Demokritos", Greece |
| Kostas Stathis | Royal Holloway, University of London, UK |
| Jeremy Pitt | Imperial College London, UK |

## OAMAS 2008 Program Committee

| | |
|---|---|
| Thomas Ågotnes | Bergen University College, Norway |
| Robert Axtell | George Mason University, USA |
| Yaneer Bar-Yam | New England Complex Systems Institute, USA |
| Guido Boella | Università degli Studi di Torino, Italy |
| Olivier Boissier | Ecole Nationale Superieure des Mines de Paris, France |
| Jeff Bradshaw | IHMC, USA |
| Jan Broersen | Utrecht University, The Netherlands |
| Keith Decker | University of Delaware, USA |
| Virginia Dignum | Utrecht University, The Netherlands |
| Paul Feltovich | IHMC, USA |
| Erol Gelenbe | Imperial College London, UK |
| Marie-Pierre Gleizes | IRIT Université Paul Sabatier, France |
| Zahia Guessoum | Laboratoire d'Informatique de Paris 6 (LIP6), France |
| Salima Hassas | Université Claude Bernard Lyon 1, France |
| Mark Hoogendoorn | VU University, The Netherlands |
| Lloyd Kamara | Imperial College London, UK |
| Eric Matson | Wright State University, USA |
| Pablo Noriega | IIIA, Spain |
| Andrea Omicini | University of Bologna, Italy |
| Olga Pacheco | University of Minho, Portugal |
| Julian Padget | University of Bath, UK |
| Paolo Petta | Austrian Research Institute for Artificial Intelligence, Austria |
| Antonino Rotolo | University of Bologna, Italy |
| Filipe Santos | ISCTE, Portugal |
| Liz Sonenberg | The University of Melbourne, Australia |
| Kostas Stergiou | University of the Aegean, Greece |

Fransesca Toni          Imperial College London, UK
Luca Tummolini          ISTC-CNR, Italy
Leon Van der Torre      University of Luxembourg, Luxembourg
Marina De Vos           University of Bath, UK
Pinar Yolum             Bogazici University, Turkey

## Additional Reviewers

James Atlas             University of Delaware, USA
Hugo Carr               Imperial College London, UK
Dorian Gaertner         Imperial College London, UK
Sachin Kamboj           University of Delaware, USA
Loris Penserini         Utrecht University, The Netherlands
Daniel Ramirez Cano     Imperial College London, UK
Gil Tidhar              University of Melbourne, Australia
Serena Villata          Università degli Studi di Torino, Italy

# Table of Contents

# Issues in Designing Logical Models for Norm Change

Jan Broersen

Department of Information and Computing Sciences, Utrecht University,
The Netherlands

**Abstract.** The aim of this paper is to raise awareness of some issues in
designing (formal) models for norm change. I start by positioning this
research in a broader context. Then I will briefly recall several concepts
and problems from deontic logic, which is the field primarily concerned
with notions like 'norm', 'obligation', 'right', etc. Then I proceed with
what I regard the main contribution of the paper: the distinction of
four categories of problems one faces when thinking about formal logical
models for norm change.

## 1 Introduction

About 20 years go, when the field emerged as a viable area of research within
computer science, the study of logical formalisms for modeling artificial agent
behavior mainly focussed on intelligent or rational behavior of *individual* agents.
For instance, the main objective of formal systems such as the one composed
by Cohen and Levesque [19], the KARO framework [43], and BDI-CTL [50,52],
is to describe the interrelations of mental attitudes of individual agents and to
give logical constraints on the evolution of mental states over time. However,
as readers familiar with these papers know, it is not the case that in these
formalisms attention is strictly limited to individual agents only. The point is
that in these logical frameworks all three pillars of modeling rational agency,
that is, modeling (1) knowledge and belief, (2) preference and intention, and (3)
action and ability, are considered from the *perspective* of single agents. Other
agents only come into the picture in as far as they are a relevant part of the
environment relative to which to make rational decisions.

A departure from this initial perspective on rational agency is embodied by
the shift in attention from what are basically decision theoretic models to game
theoretic models. A main difference between these two paradigms is that in
definitions for game theoretic solution concepts, the often subtle and complicated interactions with the preferences and beliefs of other agents are taken into
account. In decision theoretic models, traditionally, mental attitudes of other
agents are not considered.

In computer science, a development that occurred roughly in parallel with
the transition from decision theoretic models to game theoretic models was the
shift in attention, over the course of the last twenty years, from a single agent

G. Vouros et al. (Eds.): OAMAS 2008, LNAI 5368, pp. 1–17, 2009.

perspective to a multi-agent perspective on rationality *itself*. That is, the focus was no longer limited to rational behavior of individuals in the context of other individuals, but now included notions connected to rational behavior of groups. In the area of epistemic logics and game theory, notions like 'common knowledge' and 'distributed knowledge', already known since Aumann's well-known paper [5], became subject of study in computer science [49,56]. A little later, researchers working on formalisms for action and ability, also shifted attention to actions and abilities of *coalitions* of agents [4,46]. And finally, extending the thinking about single agent motivational concepts like 'desires' and 'intentions' to the multi-agent context, researchers in multi-agent systems got more and more interested in studying 'collective intentions' [53,22], 'social choice' [25], 'social laws' [45,44,57] and 'norms' [35,10].

Another development, surfacing already more than 20 years ago with the publication of the AGM postulates [2], is the progress from studying properties of the *static* relations between agent concepts to the modeling of properties concerning the *dynamics* of informational states, like knowledge and belief states, and motivational attitudes like intentions and obligations. Witness the vast literature on belief revision and knowledge update (for textbooks, see [29,7,20]), most attention was drawn towards the dynamics of informational attitudes, while motivational attitudes, yet, as suggested above, forming one of the pillars of rational agency, got very little attention.

The present paper discusses some of the issues living at the point where both independent developments sketched above meet: modeling the dynamics of norms. First, in the next section, I will do a brief Q&A on norms, since many may not be familiar with the terminology and concepts of deontic logic, which is the area occupied with the study of norms, obligations, rights, etc. Then, in section 3, I briefly sketch some of my motivations for being interested in norm change. Then, in section 4, I discuss four issue that I perceive as interesting subproblems of the general problem of designing logical models for norm change.

Admittedly, my account is a rather personal (and 'Dutch') one, disregarding many related efforts of research groups around the world. Yet I hope the reader will forgive me for that, or else point me to the blatant omissions.

## 2    Some Questions and Answers on Norms and Obligations

This section contains a brief Q&A on norms. The aim is threefold. First I hope it helps the readers who are unfamiliar with deontic logic to understand some of the standard issues in this area. Second, it enables me to convey my personal views on these issues. And third, I hope it will help readers to understand my use of terminology, some of which is likely to be new even to readers familiar with the deontic logic literature.

### What 'Kind' of Things Are Norms?

Norms are abstract. They, so to say, 'live' in the abstract world of 'ideas'. Norms can be (1) 'reified' in sentences as in written law, or (2) implicit and shared by minimally two agents as in 'promises'. Maybe norms can also be entirely private as in 'personal principles and values', but that is more controversial.

## What Are Norms for?

Norms are used for regulating multi-agent behavior. They can thus be seen as directives for groups of agents, aimed at inducing intended group behaviors. What is important here, is the origin of the norm. Either this origin lies outside the group of agents being regulated by the norm, or the norm comes from 'within'. In the former case, examples include parent-child relations, dictatorships, etc. But, also the case of a system designer formulating goals for his multi-agent system. Multi-agent systems are usually thought of as systems populated by autonomous agents equipped with their own goals. One immediately sees a potentially difficult task ahead for the designer of such a system. First of all, the overall design goal of the system has to be met. But, the designer has decided, for reasons of flexibility and robustness, that the design goal is best reached through a system populated by autonomous agents having their own goals. The challenge for the multi-agent system designer is then to find the right mechanisms for controlling the balance between the individual agent goals and the norms he imposes on the multi-agent system as a whole. This balance should result in the overall design goals being met.

The other case, where the origin of the norms comes from within, is the more 'cooperative' view. Examples include cases where norms are used to simply coordinate behavior, benefitting every member of the group, such as the rules for driving right (or left, depending on the country). A more complex example is putting together an organization, by dividing tasks over agents through assignment of 'responsibilities', and by defining 'roles', which can be seen as sets of norms turning into obligations (and sometimes even beliefs) for the agents enacting the role. In this view, an organization is seen as a structure that optimizes the division and allocation of group tasks and goals against individual capabilities and preferences, ultimately benefiting each member of the organization.

In these examples, the agents involved have a clear *incentive* to cooperate (drivers do not want to crash into each other). In this context it is clear then why norms will emerge: the norms are in line with the goals of the individuals. But, for the most interesting category of norms, this is not the case. The paradigmatic scenario is the prisoners dilemma (that we assume to be known to the reader). In this dilemma, the individuals have a clear incentive *not* to cooperate. Still, as a group, they may recognize that it is best for them to cooperate.

Most game theoretic answers to the case of the prisoners dilemma (Nash, strict dominance, etc.) say that the individuals should not cooperate. We might see these solutions as pointing to a preference not to cooperate in prisoner dilemma like situations. However, the agents may recognize that they can gain more, as a group, and thus also individually, if they install a norm giving agents an incentive for cooperation. We have many examples of such norms from everyday life. A personal favorite are the quota for fishing. Fishermen have a clear individual incentive for catching as much fish as they can. But if everybody behaves like that, the seas will be empty, and everybody loses. The society recognizes the situation, and installs norms in the form of fishing quotas. A very common one is the norm for having to pay taxes: there is a clear personal incentive not to do so, but if nobody does, there is no government and everybody will be worse off (really). An obvious one is the rule prohibiting stealing. Clearly agents have incentives to steal. But if everybody steals from everybody, all will be worse off. All these examples concern cases where a norm prevents selfishness, which may not be profitable for the agent society as a whole, and, consequently, also not for the agents that are part of it. Because of the mutually enforcing tension between the personal incentive and the incentive imposed by the norm, the norms exemplified by the above cases are the most interesting ones.

It might be a little confusing to bring up the prisoners dilemma in this context, because the Nash-answer to the prisoners dilemma is sometimes also described in terms of '(social) norms'. A Nash-equilibrium is a strategy that is always the best response in case everybody adopts that same strategy. Game theorists phrase this by saying that a strategy is a Nash-equilibrium, if in case that strategy is 'the norm', it is always the best response for everybody. So, in game theory (and sociology) one thinks of norms as 'stable expectations'. It is clear then that in these areas the term 'norm' is used under a different interpretation: it refers not so much to ideality of behaviors relative to some prescription, as to adhering to what is the most 'common' thing to do. We do not use the term 'norm' under this interpretation.

### What Kinds of Norms Are There?

The norms discussed above are all examples of 'regulative' norms. Another category distinguished in the literature (philosophical, social, computer science) are the constitutive norms [53,34,27].

An example of a constitutive norm is the law's description of what a 'father' is. The law, of course, does not identify the notion of 'father' with the notion of 'biological father'. For the law, you can be a father without being a biological father, and the other way round. The law attaches all kinds of legal consequences to the status of 'father' (custody, legal responsibility, inheritance, child allowance, etc.). So, according to the law (at least in many countries) being a biological father does not 'count as' being a father in the sense of the law. The law describes exactly which criteria have to be met for 'counting as' a father. And this description is a reification of a 'constitutive norm'.

Boella and van der Torre mention that constitutive norms "regulate the creation of institutional facts" [8]. I would rather say that they regulate the 'interpretation' of institutional terms (like 'father', in the legal sense). This interpretation then of course has to be checked against the so called 'brute facts' [53] (e.g., check whether the father is married to the mother, or else has signed a paper in which he acknowledges the child). This process of checking interpretations may come with its own regulations. And, indeed, this process can be seen as resulting in 'institutional facts' (e.g., for the law, X is the father of Y). But to define constitutional norms as norms on the process by which institutional facts are checked, is maybe too big a step to make. I admit that it may be defended under a 'meaning is use' view on constitutional norms. But, in this case, I prefer a more static view.

Another property that sets constitutive norms apart, is that they cannot be violated. For a regulative norm, it is clear what it means to say that it is violated: when the actual behavior is different from the prescribed behavior. But it is much more difficult to think about a constitutive norm being violated. Does it mean that an institutional term is used under a wrong interpretation?

### Are Norms and Obligations the Same Kind of Thing?

No they are not. And it is important to make the distinction, because there is much literature around confusing the two concepts. A norm is aimed at some general good for a society of agents. This general good may, or may not, transcend the goals of specific individual agents. Norms can thus be said to 'exist' in an agent's social environment, independent of the agent. Also, typically, a norm applies over an extended period of time.

In contrast to that, obligations are 'situated' in time and 'space'. They do not 'exist' in an agent's environment, but are part of the motivational states of individual agents. An obligation thus plays a role in the decision of a particular agent at a particular moment in time. And, obligations applying to an agent at a particular time and for particular situations originate from the norms holding for the group of agents the agent is part of and holding over the interval of time the agent is in the group.

The difference between norms and obligations is paralleled by the differences in the logical formalisms defined for both. For instance, in Input-Output logics [40,41], which are designed for reasoning about norms, there are no notions of agency or time. This contrasts with modern formalisms for reasoning about obligations, such as STIT-logics [31], and deontic versions of CTL [15] and ATL [12]. In these logics agency and time are central. Recently [17] we started to work on an approach to define the relation between norms and obligations, and between Input-Output logics and temporal deontic reasoning.

### What Do Obligations Pertain to?

Obligations are one of the factors playing a role in the decision processes of individual agents. But, obligations may pertain to different concepts. A rather well-known distinction from the deontic literature is the one between 'ought-to-be' and 'ought-to-do'. Roughly the distinction is that 'ought-to-be' is about discriminating between good or bad *states*, while 'ought-to-do' is about discriminating between good or bad *actions*. However, in the deontic logic literature there is no consensus about how actions should actually be represented in the object language. This implies that for several deontic logic operators in the literature it is actually not undisputed whether they reflect an 'ought-to-do' notion or not. Von Wright's seminal paper on, what he called, Standard Deontic Logic (SDL) [61] used propositions to talk about actions. Later he switched his view, arguing that the same formalism could actually be used to model 'ought-to-be' notions. And even today many researchers still use plain propositions to represent actions, arguing that propositions are abstract enough to hide any 'internal' structure you want. A second way to represent actions is through a modal agency operator. Such operators link an agent, or a group of agents, to certain action effects expressed by a proposition. So, these so called STIT formalisms distinguish between propositions and actions through a modal operator for 'agency'. The setting can either be temporal [31], or 'general' [47,23]. Modern formalisms for reasoning about multi-agent systems such as Coalition Logic (CL) and ATL are very closely related to STIT formalisms [16]. But, many computer scientists do not consider the STIT representation of action satisfactory. They feel that a necessary condition for logical models of action is to have names for actions in the object language. The formalism I am talking about here is Dynamic Logic [48,30]. Meyer [42] was the first to use Propositional Dynamic Logic (PDL) as the basis for a deontic logic.

### Can Norms Be True or False?

It is clear that 'beliefs' can be true or false in the sense that if a belief reflects a condition that actually holds in the environment of the agent carrying the belief, then the agent's belief is *true*. So, there are such things as true or false beliefs. But, not in the same sense there are such things as true or false norms or obligations (or desires, intentions, etc.). The reason is clear: we think of beliefs as *descriptions* of states of affairs in an agent's environment, and of their truth or falsehood as a measure for the faithfulness of the description. But norms and obligations are *prescriptions*. And there is not in the same sense as for descriptions an environment against which to measure or verify the faithfulness of a prescription.

However, prescriptions can be verified against an existing body of norms. And in that sense they can be true. For instance, it can be *true* that an agent is under the obligation of finishing a paper before midnight, because that is decreed by the organization of the conference he wants to attend. However, as Von Wright explains [62], what is true here is not the norm, but, what he calls, the 'norm proposition'.

Von Wright and Alchourrón [3] emphasize that we should take the distinction between norms and norm propositions seriously, and that logics of norms are different from logics of norm-propositions. A line of research that is motivated by the distinction between norms and norm-propositions is that by Makinson and Van der Torre on Input-Output logics [39,40].

In the deontic logic literature, the question whether a deontic logic of norms is possible even though apparently norms lack truth values has become known as "Jörgenson's dilemma" [36]. My position is that such logics are possible. I take the standpoint of Von Wright [62] who says that maybe 'logic has a wider reach than truth'. I think we do not even have to adhere to the view that logic is about truth, it is enough just to say that logic is about entailment relations between meaningful sentences. Truth can be regarded an 'internal' variable of reasoning, a variable that can be hidden from the reasoner altogether.

A category of sentences often mentioned in this context are the so called 'imperatives'. An example of an imperative sentence is "leave the room!". Also linguists doing formal semantics are puzzled by the fact that such sentences have no truth values. But, with imperatives I see two reasons for this. Not only do they express a prescription, they also reflect speech acts. And assigning truth values to acts as such is already problematic.

# 3   Motivations for Modeling Norm Change

Now that I have tried to explain what norms are, and what they are used for, I want to give some reasons for being interested in modeling norm *change.*

As already sketched in the introduction, looking at the dynamics of agent concepts is not something new. In 1985 the AGM postulates for theory revision were published [2]. Actually, Alchourrón and Makinson, two of the fathers of these postulates (the 'A' and 'M'), were originally interested in axioms governing the derogation (contraction) of norms. Later they found that there was a great overlap with similar ideas about the dynamics of beliefs, as proposed by Gärdenfors (the 'G'). Both worked with only propositional logic for the object language, which is why they joined forces. Although 'AGM' was thus presented as a series of postulates for belief revision, Alchourrón and Makinson still also had the applicability to norms in mind.

In 1997 van Benthem's book 'Exploring Logical Dynamics' [55] appeared. The book promotes taking a different view on logics and in particular their semantics. Inspired by similar ideas from linguistics [59], the idea was put forward that the meaning of logical sentences might better be expressed in terms of the effect they have on the state of the interpreter of a sentence than in terms of the traditional static models. For instance, logicians preferred to see the notion of 'logical truth' not as a relation between a logical sentence and its model, but as the result of a strategic game between a proponent and an opponent where the first attempts to make the formula true, while the second tries to make it false.

Already, in itself, the above described circumstances are enough to justify being interested in logical models for norm change. However, I also want to formulate some independent reasons. To be able to do so I first need to be more explicit about a distinction already made in section 2, between norms originating outside the regulated group of agents, and norms 'coming from within'. The first I referred to as a *'dictatorship'* situation The other situation is where the source of, at least, part of the norms governing a multi-agent system lies within the system itself. So, we are dealing with a system where the designer of the system does not only try to meet his design goals by explicitly giving norms for the system, but where, to a certain extent, he allows the system to come up with its own norms. So we think of the system as having a *self-regulating* capacity.

The reason to be interested in norm change in 'dictatorship' situations, such as the one where the designer of a multi-agent system is at the same time its 'dictator', is the following. System designers have to find the right balance between autonomy and norm susceptibility of agents in order to realize the overall system goals. Finding the right balance can be a matter of finding the right norms. In this view, optimization of the system against the goals of the designer is a matter of norm adaptation, and thus, of norm change.

Norms need changes because the balance between individual agent goals and system norms can be 'threatened' by unexpected changes in the environment and changes in the abilities and powers of agents. To restore the balance, norms might have to be changed. And to understand *how* the norms have to be changed, it has to be studied how norms, agent goals and preferences, and agent powers and strategies, are interrelated.

Now, consider the second situation: the 'self-regulatory' one. Here we have, that part of the norms governing the system come from within. In particular, the norms partially originate from the preferences of the individuals inhabiting the multi-agent system. We get the situation that on the one hand, the norms emerging in a system find their origin in the preferences of the individual agents, while on the other hand, the norms give rise to obligations that affect the preferences of these same agents. So, here it is clear that there is a certain amount of circularity in the interaction between norms and preferences. This mutual dependency between norms and preferences was discussed by Boella and van der Torre in terms of what they call 'the social delegation cycle' [9]. Fig 1. depicts this cycle.

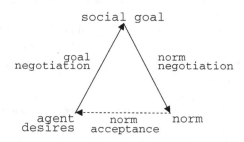

**Fig 1.** The social delegation cycle

As I see it, the social delegation cycle takes an essentially cooperative view on norm emergence. Individual preferences (desires) are aggregated into common goals (social goals) by a process of social choice. In figure 1 this process is labeled 'goal negotiation'. Then, the norms result from the established common goals by a process of norm negotiation. The goal and norm negotiation steps together embody the emergence of norms out of the preferences of individual agents. The cycle is closed by the dotted line representing the opposite direction: the influence of norms on the preferences of individual agents. Here the issue is that agents can either accept or reject norms.

The cycle promotes a clear motivation for being interested in norm change. The mutual dependency between preferences and norms means that changes in preferences cause changes in norms. And agents change preferences (interpreted in the broadest sense, covering 'desires', 'goals', 'wishes', etc.) quite often.

# 4   Issues in Logically Modeling Norm Change

In this section I will mention four issues that I consider to be significant sub-problems of the general problem of designing logical models for norm change.

## 4.1   Issue 1: How Do Norms Depend on Abilities?

Recently several formalisms have been proposed for multi-agent abilities. In computer science several logicians work on variants and extensions of Alternating time Temporal Logic (ATL [4]), which is best interpreted as a logic whose central operator expresses 'strategic ability'. ATL has a non-extensive fragment in 'Coalition Logic' (CL [46]), which was formulated independently. Also in the philosophical literature essentially the same concepts were studied and formalized [18,31], again independently (and earlier).

Now, the abilities of the agents populating a multi-agent system determine the possible courses of events within the system. What is more, in logics like CL and ATL abilities are defined as 'what can be brought about independent of what other agents do'. Under this notion of 'ability', if an agent gives preference to a goal for which it has the ability to bring it about, it guarantees the system evolves in a certain direction. This is very strong, and one might thus ask whether ATL and CL study the notion of ability that is most relevant for normative multi-agent systems. But what it also shows is that abilities play a crucial role in the balance between individual goals and norms of the system. Abilities change. Agents run out of power, get access to powers they did not have before, get damaged, learn things they could not do before, etc. So, to ensure the right behavior, if abilities change, norms should very likely also be changed. In particular, there is no use to specify norms aimed at behaviors that will not occur anyway. This is closely related to the deontic concept of 'ought implies can' [33]. On the other hand, new, unforeseen behaviors due to newly obtained abilities of agents may require adaptations of existing norms.

The open issues are multiple. Can we conditionalize the strong notion of ability as modeled by ATL and CL to the 'normal' circumstances, such that 'ability' is only associated with the possibility to bring about a condition under normal circumstances, but not under all circumstances (note that here there is an interesting parallel with what in theories of action is called the 'qualification problem' [54])? Can we design logical models for 'ability change', maybe in the same way as is done for changes in knowledge and belief states [58,6]? And if so, how can we connect these formalisms to ones that model the dynamics of norms based on the dynamics of abilities? In what sense do abilities intermediate between deontic notions of 'ought-to-be' and 'ought-to-do'? Partial answers to some of these questions have been given [31,12]. But most questions remain open.

## 4.2   Issue 2: How Do Norms Depend on Preferences?

In section 3, we explained that for self regulatory multi-agent systems that can come up with their own norms, there is a mutual dependency between norms and preferences of the agents. We consider both dependencies as issues that, in principle, can be studied independently. In this section we discuss the first one.

The main issue is that to understand the dynamics of norms, and in particular, the reason why a norm emerges or is useful for an agent society, one has to understand in what sense norms are related to the social preferences and abilities of coalitions of agents. In section 2, I explained that one can distinguish between situations where the norms are in-line with the individual preference, like in coordination problems, and situations where the norms and the preferences oppose each other. Let us here focus on the second case. Fig 2. gives the prisoners dilemma ('PD', for short).

| Column Row | Cooperate | Defect |
|---|---|---|
| Cooperate | $(4, 4)$ | $(1, 5)$ |
| Defect | $(5, 1)$ | $(2, 2)$ |

**Fig 2.** The prisoners dilemma (PD)

The situation is symmetric in both agents. For either agent defecting is the best option according to a majority of game theoretic solution concepts. So, we might say that agents confronted with the PD will 'prefer' to defect. However, in situations like these, agents are very likely to come up with a norm putting a fine on defecting (see the examples in section 2). Let us say, the fine is 2 points. Now, under the assumption that the agents simply accept the norm, or do not have a choice but to accept the norm (i.e. in case of violations, payment of the fine is solidly enforced), it follows that the norm is 'internalized' and merged into the agents' preferences. So, a new game results. The game is depicted in fig. 3. It results from the game in fig. 2 by simply subtracting the fines from the numbers associated with defecting in fig. 2. The subtraction reflects the internalization of the norm. Now, for the new game, all solution concepts point to cooperation as the preferred action.

| Column Row | Cooperate | Defect |
|---|---|---|
| Cooperate | $(4, 4)$ | $(1, 3)$ |
| Defect | $(3, 1)$ | $(0, 0)$ |

**Fig 3.** The PD after a 2-point fine on defecting is solidly enforced

Now the point of the example is not that the preferences of the agents change as the result of their acceptance of the norm. This is the subject of the next section, and indeed, there I will come back to this same example. The point here is that under the *assumption* that it is fully accepted, the norm is chosen in such a way that a socially optimal outcome is promoted in the new game.

The mechanism of norm creation exemplified by the issuing of the 2 point fine on defecting in the PD example, is one of the things we are interested in in the context of norm change. Clearly if in situations like these the preferences change, also the norms might have to change to ensure a socially optimal outcome. We already made first steps [11] of modeling the dependency of socially optimal norms on the underlying preferences, in the context of Coalition Logic [46]. In [11] we investigate the relation between norms and preferences by defining an operator for coalitional rational choice, and by considering situations where what is rational for sub-groups may conflict with what is rational for the whole group; the situation the prisoners dilemma is the typical example of. Then it is assumed that the reachability of outcomes optimal for the whole group, gives rise to a social norm saying that sub-groups should not pursue their own best interest if that conflicts with the group's interest. Norms are not represented explicitly. Instead, a semantics for deontic operators for permission, prohibition and obligation is defined, in terms of the implicit socially optimal norms determined by the preferences and abilities of agents.

However, the work we did in [11] is only a first step. There is much research ahead. There are close connections with other work in deontic logic [37] that have to be explored, and many generalizations have to be investigated, like for instance the generalization to the fully strategic case (i.e., from normal game forms to extensive game forms), and the connection with logical models for the dynamics of preferences [38].

### 4.3   Issue 3: How Do Preferences Depend on Norms?

This issue is about modeling the influence of changes in norms on the preferences of the individual agents inhabiting the system. We have studied this relation within the so called 'BOID' architecture [14,13]. We develop a theory for determining agent's goals from the interplay between beliefs, obligations, intentions and desires. One of the issues discussed in the context of BOID is that the interplay between 'internal' motivations and 'external' ones originating from norms of an agent's social context, enables us to distinguish between several agent types. For instance, a benevolent agent will give priority to norms, while an egocentric agent will not.

The difference between benevolent agents and egocentric agents shows that the main issue here is 'norm acceptance'. Benevolent agents are more willing to internalize, or accept norms than egocentric ones.

But, let us first go back to the PD example of the previous section, as depicted in figures 2 and 3. Subtraction of the 2 point fine on defecting corresponds with full acceptance of the norm. As said, this can either be because the norm is solidly enforced, or because the agent, for some reason or another (maybe it is very benevolent), simply accepts the norm. But, of course, in many concrete examples acceptance is not full, but only partial. For, instance, you will only be fined if your wrongdoing is detected by some imperfect control mechanism (think about human police agents). Or, you will only want to accept the norm if you can be fairly sure that others accept it as well. Our human society is full of examples of this phenomenon. If nobody waits for the traffic lights, it would be irrational to do so yourself. If nobody pays taxes, you will probably decide also not to do so.

It is an interesting observation, motivated be these examples, that apparently also norm acceptance is a game played with other agents subject to the same norm. Only if a certain number of other agents obey the norm, it is rational for you to do so also. That norm-acceptance is a game in this sense, is the central observation in a work [1] by Ågotnes, van der Hoek and Wooldridge. These authors define a normative system as a *strict* constraint on behavior (a choice I will argue against below), and consider the decision of accepting it or not. Each agent is assumed to have a prioritized list of goals represented as formulae of Computation Tree Logic (CTL [24]). Different normative systems may realize different goals. Then, given its goals, an agent must determine whether or not it is rational to act according to one of the suggested normative systems (i.e., in this setting, a set of possible behaviors, each of which is strictly enforced if accepted). Whether or not it is better to agree to a behavior depends on which of the other agents agree. Thus, in the light of the agents' goals we can interpret the situation as a standard strategic game. This makes it possible to consider questions like the complexity of deciding whether or not a normative system (in the sense of Ågotnes et al.) is a Nash-equilibrium (or 'Nash-implementation'), relative to a set of other normative systems.

So, Ågotnes et al. define norms as hard constraints on multi-agent behavior. In their normative systems, if a norm is 'active', agents simply cannot perform behaviors that are not according to the norm. In other words: there can not be any violations. This promotes a rather different view on norms than the one I described in this paper. The dominant view in deontic logic is that it deals with modeling the reasoning about violations, and that it is not about excluding them altogether. In particular, in the PD example I discussed in the previous section, the norm is a *disincentive* (2 points) on defecting, and not a *hard constraint* making defecting impossible. Accepting this norm, or partially accepting it, means the disincentive is subtracted, or partially subtracted, from the preference values for the different choices. But, this does not mean that agents have no choice but to obey the norm: clearly, they can still decide to violate it.

It is fascinating that in both the process of norm emergence (the previous section) and the process of norm acceptance (the present section) similar game theoretic considerations seem to play a role. We might even say that the problems reveal a certain duality, which is not too strange given that they model opposite directions in the social delegation cycle we discussed in section 3. More research is required to reveal the full extent of this duality.

## 4.4   Issue 4: How Is 'Change' Best Represented?

The final issue I want to discuss is a little different from the previous three in that it is not so much about how agent concepts are related as about the more general problem of 'representation'. AGM style theory revision takes the perspective that for modeling change we have to consider how (sets of) formulas are updated to other (sets of) formulas. So change is represented as a difference between theories. The main characteristic of this form of representing change is that the policies or postulates for change are formulated in a meta-language, while the object language is only used to talk about the states that change. Alternatively, we can try to model the policies for change as axioms within the object language. In the case of belief or theory revision, this part of the spectrum is covered by the so called 'dynamic epistemic logics' [6,20]. So one of the representational questions we have to answer when modeling norm change is 'do we want an object language that is strong enough to express change postulates, and if so, why?'.

But there are more representational questions to answer. In the introduction we already mentioned there is quite a discrepancy between formalisms for norms and formalisms dealing with obligations. Since norms are more abstract in the sense that they are not relative to particular moments or particular agents, they can be suitably modeled using propositional conditional formulas, such as, again, Input-Output logics [40]. One of the questions this gives rise to is how these more abstract representations of norms relate to the often more concrete representations of obligations, prohibitions and permissions, such as in, for instance, temporal deontic logics, and in logics of (multi-)agency, such as STIT logics and their deontic extensions. First steps to solve these questions have been made [17], but again, also on this subject many questions remain unresolved.

The final representational question I want to address is linked to the representation of norms as conditional formulas (often 'rules') over a propositional language, as in Input-Output logics. The question is how, under this representation, we account for change of the norms. One idea could be to simply apply AGM-like postulates to theories consisting of rules (see [28]). First observations concerning this problem seem to suggest that AGM's recovery postulate does not work under all norm semantics. Also, there seem to be obvious connections with the problem of revision of non-monotonic theories [60], but the links still have to be investigated.

However, if norms are modeled by rules, we can also model change by non-monotonic inference instead of revision. It was already recognized quite early that belief revision and non-monotonic inference are actually very similar processes [26]. In particular, for the case where norms are represented by rules, change can also be modeled by giving a non-monotonic interpretation of the rules, and define any change of the norms in terms of the addition of new rules. Due to the non-monotonic semantics, new rules may cause that earlier conclusions can no longer be derived. In principle we can get all the effects known from semantics of 'argumentation frameworks' [21], like 'reinstatement' and 'rebuttal' of rules. One problem for this view is however that to account for all necessary revision effects, we need prioritized rules. And for such rules, the problem of finding good non-monotonic semantics has resulted in even more controversy than for the non-prioritized rules [32]. One of the underlying representational questions in the decision between revision strategies or non-monotonic strategies is whether or not changes should always be recollected by the system or not. If so, we can simply store all norms in the system, and derive the meaning of the norms through a non-monotonic inference procedure. An example of such a system for the dynamics of beliefs is [51]. If we do not want to recollect which norms entered the system at which moment, we can throw away this information by performing revisions.

## 5 Conclusion

In this paper I discuss four issues that I think are important to focus on for eventually obtaining formal models of norm change for multi-agent systems. The four issues concern separate sub-problems. From the lack of satisfactory answers to each of the sub-problems, it is clear that a full model of norm change is still far ahead of us. Yet, all the issues raised are also worth studying individually. I hope the broader context in which I put them here helps to keep an overview and to connect the separate issues to the greater aim.

## Acknowledgements

Thanks to the two anonymous referees and John-Jules Charles Meyer and Leendert van der Torre for commenting on the pre-final version of this paper.

## References

1. Ågotnes, T., Wooldridge, M., van der Hoek, W.: Normative system games. In: Huhns, M., Shehory, O. (eds.) Proceedings of the Sixth International Conference on Autonomous Agents and Multiagent Systems (AAMAS 2007), May 2007, pp. 876–883. IFAMAAS (2007)
2. Alchourrón, C., Gärdenfors, P., Makinson, D.: On the logic of theory change: partial meet contraction and revision functors 50, 510–530 (1985)
3. Alchourrón, C.E.: A sketch of logic without truth. In: The 2nd International Conference on Artificial Intelligence and Law, pp. 165–179. ACM Press, New York (1989)
4. Alur, R., Henzinger, T.A., Kupferman, O.: Alternating-time temporal logic. In: FOCS 1997: Proceedings of the 38th Annual Symposium on Foundations of Computer Science (FOCS 1997), pp. 100–109. IEEE Computer Society, Los Alamitos (1997)
5. Aumann, R.J.: Agreeing to disagree. The Annals of Statistics 4(6), 1236–1239 (1976)
6. Baltag, A., Moss, L.S.: Logics for epistemic programs. Synthese 139, 165–224 (2004)
7. Bochman, A.: A logical theory of nonmonotonic inference and belief change. Springer, New York (2001)
8. Boella, G., van der Torre, L.: Fulfilling or violating norms in normative multiagent systems. In: Proceedings of IAT 2004, pp. 483–486. IEEE, Los Alamitos (2004)
9. Boella, G., van der Torre, L.W.N.: Delta: The social delegation cycle. In: Lomuscio, A., Nute, D. (eds.) DEON 2004. LNCS, vol. 3065. Springer, Heidelberg (2004)

10. Boella, G., van der Torre, L.W.N., Verhagen, H.: Introduction to normative multia-
    gent systems. Computational & Mathematical Organization Theory 12(2-3), 71–79
    (2006)
11. Broersen, J., Mastop, R., Meyer, J.-J.C., Turrini, P.: A deontic logic for socially
    optimal norms. In: van der Meyden, R., van der Torre, L. (eds.) DEON 2008.
    LNCS, vol. 5076, pp. 218–232. Springer, Heidelberg (2008)
12. Broersen, J.M.: Strategic deontic temporal logic as a reduction to ATL, with an
    application to chisholm's scenario. In: Goble, L., Meyer, J.-J.C. (eds.) DEON 2006.
    LNCS, vol. 4048, pp. 53–68. Springer, Heidelberg (2006)
13. Broersen, J.M., Dastani, M., Hulstijn, J., van der Torre, L.W.N.: Goal generation
    in the BOID architecture. Cognitive Science Quarterly Journal 2(3-4), 428–447
    (2002)
14. Broersen, J.M., Dastani, M., van der Torre, L.: Beliefs, obligations, intentions and
    desires as components in an agent architecture. International Journal of Intelligent
    Systems 20(9), 893–920 (2005)
15. Broersen, J.M., Dignum, F., Dignum, V., Meyer, J.-J.: Designing a deontic logic
    of deadlines. In: Lomuscio, A., Nute, D. (eds.) DEON 2004. LNCS, vol. 3065, pp.
    43–56. Springer, Heidelberg (2004)
16. Broersen, J.M., Herzig, A., Troquard, N.: Embedding Alternating-time Temporal
    Logic in strategic STIT logic of agency. Journal of Logic and Computation 16(5),
    559–578 (2006)
17. Broersen, J.M., van der Torre, L.: Reasoning about norms, obligations, time and
    agents. In: Ghose, A., Governatori, G., Sadananda, R. (eds.) PRIMA 2007. LNCS,
    vol. 5044, pp. 171–182. Springer, Heidelberg (2008)
18. Brown, M.A.: Normal bimodal logics of ability and action. Studia Logica 51(3/4),
    519–532 (1992)
19. Cohen, P.R., Levesque, H.J.: Intention is choice with commitment 42(3), 213–261
    (1990)
20. van Ditmarsch, H., van der Hoek, W., Kooi, B.: Dynamic Epistemic Logic. Synthese
    Library, vol. 337. Springer, New York (2007)
21. Dung, P.M.: On the acceptability of arguments and its fundamental role in non-
    monotonic reasoning, logic programming and n-person games. Artificial Intelli-
    gence 77(2), 321–358 (1995)
22. Dunin-Keplicz, B., Verbrugge, R.: Collective intentions. Fundamenta Informati-
    cae 51(3), 271–295 (2002)
23. Elgesem, D.: The modal logic of agency. Nordic Journal of Philosophical Logic 2(2),
    1–46 (1997)
24. Emerson, E.A.: Temporal and modal logic. In: van Leeuwen, J. (ed.) Handbook of
    Theoretical Computer Science. Formal Models and Semantics, vol. B, ch. 14, pp.
    996–1072 (1990)
25. Endriss, U.: The 1st international workshop on computational social choice. Knowl-
    edge Engineering Review 23(2), 213–215 (2008)
26. Gärdenfors, P.: Belief revision and nonmonotonic logic: two sides of the same coin?
    In: van Eijck, J. (ed.) JELIA 1990. LNCS, vol. 478, pp. 52–54. Springer, Heidelberg
    (1991)
27. Grossi, D., Meyer, J.-J.C., Dignum, F.: Classificatory Aspects of Counts-as: An
    Analysis in Modal Logic. J. Logic Computation 16(5), 613–643 (2006)
28. Hansen, J., Pigozzi, G., van der Torre, L.W.N.: Ten philosophical problems in
    deontic logic. In: Normative Multi-agent Systems (2007)
29. Hansson, S.O.: A Textbook of Belief Dynamics. Kluwer Academic Publishers, Dor-
    drecht (1999)

30. Harel, D., Kozen, D., Tiuryn, J.: Dynamic Logic (2000)
31. Horty, J.F.: Agency and Deontic Logic (2001)
32. Horty, J.F.: Defaults with priorities. Journal of Philosophical Logic 36(4), 367–413 (2007)
33. Jacquette, D.: Moral dilemmas, disjunctive obligations, and Kant's principle that 'ought' implies 'can'. Synthese 88(1), 43–55 (2004)
34. Jones, A., Sergot, M.: A formal characterization of institutionalized power. Journal of the IGPL 4(3), 429–445 (1996)
35. Jones, A.J.I., Sergot, M.: On the characterization of law and computer systems: The normative sytems perspective. In: Meyer, J.-J.C., Wieringa, R.J. (eds.) Normative System Specification. Deontic Logic in Computer Science, pp. 275–307. John Wiley and Sons, Chichester (1993)
36. Jorgensen, J.: Imperatives and logic. Erkenntnis 7, 288–296
37. Kooi, B., Tamminga, A.: Moral conflicts between groups of agents. Journal of Philosophical Logic 37(1), 1–21 (2008)
38. Liu, F.: Changing for the Better: Preference Dynamics and Agent Diversity. PhD thesis, ILLC Dissertation Series, Amsterdam (2008)
39. Makinson, D.: On a fundamental problem of deontic logic. In: McNamara, P., Prakken, H. (eds.) Norms, Logics and Information Systems. New Studies on Deontic Logic and Computer Science, pp. 29–53. IOS Press, Amsterdam (1998)
40. Makinson, D., van der Torre, L.W.N.: Input-output logics. Journal of Philosphical Logic 29, 383–408 (2000)
41. Makinson, D., van der Torre, L.W.N.: Permission from an input-output perspective. Journal of Philosophical Logic 32, 391–416 (2003)
42. Meyer, J.-J.C.: A different approach to deontic logic: Deontic logic viewed as a variant of dynamic logic. Notre Dame Journal of Formal Logic 29, 109–136 (1988)
43. Meyer, J.-J.C., van der Hoek, W., van Linder, B.: A logical approach to the dynamics of commitments (1999)
44. Minsky, N.H., Ungureanu, V.: Law-governed interaction: a coordination and control mechanism for heterogeneous distributed systems. ACM Trans. Softw. Eng. Methodol. 9(3), 273–305 (2000)
45. Moses, Y., Tennenholtz, M.: Artificial social systems. Computers and AI 14, 533–562 (1995)
46. Pauly, M.: A modal logic for coalitional power in games. Journal of Logic and Computation 12(1), 149–166 (2002)
47. Pörn, I.: The logic of power. Basil-Blackwell, Malden (1970)
48. Pratt, V.R.: Semantical considerations on Floyd-Hoare logic. In: Proceedings 17th IEEE Symposium on the Foundations of Computer Science, pp. 109–121 (1976)
49. Moses, Y., Fagin, R., Halpern, J.Y., Vardi, M.Y.: Reasoning about Knowledge (1995)
50. Rao, A.S., Georgeff, M.P.: Formal models and decision procedures for multi-agent systems 8(3), 293–342 (1998)
51. Roorda, J.W., van der Hoek, W., Meyer, J.-J.: Iterated belief change in multi-agent systems. Logic Journal of the IGPL 11(2), 223–246 (2003)
52. Schild, K.: On the relationship between BDI-logics and standard logics of concurrency. Autonomous agents and multi-agent systems 3, 259–283 (2000)
53. Searle, J.: The Construction of Social Reality. Free Press, New York (1995)
54. Thielscher, M.: The qualification problem: A solution to the problem of anomalous models. Artificial Intelligence 131(1-2), 1–37 (2001)
55. van Benthem, J.: Exploring logical dynamics. Center for the Study of Language and Information, Stanford (1997)

56. van der Hoek, W., Meyer, J.-J.C.: Epistemic Logic for AI and Computer Science (1995)
57. van der Hoek, W., Roberts, M., Wooldridge, M.: Knowledge and social laws. In: AAMAS 2005: Proceedings of the fourth international joint conference on Autonomous agents and multiagent systems, pp. 674–681. ACM, New York (2005)
58. van Ditmarsch, H., van der Hoek, W., Kooi, B.: Public announcements and belief expansion. Advances in Modal Logic, vol. 5 (2005)
59. Veltman, F.: Defaults in update semantics. Journal of Philosophical Logic 25, 221–261 (1996)
60. Witteveen, C., van der Hoek, W.: Recovery of (non)monotonic theories. Artif. Intell. 106(1), 139–159 (1998)
61. von Wright, G.H.: Deontic logic. Mind 60, 1–15 (1951)
62. von Wright, G.H.: Deontic logic - as I see it. In: McNamara, P., Prakken, H. (eds.) Norms, Logics and Information Systems. New Studies on Deontic Logic and Computer Science, pp. 15–25. IOS Press, Amsterdam (1999)

# Adapting Autonomic Electronic Institutions to Heterogeneous Agent Societies

Eva Bou[1], Maite López-Sánchez[2], J.A. Rodríguez-Aguilar[1],
and Jaime Simão Sichman[3]

[1] IIIA, Artificial Intelligence Research Institute
CSIC, Spanish National Research Council, Campus UAB 08193 Bellaterra, Spain
{ebm,jar}@iiia.csic.es
[2] WAI, Volume Visualization and Artificial Intelligence,
MAiA Dept., Universitat de Barcelona
maite@maia.ub.es
[3] LTI, Intelligent Techniques Laboratory, Computer Engineering Department,
University of São Paulo, Brazil
jaime.sichman@poli.usp.br

**Abstract.** Electronic institutions (EIs) define the rules of the game in
agent societies by fixing what agents are permitted and forbidden to
do and under what circumstances. Autonomic Electronic Institutions
(AEIs) adapt their rules to comply with their goals when regulating agent
societies composed of varying populations of self-interested agents. We
present a self-adaptation model based on Case-Based Reasoning (CBR)
that allows an AEI to yield a dynamical answer to changing circumstances. In order to demonstrate adaptation empirically, we consider a
traffic control scenario populated by heterogeneous agents. Within this
setting, we demonstrate statistically that an AEI is able to adapt to
different heterogeneous agent populations.

## 1 Introduction

Electronic institutions (EIs) [1] have been proved to be valuable to regulate open
agent systems. The idea behind EIs is to mirror the role traditional institutions
play in the establishment of "the rules of the game" –a set of conventions that
establish what agents are permitted and forbidden to do and under what circumstances. According to North [2] human institutions are not static; they may
evolve over time by altering, eliminating or incorporating norms. Thereby, Bou
et al. [3] have defined Autonomic Electronic Institutions (AEIs) as EIs with
autonomic capabilities. The vision of autonomic computing [4] constitutes an
approximation to computing systems with a minimal human interference. One
main challenge of autonomic computing is the development of adaptive algorithms that allow a system to deal with changing, heterogeneous and open environments. In this way, AEIs use learning techniques to be capable of dynamically
adapting their rules to social changes –changes in the agent's behaviours.

Notice that adaptation of Multi-Agent Systems (MAS) has been usually envisioned as an agent capability, where the agents composing the system learn how

G. Vouros et al. (Eds.): OAMAS 2008, LNAI 5368, pp. 18–35, 2009.

to adapt to the whole system in order to accomplish some organisational goals. It has been largely approached either as a coordination problem, a reorganisation problem, and an organisation formation problem [5] [6] [7] [8]. However, in AEIs the adaptation is addressed as a system capability: an AEI self-adapts to social changes. To the best of our knowledge, adaptation in EIs have been only previously approached by Sierra et al. [9]. However, they search the best population of agents that helps achieve some institutional goals instead of adapting the institution itself.

In previous work [3] we have learnt those regulations that best accomplished the institutional goals for a collection of simulated agent populations. We have proposed a Case-Based Reasoning (CBR) approach that allows an AEI to self-configure its regulations for any homogeneous agent population. In this paper we focus in AEIs that use learning algorithms in order to adapt its regulations to comply with institutional goals despite varying agent's behaviours. Thus, this paper extends previous work by using the CBR approach to self-adapt AEI regulations to any heterogeneous agent society. By heterogeneous, we mean agent societies where agents behave in different ways. In this manner, if we take a population as being a set of agents behaving similarly, then we can compose an heterogeneous agent society by including several populations with a given proportion. Therefore, we study how the AEI adapts to heterogeneous agent societies by combining different populations of agents in different proportions.

Our CBR approach helps an AEI to identify agent populations that behave similarly and subsequently retrieve the rules that best regulate them. We present a traffic case study to empirically test the proposed CBR approach. A statistical analysis of results allows us to conclude that an AEI is able to adapt to heterogeneous agent populations.

The paper is organised as follows. First, section 2 presents an overview of the related work. In section 3 we recall the notion of autonomic electronic institution as introduced by Bou et al. [3]. Section 4 describes the learning model that we propose and how an AEI uses CBR. Section 5 describes the case study employed as a scenario wherein we have tested AEI's adaptation. Section 6 provides some empirical results. Finally, section 7 draws some conclusions and sets paths to future research.

## 2   Related Work

Within the area of multi-agent systems, system adaptation has been usually envisioned from an agent point of view where agents learn how to reorganise or coordinate themselves [10] [11]. Along this direction, Hübner et al. [12] propose a model for controlling adaptation by using the $\mathcal{M}$OISE+ organisation model. Gâteau et al. [13] propose $\mathcal{M}$OISE$^{Inst}$ as an extension to $\mathcal{M}$OISE+ as an institution organisation specification of the rights and duties of agents' roles. In both models agents adapt their MAS organisation to both environmental changes and their own goals. Vecht et al. [14] also take an agent point of view, where agents must coordinate to accomplish some organisational goals. They introduce adjustable autonomy as a concept that allows dynamically switching between co-ordination types. They propose a way to implement adjustable autonomy in the agents in order to achieve the dynamic coordination. The approach proposed by Kota et al. [11] also enables the agents to modify the organisational structure. The fact that adaptation is carried out by the agents composing the MAS is the most significant difference with the approach presented in this paper. Our approach is centred on an organisational point of view, since the institution adapts its regulations to accomplish its institutional goals. The most similar work to ours is [15], where Hoogendoorn addresses the dynamical adaptation of organisations to environment changes by translating the organisational model into a max flow network. Therefore, his purposes differ from ours because they only focus on adapting to environment fluctuation.

Regarding the traffic domain, it has been previously used in MAS research [16] [17]. For example, Bazzan et al. [18] discuss the effects of integrating co-evolution in traffic networks. They design the control to achieve the system goal via decentralised traffic lights (modelled as agents). In this framework, they test the use of different strategies when both road agents and traffic light agents adapt, each one having its own goal.

Additionally, Case-Based Reasoning has been applied before in MAS where agents use different CBR approaches to individual learning and to cooperative learning for distributed systems. For example, Ros and Veloso [19] propose a case-based coordination mechanism where they use a case-based reasoning approach to coordinate a multi-robot system.

## 3  Autonomic Electronic Institutions

Basically, an EI [1] is composed of three components: a dialogical framework (DF) that represents the context of interaction between agents; a performative structure (PS) that defines the activities among the agents; and a set of norms (N) defining the consequences of agent's actions. In general, an EI [1] involves different groups of agents playing different roles within scenes in a so called performative structure. Each scene is composed of a coordination protocol along with the specification of the roles that can take part in the scene. Typically, there are specific scenes —such as admission and clear scenes in auctions— devoted to allow agents to join in and leave the institution. In fact, these scenes enable the institution to deal with open systems. Nonetheless, the current definition of EI does not support the adaptation at run-time in the face of a changing environment and changing agents behaviour. In a previous work, we extend the notion of EI to define *autonomic electronic institutions* (AEIs), namely EIs capable of dynamically adapting their rules under changing circumstances. We do it by incorporating the notions of institutional goals and self-configuration to the definition of an EI to support self-adaptation, in the sense of regulation adaptation. The basic idea is that an institution can adapt to agents' behaviours at run-time by means of learning techniques. Next, we just provide an intuitive idea about the elements of an AEI, which is defined as a tuple: $\langle PS, N, DF, G, P_i, P_e, P_a, V, \delta, \gamma \rangle$ (further details can be found in [3]).

The main objective of an AEI is to accomplish its institutional goals $(G)$. For this purpose, an AEI will adapt its rules to the agents it regulates. The institution can observe some information to assess whether its goals are accomplished or not. We specify this information in terms of the following properties $(P)$: institution's own state $(P_i)$, the environment where agents interact $(P_e)$, and the institutional state of the agents participating in the institution $(P_a = \langle a_1, \ldots, a_n \rangle)$. An AEI is only aware of the *institutional (social) state* of a participating agent $a_i$ because an AEI has no access whatsoever to the inner state of any agent. Therefore, an AEI characterises each agent by its institutional state $a_i = \langle a_{i_1}, \ldots, a_{i_m} \rangle$ where $a_{i_j} \in \mathbb{R}$, $1 \le j \le m$. From all this observable information an AEI obtains a set of reference values $(V)$ required to determine the fulfilment of goals. Formally, these reference values are defined as a vector $V = \langle v_1, \ldots, v_q \rangle$, where each $v_j$ results from applying a function $h_j$ upon the information observed by the institution $(v_j = h_j(P_a, P_e, P_i), \ 1 \le j \le q)$.

The goals of an AEI are fixed and are defined as a finite set of constraints. Formally, institutional goals are defined as $G = \{c_1, \ldots, c_p\}$ where each $c_i$ is defined as an expression $g_i(V) \lhd [m_i, M_i]$ where $m_i, M_i \in \mathbb{R}$, and $\lhd$ stands for either $\in$ or $\notin$. Additionally, $g_i$ is a function over the reference values. Thus, each goal is a constraint upon the reference values where each pair $(m_i, M_i)$ defines an interval associated to some constraint $c_i$. The institution achieves its goals if all $g_i(V)$ values satisfy their corresponding constraints of belonging (at least to a certain degree) to their associated intervals. This is measured by means of a satisfaction function that computes the goal satisfaction degree (see [3] for further details).

Finally, *norm transition function* $(\delta)$ and *PS transition function* $(\gamma)$ are the mechanisms to support the adaptation of an AEI to the agent populations it regulates. From all components that an AEI uses to constraint agents' behaviours, and AEI only adapts at run-time norms and roles. Norms are employed to constrain agents' behaviours and to assess the consequences of their actions within the scope of the institution. An AEI does not create or eliminate norms to adapt, but the adaptation of norms is made by using parameters values. Each norm $N_i \in N$ $(i = 1, \ldots, n)$ has a set of parameters $\langle p_{i,1}^N, \ldots, p_{i,m_i}^N \rangle \in \mathbb{R}^{m_i}$. The *norm transition function* $(\delta)$ changes the values norms' parameters to adapt. On the other hand, each scene in the performative structure, $S_i \in PS$, $i = 1, \ldots, t$, is defined as having a set of parameters $\langle p_{i,1}^R, \ldots, p_{i,q_i}^R \rangle \in \mathbb{N}^{q_i}$ where $p_{i,j}^R$ stands for the number of agents playing role $r_j$ in scene $S_i$. Notice that an AEI does not create or eliminate roles to adapt. Thus, adapting a PS involves changing the values of these parameters, whose values are changed by the *PS transition function* $(\gamma)$.

Since both *norm transition function* $(\delta)$ and *PS transition function* may be difficult to define mathematically, we propose to use learning methods to approximate them. Next section details the learning model used to adapt an AEI by changing the values of the norms' parameters and the PS' parameters.

## 4    Learning Model

With the aim of adapting AEI's regulations to any population at run-time, we propose to learn the *norm transition function* ($\delta$) and the *PS transition function* ($\gamma$) in two different steps in an overall learning process. As Figure 1 shows, first learning step corresponds to learning the best parameters for a collection of predefined agent populations. Learning is performed using an evolutionary approach. Each individual ($I_i$) represents a specific AEI's parameter configuration. For a given population of agents ($A$), a genetic algorithm explores the space of parameter values ($I_1, .., I_k$) in search for the ones that lead the AEI to best accomplish its goals ($G$) for this population. Our AEI learns the best parameters for a collection of predefined agent populations by repeating a genetic algorithm for each population. These best parameters will be used by subsequent step in the learning process.

As a second learning step, we propose to use a Case-Based Reasoning (CBR) approach, as shown in Figure 1. CBR [20] is based on learning from experience. Its basic idea is to search in the system's experience for similar situations - called cases. In general, a new problem in a CBR system is solved by retrieving similar cases, reusing the case solution, revising the reused solution, and retaining the new experience. We assume that agent populations that behave in similar way may require similar solutions (i.e. regulations). Therefore, we expect the CBR will allow an AEI to solve situations at run-time that are similar to the ones learnt during the first learning step. Thus, whenever goals are not achieved, our AEI uses CBR to retrieve a solution (regulation parameters) from the most similar situation in the knowledge base. The knowledge base is generated by simulating the same agent populations used in first learning step. So that the cases' solution correspond to the best parameters learnt at first learning step for each population.

In this work we focus on the second learning step, namely how to adapt the parameters to any population at run-time. The way the first learning step is carried out is fully detailed by Bou et al. in [3].

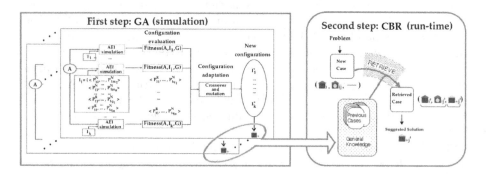

**Fig. 1.** Learning Model in two steps

## 4.1   Applying CBR

In this section we describe the representation of cases we propose to be used by an AEI. We also describe how to compute the similarity function used for comparing two cases. We assume that the set of all cases approximates both the *norm transition function* ($\delta$) and the *PS transition function* ($\gamma$).

Intuitively, a case represents how an AEI using some parameters' values for regulating a given population of agents should change its regulations (to the best parameters' values). However, notice that an institution can only use observable information for representing cases because it has no access to the inner characterisation of the agents that populate it. Therefore, the agent population can not be explicitly represented in the cases. With all of this in mind, we differentiate three main features to represent cases that we define as a tuple ($N^p$,$PS^p$,$V$,pop,$N^{p*}$,$PS^{p*}$):

- **AEI parameters' values: ($N^p$,$PS^p$).** They represent the parameters' values of the institution, namely norm parameters' values and performative structure parameters' values that it uses for regulating agents.
  - $N^p$ stands for the current norm parameters' values; and
  - $PS^p$ stands for the current performative structure parameters' values.
- **Run-time behaviour: ($V$,pop).** They represent the global behaviour of the institution at run-time for a given agent population when the institution uses the previous *AEI parameters' values*. In other words, the effect of the parameters in the behaviour of agents at run-time.
  - $V$ stands for the current set of reference values; and
  - **pop** stands for statistical data that characterises the behaviour of the agents' population at run-time[1].
- **Best AEI parameters' values: ($N^{p*}$,$PS^{p*}$).** They represent the learnt parameters' values of the institution for the previous agent population. In other words: the solution (learning by simulation at first learning step). Thus, they correspond to the parameters that the institution must apply in order to accomplish its institutional goals given both previous AEI parameters' values and run-time behaviour.
  - $N^{p*}$: represents the best values for the norm parameters given the current norm parameters values ($N^p$) and the run-time behaviour ($V$,pop); and
  - $PS^{p*}$: represents the best values for the performative structure parameters given the current performative structure parameters values ($PS^p$) and the run-time behaviour ($V$,pop).

In order to compare two cases, we use an aggregated distance function to compute the degree of similarity $S(C^i, C^j)$ between a new case $C^i$ and a case $C^j$ in the case base:

$$S = w_1 \cdot S_{AEI}(C^i, C^j) + w_2 \cdot S_V(C^i, C^j) + w_3 \cdot S_{pop}(C^i, C^j) \qquad (1)$$

---

[1] Notice that this data corresponds to reference values.

where $S_{AEI}$ corresponds to the distance of the AEI parameters' values ($N^p$, $PS^p$), $S_V$ and $S_{pop}$ correspond to the distance of the run-time behaviour (V,pop), and $w_1, w_2, w_3 \leq 0$ are weighting factors such that $w_1 + w_2 + w_3 = 1$. The $S_{AEI}$, $S_V$ and $S_{pop}$ distance functions are computed as the distance average of their attributes. The distance between the values of an attribute is computed as:

$$sim(attr^i, attr^j) = \frac{|attr^i - attr^j|}{max(attr) - min(attr)} \quad (2)$$

where $min(attr)$ and $max(attr)$ correspond to the limits of the interval of values of the attribute considered in the domain.

**The Retrieval process.** In order to retrieve the most similar case to the problem case $C^i$ without comparing all cases in the case base, we propose to perform this process in two steps:

1. Compare the AEI parameters' values, ($N^p$,$PS^p$), of the problem case $C^i$ with the collection of all the AEI parameters' values in the case base using $S_{AEI}$ and select the set of AEI parameters' values that best match.
2. Access the set of examples in the case base with these AEI parameters' values. Afterwards, we compare case $C^i$ with these examples and select the case that best matches it based on distance function $S$.

We use the first step with the idea that the most similar case must have similar AEI values because the run-time behaviour depends a lot of the AEI parameters' values. In fact, this is our hypothesis since we want to change the AEI parameters' values to change in some way the population behaviour and thus modify the run-time behaviour in order to achieve the institutional goals. The first step makes easy and fast the access to the most similar cases because we concentrate on only comparing the cases with similar AEI parameters' values. Thus, we do not need to compare all the cases of the case base. Moreover, we only need to compute once the distance function $S_{AEI}$ for all cases with the same values of AEI parameters' values.

## 5  Case Study: Traffic Control

This section introduces the case study we use to test our learning model. As case study we have extended the Traffic Regulation Authority presented in [3] as an Autonomic Electronic Institution. The environment is modelled as a 2-lane road junction where no traffic signals are considered. This case study considers the performative structure to be a single traffic scene with two agent roles: one institutional role played by police agents (that detect norm violations); and one external role played by car agents. The performative structure is parametrised by the number of agents playing the police role. Each police agent is able to detect only a portion of the total number of norm violations that car agents actually do. Although we deal with open MAS, we are focused in the learning process, and thus, the definition of a scene that allows external agents to join the institution becomes out of the scope of this paper. Nevertheless, it is worth mentioning that, when entering the institution, agents are assigned a set of points associated to its driving license and this could be modelled in a driving license scene. On the other hand, leaving the institution is partially considered, since cars running out of points are expelled from it.

Norms within this normative environment are related to actions performed by cars. There are two priority norms: the 'right hand-side priority norm', that prevents a car reaching the junction to move forward or to turn left whenever there is another car on its right; and the 'front priority norm', that applies when two cars reaching the junction are located on opposite lines, and one of them intends to turn left. Additionally, norms are parametrised by the associated penalties that are imposed to those cars refusing or failing to follow them. Cars do have a limited amount of 40 points each so that norm offences cause points reduction. Moreover, the institution forbids external agents to drive without points in their accounts. In our setting, the environment is populated with 10 cars interacting inside the traffic scene and moving along the road network. During each discrete simulation, the institution replaces these cars running out of points by new cars so that the cars' population is kept constant.

Car agents only coordinate by following the traffic norms imposed by the AEI. Cars do not have learning skills. They just move based on their random trajectories and the probability of complying with a norm (based on function 3). Each car is modelled by their *agent norm compliance parameters*: $\langle fulfill\_prob,$ $h\_p, inc\_prob \rangle$; where $fulfill\_prob \in [0,1]$ stands for the probability of complying with norms that is initially assigned to each agent; $h\_p \in \mathbb{N}$ stands for the fine threshold that causes an agent to consider a fine to be high enough to reconsider norm compliance; and $inc\_prob \in [0,1]$ stands for the probability increment that is added to $fulfill\_prob$ when the fine norm is greater than the fine threshold ($h\_p$). Thus, car agents decide whether to comply with a norm based on their norm compliance parameters along with the percentage (between 0 and 1) of police agents that the traffic authority has deployed on the traffic environment. To summarise, agents decide whether they keep on moving –regardless of violating norms– or they stop –in order to comply with norms– based on a probability that is computed as:

$$prob \begin{cases} police \cdot fulfill\_prob & fine \leq h\_p \\ police \cdot (fulfill\_prob + inc\_prob) & fine > h\_p \end{cases} \qquad (3)$$

Notice that to use the norm compliance parameters to model cars allows us to generate homogeneous and heterogeneous agent populations. We refer to homogeneous agent population when agents in this population have the same compliance parameter values. Thus, all agents from homogeneous populations decide to comply with norms based in the same probability and therefore behave in a similar way. On the other hand, if in a population there are cars with different norm compliance parameters we consider it as an heterogeneous agent population, because agents have different behaviours.

The reference values the institution can observe along time are $V = \langle col, off,$ $crash, block, expel, police \rangle$ where $col$ indicates total number of collisions for the last $t_w$ ticks ($0 \le t_w \le t_{now}$), $off$ indicates the total number of offences accumulated by all agents [2], $crash$ counts the number of cars involved in accidents, $block$ describes how many cars have been blocked by other cars, $expel$ indicates the number of cars that have been expelled out of the environment due to running out of points, and finally, $police$ indicates the percentage of police agents that the institution deploys in order to control the traffic environment.

On the other hand, the institution has four conflicting institutional goals: (i) minimise the number of collisions; (ii) minimise the number of offences; (iii) minimise the number of expelled cars; (iv) and minimise the percentage of police agents to deploy to control the traffic environment. Goal satisfaction is measured by combining the degree of satisfaction of these four institutional goals. They are combined in a weighted addition function, with weights 0.4, 0.4, 0.1, and 0.1 respectively. Thus, the first two goals are considered to be most important. The institution tries to accomplish its institutional goals by specifying the penalties of both priority norms and by specifying how many police agents should be deployed in the traffic scene.

Following the tuple case definition introduced in section 4.1, $(N^p, PS^p, V, pop,$ $N^{p*}, PS^{p*})$, a case $C^i$ in the traffic scenario is defined as follows:

- $N^p = (fine_{right}, fine_{front})$ are the values of both norms' parameters;
- $PS^p = (police)$ is the value of the performative structure parameter;
- $V = (col, crash, off, block, expel)$ are the reference values;
- $pop = (mean\_off, median\_off, mean\_frequency\_off, median\_frequen$-$cy\_off)$ contains the mean number of offences, the median number of offences, the mean of the frequency of offences, and the median of the frequency of offences carried out by agents for the last $t_w$ ticks ($0 \le t_w \le t_{now}$);
- $N^{p*} = (fine^*_{right}, fine^*_{front})$ are the best values for both norms' parameters;
- $PS^{p*} = (police^*)$ is the best value for the parameter of the performative structure.

To compute the degree of similarity between two cases, we use aggregated distance function (1), $S(C^i, C^j)$. We have set the weights as follows: $w_1 = 0.1$, $w_2 = 0.5$, and $w_3 = 0.4$. Regarding the attributes of the AEI parameters' values, $fine_{front}$ and $fine_{right}$ values are in the interval $[0, 15]$, and $police$ values are in the interval $[0, 1]$. Although the attributes of the run-time behaviour have not known limited values, we have established limits based on the values of the initial generated cases. Thus, we have established that $col$ values are in the interval $[0, 300]$, $crash \in [0, 400]$, $off \in [0, 500]$, $block \in [0, 200]$, $expel \in [0, 900]$, $mean\_off \in [0, 30]$, $median\_off \in [0, 30]$, $mean\_frequency\_off \in [0, 2]$, and $median\_frequency\_off \in [0, 2]$. Since the values of these attributes can be out of the proposed interval, we force distance to be 1 when $|attr^i - attr^j| > max(attr) - min(attr)$.

---

[2] Notice, though, that these offences do not refer to offences detected by police agents but to the real offences that have been actually carried out by car agents.

## 5.1   Case Base Generation

As mentioned in section 4, (during training period) an AEI generates an initial base of cases from simulations of a set of prototypical populations. In this work, our aim is to test if the proposed CBR approach is suitable to help the AEI to adapt its parameters to heterogeneous agent populations. Notice the importance of the case base, because the adaptation of an AEI largely depends on the cases it uses. Notice that an AEI needs to retrieve a similar case whose values, when applied to the current population, help the AEI fulfil its institutional goals. If the AEI has not any good, similar cases in the case base, it would be not able to adapt its parameters to the population. Therefore, the more representative a case is (i.e., the more coverage it has), the more useful it becomes for solving new cases. Case coverage is related to similarity but also to generality. In order to study if case coverage is affected by population heterogeneity, we have considered two ways of generating the case base. First, we want to test how well the AEI adapts to heterogeneous populations when it uses a case base whose cases have been created from homogeneous agent populations. Moreover, we want to test the AEI adaptation performance to heterogeneous agent populations when heterogeneous populations are also used for creating the cases, so that cases will be more similar. The idea is to compare the adaptation of the AEI to different heterogeneous populations when it uses each case base. Thus, we have considered two settings, one for each case base.

**Setting 1.** This setting has a case base generated from homogeneous agent populations. Table 1 shows the features of the seven homogeneous populations (Pop) we have considered to generate this case base. They are characterised by the norm compliance parameters of the agents, being $fulfill\_prob = 0.5$ and $inc\_prob = 0.4$ for all of them, whereas $h\_p$ varies from 0 to 14. Table 1 also shows the best AEI parameters' values $(N^*, PS^*)$ the institution has learnt by using genetic algorithms for each population $(fine^*_{right}, fine^*_{front}$ and $police^*)$.

In order to create the case base we have combined all values of the AEI parameters' values. We have considered to cover the range of all possible parameters' values ($fine_{front}$ and $fine_{right}$ values are in the interval $[0, 15]$, and $police$ values are in the interval $[0.8, 1]$). Thus, we have used $fine_{right} \in \{0, 3, 6, 9, 12, 15\}$, $fine_{front} \in \{0, 3, 6, 9, 12, 15\}$, and $police \in \{0.8, 0.9, 1\}$. Thus, overall we have

**Table 1.** Homogeneous agent populations employed to generate the case base in setting 1

| Populations | Pop1 | Pop2 | Pop3 | Pop4 | Pop5 | Pop6 | Pop7 |
|---|---|---|---|---|---|---|---|
| $fulfill\_prob$ | 0.5 | 0.5 | 0.5 | 0.5 | 0.5 | 0.5 | 0.5 |
| $h\_p$ | 0 | 3 | 5 | 8 | 10 | 12 | 14 |
| $inc\_prob$ | 0.4 | 0.4 | 0.4 | 0.4 | 0.4 | 0.4 | 0.4 |
| $fine^*_{right}$ | 2 | 8 | 13 | 12 | 13 | 14 | 15 |
| $fine^*_{front}$ | 3 | 13 | 8 | 13 | 11 | 13 | 15 |
| $police^*$ | 1 | 1 | 1 | 1 | 1 | 1 | 1 |

obtained 108 different AEI parameters' values. To create cases for this case base, we have simulated the seven populations in Table 1 with all 108 AEI parameters' values. So, we have generated a total of 756 cases for the seven agent populations. To create each case, we have simulated the traffic model during 2000 ticks. Once finished the simulation, we generated a case by saving the AEI parameters' values ($N^p$, $PS^p$) used in this simulation, the run-time behaviour for the 2000 ticks ($V, pop$), and the best AEI parameters' values ($N^{p*}$, $PS^{p*}$) corresponding to the population used in this simulation.

**Setting 2.** Here we have combined homogeneous and heterogeneous agent populations to generate the case base. In order to create heterogeneous agent populations (or societies), we have combined agents from different homogeneous populations in Table 1 with different proportions. Thus, to create cases for this case base, we have considered two types of heterogeneous populations. The first one has two kinds of agents that are equally distributed (50 percent each, i.e., 5 cars from a certain homogeneous populations and 5 cars from another one). The second heterogeneous population is composed of seventy percent agents of one kind and a thirty percent of another one. With the aim of covering the range of all $h\_p$ values, the agents we have combined to generate both types of heterogeneous populations are agents from populations Pop2, Pop4, Pop6, Pop7 in Table 1 (with $h\_p$ values 3,8,12 and 14 respectively). Thus, in total we have considered 32 populations, 16 (=4 × 4) populations equally distributed along with other 16 populations distributed in a 70-30 percentage. Notice that some population combinations are in fact homogeneous (e.g.combining Pop2 with Pop2). Furthermore, notice also that there are repeated populations (i.e., first combining Pop2 with Pop4 and afterwards Pop4 with Pop2). These repetitions are allowed to increase case coverage, because the same combination results in different cases when observing the overall behaviour (since agents' behaviour is based on probabilities). Likewise the first setting, to create the case base we have simulated each of 32 populations (homogeneous and heterogeneous) with the 108 different AEI parameters' values, generating 3456 cases overall. Cases from each 2000 ticks have also been created likewise in the first setting.

## 6    Empirical Evaluation

We have designed an experiment to test if an AEI is able to self-configure at run-time for different heterogeneous agent populations by using the proposed CBR approach. Figure 2 shows a scheme of an experiment using the case study in section 5. We run this experiment several times so that each experiment corresponds to the simulation of a different heterogeneous population. As Figure 2 shows, each experiment is composed of 20000 ticks that we divide into 10 steps. At each step (every 2000 ticks), the AEI checks the fulfilment of the institutional goals by means of its goal satisfaction degree. At the end of each step the AEI uses the CBR approach to change its parameters' values, if required. In other words, the institution analyses agents' behaviour along 2000 ticks. At the end

**AEI traffic (20000 ticks execution divided in 10 steps of 2000 ticks each)**

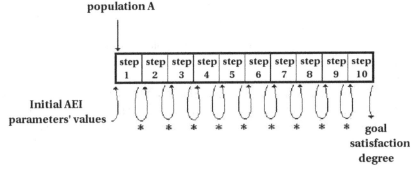

\* 1)The AEI checks the goal satisfaction degree in last 2000 ticks.
2)If required the AEI uses the CBR approach to change the
AEI parameters' values.

**Fig. 2.** Scheme of an AEI traffic experiment

of these ticks, the AEI generates a case from these observation, considering the behaviour of all agents as a single heterogeneous population, and tries to adapt accordingly. The length of this observation interval is a parameter that depends on the frequency of the changes in the environment and on agents' behaviour. Therefore, if societal changes happen with a higher frequency than this parameter, then the institution will consider the combination of all changes as a single —more complex— one.

In the context of CBR, the AEI generates each new problem case by considering its current configuration values and the population's run-time behaviour at the end of the current step. As mentioned above, after each step, the AEI decides if it needs to retrieve a case or not. The decision is based on the goal satisfaction and a threshold value. This threshold is computed as a desired goal satisfaction value $(G^*)$ with some deviation $(\epsilon)$. In our experiments, we have set $\epsilon = 0.04$ and $G^* = 0.67$, which corresponds to the minimum of the best goal satisfaction degrees for the populations in Table 1. Therefore, we set the threshold value to 0.63. If the goal satisfaction is greater than the threshold, the AEI keeps the same parameters during 2000 more ticks (that is, until the next step is reached). Otherwise (when the goal satisfaction is lower than the threshold) the AEI launches its CBR engine to retrieve the most similar case from its case base so that the AEI can use its solution (i.e., best parameters' values) at the next step.

In order to test if the AEI is able to self-adapt its regulations at run-time, we start each experiment with parameter values that prevent the institution from accomplishing its goals. Thus, for all experiments, the AEI starts with (0,0,0.8) parameters, causing no agent to follow the norms. These parameters correspond to no fine for both right-hand side and front priority norms, and a deployment of 80% of police agents. Thus, we expect the AEI to start with a low goal satisfaction degree. However, we also expect the AEI to be able to progress towards its goals in a few steps by retrieving a similar case whose parameters help the AEI to fulfil its institutional goals. Notice that if the AEI does not manage to retrieve a case whose parameters help it obtain a goal satisfaction higher than 0.63, the AEI will not adapt. Therefore, an AEI keeps retrieving cases trying to adapt better to each population it regulates. Thus, it is natural to think of computing the number of steps an AEI needs to adapt (i.e., to achieve its goals), namely to reach a goal satisfaction higher than the threshold value 0.63. At this aim, we compute the step at which an AEI achieves its goals for each experiment. We consider that an experiment is successful at some step if the goal satisfaction degree during the last 2000 ticks is equal or greater than the threshold value. Otherwise, we consider that the experiment is not successful at this step. That is, we consider that an experiment is successful at a specific step if the AEI fulfils its institutional goals during that step.

The experiment we have designed (see Figure 2) helps us testing if an AEI can retrieve a case out of the case base in order to adapt its parameters to different heterogeneous agent populations at run-time. To test our approach we have used different heterogeneous populations. As before, to create heterogeneous populations we have combined two different cars' behaviours. Cars to be combined are characterised by their norm compliance parameters, being $fulfill\_prob = 0.5$ and $inc\_prob = 0.4$ for all of them, whereas $h\_p$ varies from 0 to 14. In this work, trying to cover a wide range of heterogeneous populations, we have performed experiments combining cars with $h\_p \in \{2, 4, 8, 10, 12, 14\}$ in percentages of 50, 60, 70 and 80 percent with cars with $h\_p \in \{5, 9, 13\}$ in percentages of 50, 40, 30 and 20 percent respectively. We have used the 72 ($= 6 \times 4 \times 3$) heterogeneous populations resulting of all these combinations to test both experimental settings 1 and 2. It is important to notice that we are testing with different populations than the ones used to create the case base. In order to obtain statistical results we have run each experiment 50 times for each heterogeneous agent population. Thus, overall we have performed a total of 3600 experiments for each setting (50 runs of the 72 populations).

## 6.1   Results

**Setting 1.** In these experiments, although we use heterogeneous populations, the AEI retrieves cases from a case base created from homogeneous populations. The idea is to test how well the AEI adapts to heterogeneous agent populations when it uses cases created from information of homogeneous agent populations.

Figure 3 shows the percentage of successful experiments at each step from the total of 3600 experiments. In Figure 3 we can see how the curve of the percentage of successful experiments corresponding to setting 1 stabilises around 70 percent at step 5. Thus, we can state that, in these experiments, after five steps (10000 ticks) our AEI manages to adapt its parameters to approximately 70 percent of heterogeneous populations when using a case base created from homogeneous populations.

In order to analyse how many steps the AEI needs to adapt, we have computed for each experiment at which step the experiment starts to succeed (that is, the

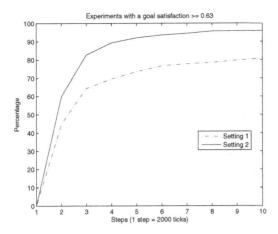

**Fig. 3.** Percentage of successful experiments

**Table 2.** Number of successful at each step

| Steps | 2 | 3 | 4 | 5 | 6 | 7 | 8 | 9 | 10 | No adaptation |
|---|---|---|---|---|---|---|---|---|---|---|
| **Setting 1 First time successful** | **1612** | **908** | **276** | **157** | **119** | **67** | **56** | **44** | **52** | **309** |
| Percentage | 44.8 | 25.2 | 7.7 | 4.3 | 3.3 | 1.9 | 1.6 | 1.2 | 1.4 | 8.6 |
| Accumulated percentage | 44.8 | 70 | 77.7 | 82 | 85.3 | 87.2 | 88.8 | 90 | 91.4 | |
| **Setting 2 First time successful** | **2156** | **900** | **261** | **103** | **60** | **40** | **31** | **16** | **7** | **26** |
| Percentage | 59.9 | 25 | 7.3 | 2.9 | 1.7 | 1 | 0.9 | 0.4 | 0.2 | 0.7 |
| Accumulated percentage | 59.9 | 89.4 | 92.2 | 95.1 | 96.8 | 97.8 | 98.7 | 99.1 | 99.3 | |

first step for which the AEI has obtained a goal satisfaction $>= 0.63$). Table 2 shows the number of experiments of this setting that were successful for the first time at each step, together with the corresponding percentage they represent and the accumulated percentage. We can see that, although at step three (6000 ticks) the AEI has adapted to a 70 percent of experiments, for 8.6 percent of the experiments the AEI did not manage to adapt its parameters (i.e., at ten steps the AEI obtained a goal satisfaction lower than 0.63).

**Setting 2.** Like in the previous setting, we have run a total of 3600 experiments using heterogeneous populations. However, in these experiments the AEI retrieves cases from a case base created from both homogeneous and heterogeneous populations.

Figure 3 shows the percentage of successful experiments at each step. We can see how the curve of the percentage of successful experiments corresponding to setting 2 stabilises around 90 percent at step 5. Comparing both curves, we can state that our AEI adapts better its parameters to heterogeneous populations when using a case base created from homogeneous and heterogeneous

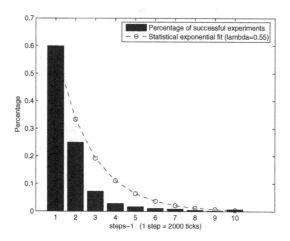

**Fig. 4.** Percentage of experiments initially successful

populations. That is because in this setting cases are more representative of heterogeneous populations than the previous setting's.

In the same way that in the previous setting, we have computed the required number of steps to reach adaptation for a given initial heterogeneous population of agents. The number of experiments of this setting that have been successful for the first time at each step are shown in Table 2, together with the corresponding percentage they represent and the accumulated percentage. In order to obtain statistical results, we have performed the chi-square test to test if the data (the percentage of experiments that have been successful for first time at each step) follows an exponential distribution. The chi-square test allows us to say that our data follows an exponential distribution with lambda = 0.55 (chi-square value=6.78, with a significance level of 0.01 and 4 degrees of freedom). Figure 4 shows the percentage of experiments that have started to succeed at each step and the fitted exponential[3]. Finally, we have computed the accumulated function of the fitted exponential in order to compute the number of steps an AEI needs to adapt to heterogeneous agent populations when using cases from homogeneous and heterogeneous populations. We have found that an AEI needs 6 steps (12000 ticks) to adapt for the very first time to the 95 percent of population -in the statistical sense- (significance level of 0.01).

## 7    Conclusions

This paper presents a Case-Base Reasoning approach which allows an AEI to self-adapt at run-time. This CBR approach performs a previous selection of cases where agent populations behave similarly and helps the AEI to retrieve the best

---

[3] Notice that we have performed a correction in the steps because in first step there is a zero percentage.

regulations at run time by identifying similar agents' behaviour. We have tested the retrieval process of the approach on a case study, where the AEI learns two traffic norms and the number of institutional agents it requires in order to adapt the norms and the performative structure to heterogeneous agent populations. Due to the importance of the base of cases to the adaptation, we have tested the approach in two settings, one for each case base. As to the first setting, we have used homogeneous agent populations to create the cases, whereas for the second setting we have used both homogeneous and heterogeneous agent populations. Since we have run experiments with heterogeneous agent populations, the case base of the second setting is more suitable for the AEI adaptation because cases are more representative (even though they come from different populations combined in different proportions). We have performed statistical analysis about the time (in steps of 2000 ticks) an AEI needs to adapt its parameters to heterogeneous populations. The results in this paper look promising since they show that our traffic AEI can indeed adapt to heterogeneous populations. However, the degree of adaptation depends on the case base an AEI uses. The adaptation to heterogeneous populations is better when the cases the AEI uses are generated from homogeneous and heterogeneous agent populations than when they are only generated from homogeneous agent populations. Statistical results show that an AEI needs 6 steps (12000 ticks) to adapt to the 95 percent of population (significance level of 0.01), when it uses cases generated from homogeneous and heterogeneous agent populations. Nevertheless, it is important to notice that distribution percentage does not need to be equal in order for a case to be representative. In fact, we have generated a case base of 32 populations with distributions 50%-50% and 70%-30% and tested 72 different populations with distributions 50%-50%, 60%-40%, 70%-30% and 80%-20%. Therefore, our experimental results show that there is no need for the case base to include all possible distributions in order to provide useful cases.

As future work, we plan to develop a more complex traffic network. Additionally, we are interested in studying how institutional parameters and agent strategies may co-evolve. Nevertheless, this will require to extend the agents so that they become able to adapt to institutional changes. We are also interested in modifying the approach to include institutional goals in the definition of the cases in order to allow the AEI to change its goals at run-time.

## Acknowledgements

The authors want to thank Pere García and Lluis Godo for their comments and advice. This work was partially funded by the Spanish Education and Science Ministry as part of the IEA (TIN2006-15662-C02-01) and the 2006-5-0I-099 projects. Research partially supported by the Generalitat de Catalunya under the grant 2005-SGR-00093 and the Spanish project "Agreement Technologies" (CONSOLIDER CSD2007-0022, INGENIO 2010). The first author enjoys an FPI grant (BES-2004-4335) from the Spanish Education and Science Ministry.

# References

1. Esteva, M.: Electronic Institutions: from specification to development, vol. 19. IIIA PhD Monography (2003)
2. North, D.C.: Institutions, Institutional Change and Economics Perfomance. Cambridge U. P (1990)
3. Bou, E., López-Sánchez, M., Rodríguez-Aguilar, J.A.: Adaptation of autonomic electronic institutions through norms and institutional agents. In: O'Hare, G.M.P., Ricci, A., O'Grady, M.J., Dikenelli, O. (eds.) ESAW 2006. LNCS (LNAI), vol. 4457, pp. 300–319. Springer, Heidelberg (2007)
4. Kephart, J.O., Chess, D.M.: The vision of autonomic computing. IEEE Computer 36(1), 41–50 (2003)
5. Norman, T.J., Preece, A., Chalmers, S., Jennings, N.R., Luck, M., Dang, V., Nguyen, T., Deora, V., Shao, J., Gray, A., Fiddian, N.: Conoise: Agent-based formation of virtual organisations. In: Research and Development in Intelligent SystemsXX: Proceedings of AI 2003, the Twenty-third SGAI International Conference on Innovative Techniques and Applications of Artificial Intelligence, pp. 353–366. Springer, Heidelberg (2003); 353–366 Best Paper Award at AI-2003, ©Springer Verlag
6. Excelente-Toledo, C.B., Jennings, N.R.: The dynamic selection of coordination mechanisms. Autonomous Agents and Multi-Agent Systems 9(1-2), 55–85 (2004)
7. Verhagen, H.: Norm Autonomous Agents. PhD thesis, Stockholm University (2000)
8. Sen, S., Airiau, S.: Emergence of norms through social learning. In: IJCAI, pp. 1507–1512 (2007)
9. Sierra, C., Sabater, J., Agustí, J., Garcia, P.: Integrating evolutionary computing and the sadde methodology. In: AAMAS 2003: Proceedings of the second international joint conference on Autonomous agents and multiagent systems, pp. 1116–1117. ACM Press, New York (2003)
10. Artikis, A., Kaponis, D., Pitt, J.: Dynamic Specifications of Norm-Governed Systems. In: Multi-Agent Systems: Semantics and Dynamics of Organisational Models. IGI Global (2009)
11. Kota, R., Gibbins, N., Jennings, N.: Decentralised structural adaptation in agent organisations. In: Vouros, G., Artikis, A., Stathis, K., Pitt, J. (eds.) OAMAS 2008. LNCS (LNAI), vol. 5368. Springer, Heidelberg (2008)
12. Hübner, J.F., Sichman, J.S., Boissier, O.: Using the 𝓜oise+ for a cooperative framework of mas reorganisation. In: Bazzan, A.L.C., Labidi, S. (eds.) SBIA 2004. LNCS, vol. 3171, pp. 506–515. Springer, Heidelberg (2004)
13. Gâteau, B., Boissier, O., Khadraoui, D., Dubois, E.: Moiseinst: An organizational model for specifying rights and duties of autonomous agents. In: Gleizes, M.P., Kaminka, G.A., Nowé, A., Ossowski, S., Tuyls, K., Verbeeck, K. (eds.) EUMAS, Koninklijke Vlaamse Academie van Belie voor Wetenschappen en Kunsten, pp. 484–485 (2005)
14. van der Vecht, B., Dignum, F., Meyer, J.J.C., Neef, M.: A dynamic coordination mechanism using adjustable autonomy. In: Coordination, Organization, Institutions and Norms in agent systems (COIN@Durham 2007). Co-held in Multi-Agent Logics, Languages, and Organisations Federated Workshop, Durham, UK (2007)
15. Hoogendoorn, M.: Adaptation of organizational models for multi-agent systems based on max flow networks. In: Veloso, M.M. (ed.) IJCAI, pp. 1321–1326 (2007)
16. Luke, S., Cioffi-Revilla, C., Panait, L., Sullivan, K.: Mason: A new multi-agent simulation toolkit. In: Proceedings of the 2004 SwarmFest Workshop, p. 8 (2004)

17. Camurri, M., Mamei, M., Zambonelli, F.: Urban traffic control with co-fields. In: Proc. of E4MAS Workshop at AAMAS 2006, pp. 11–25 (2006)
18. Bazzan, A.L.C., de Oliveira, D., Klügl, F., Nagel, K.: Effects of co-evolution in a complex traffic network. In: Proceedings of the AAMAS 2007 Workshop on Adaptive and Learning Agents (ALAg 2007) (2007)
19. Ros, R., Veloso, M.: Executing Multi-Robot Cases through a Single Coordinator. In: Proc. of Autonomous Agents and Multiagent Systems, pp. 1264–1266 (2007)
20. Aamodt, A., Plaza, E.: Case-based reasoning: Foundational issues, methodological variations, and system approaches. AI Commun. 7(1), 39–59 (1994)

# Adaptation of Voting Rules in Agent Societies

Hugo Carr and Jeremy Pitt

Department of Electrical & Electronic Engineering,
Imperial College London, Exhibition Road, London SW7 2BT, UK
h.carr@imperial.ac.uk, j.pitt@imperial.ac.uk

**Abstract.** We are concerned with multi-agent systems which are open, volatile, and decentralised, and which require collective use of a limited common resource. We define an institution to regulate access to the resource through a vote. We then investigate the adaptation of the voting rules to deal with the volatility of the agent presence, with the aim of achieving some semblance of 'satisfaction' without depleting the resource. Progress towards implementation of an experimental testbed, for animating this type of multi-agent system, is described and preliminary results are presented.

## 1   Introduction

Let $\mathcal{M}$ be a multi-agent system (MAS) which is *open*. Since $\mathcal{M}$ is open, then the agents are heterogeneous, may have competing and even conflicting goals, and intereactions between them may have unpredicted and/or undesirable outcomes. Now let $\mathcal{M}$ be *volatile*, in the sense that agents join and leave the system, where both arrival and departure may also be unpredicted. Finally, let $\mathcal{M}$ be *decentralised*, i.e. it has no centralised mechanisms for either knowledge or control. In other words, each agent only has partial knowledge of the environment and limited control over it, and there is no entity which has either full knowledge, or total control.

Now suppose that the goal of $\mathcal{M}$ is to provide a service, either to some external agency or to each agent individually, that can only be successfully supplied collectively and could not be supplied by each acting individually. Furthermore, suppose that service delivery, and the system functionality, is dependent on a resource that everybody uses but nobody owns; moreover that resource is, partially or wholly, stocked by contributions from the members of $\mathcal{M}$. This abstract description is representative of many situations where resources are limited, for example, ad hoc networks, traffic management systems and distributed computing problems.

In domains of human activity, faced with such a situation, either the population fails to protect the resource, for example by over-consumption or under-contribution, and the whole system fails; or they construct an *institution*, with roles, actions, rules and sanctions, a set of agreed conventions for managing the common resource and undertaking collective action. The notion of an institution has been introduced to multi-agent systems in a number of ways, either by

G. Vouros et al. (Eds.): OAMAS 2008, LNAI 5368, pp. 36–53, 2009.

organisational models, such as [9, 11] and electronic institutions [27], or norm-governed systems, such as [3], which are derived from the study of social and legal systems.

Although we choose to model $\mathcal{M}$ as an institution, the central problem remains: to ensure that the institution for $\mathcal{M}$, with $\mathcal{M}$ being open, volatile and decentralised, continues to operate in the presence of any number of its members with satisfactory 'fairness' and/or quality of service, yet tolerates the absence of any number (possibly all) of its members, without losing consistency.

Phrased like this, the problem is not dissimilar to the problem of designing and implementing rules and protocols for distributed systems operating in an asynchronous environment, as established by Lamport [16, 17]. However, while we need to leverage such results, in the more general context of $\mathcal{M}$, we also need to take into account the set of common problems which confront any effort to cope with efforts to organise collective actions: Ostrom [20], for example, specifies coping with free riding, solving commitment problems, supplying new institutions, and monitoring individual compliance with a set of rules.

Ostrom also identified a number of key properties whereby groups which formed institutions to organise and regulate their behaviour did so most successfully. Of these, two were, firstly, that the individuals affected by the rules can participate in the modification of the rules; and, secondly, that the group members (rather than any external agency) had the 'right' to devise and modify their own rules. In other words, a key pre-requisite for $\mathcal{M}$ is *participatory adaptation*: the ability of the group members to change the rules according to their own requirements, based on an awareness of the rules and of the effects of rules.

This paper aims to present our motivation for investigating organised adaptation in agent societies, but also provides an illustration of our approach through participatory adaptation of voting rules for multi-agent systems like $\mathcal{M}$. We expand further on the background and motivation for this work in Section 2, and then describe our experimental scenario in Section 3. Progress towards implementation of an experimental testbed, for animating this type of multi-agent system, is described in Section 4, the results of which can be found in Section 5, and finally we summarise and draw some conclusions in Section 6.

# 2    Background and Motivation

## 2.1    Background

Networked computers are the driving force of modern industry and commerce, providing powerful, and inter-connected, infrastructures for business organisations (through eCommerce, holonic manufacturing and agile enterprises). Increasingly, there is an emphasis on wireless communications, with particular attention drawn to pervasive computing and autonomic communications, and the types of ad hoc and sensor networks required to realise their respective objectives. Research in networked computing also needs to take into consideration the three following features:

- Local information, partial knowledge and inconsistent union: What each network node 'sees' is the result of actions by (possibly millions) of actors, some
  of which are not known, and even those actions which are known, the actor's
  motive may be unknown. Moreover, what a node 'thinks' it 'sees' may not
  be consistent with the 'opinion' of other nodes.
- Decentralised control: it follows from this that there is no single central
  authority that is controlling or co-ordinating the actions of others. The emphasis is on local decision-making based on locally available information and
  the perception of locally witnessed events.
- Heterogeneous constituency: the internal architectures of this 'population'
  (each member's needs or strategies) may not be publicly known; furthermore
  each member is self-interested (i.e. they do not necessarily share a notion of
  global utility); and as a result the members' interaction may be subject to
  unanticipated outcomes.

From these features, it follows that in the absence of an individual node with
complete knowledge and power and a uniform, compliant and predictable 'population', there is no perfect form of government: therefore the next best thing is a
government prepared to modify its policies according to the needs, requirements
and expressed opinions of its 'population'. A group of nodes conforming to a
mutually agreed set of governing conventions, and institutions for forming those
conventions, satisfies a partial requirement for a society (other requirements including language and culture).

In other words, social organisation is both a necessary and sufficient condition of any programmable ad hoc peer-to-peer network of autonomous nodes,
for which the additional demand to have sufficient intelligence or complexity
to understand and follow the conventions suggests these are, in the software
engineering sense, agents. Thus we are concerned with societies of agents.

Furthermore, if this agent society intrudes into or impinges on the 'real' world
of conventional facts, then understanding and applying conventional rules is both
the requirement for and consequence of any networked computing system which
impacts on legal or commercial relationships between real-world entities (people
or organisations). In such circumstances, it is also necessary to acknowledge
that 'things can go wrong', whether from accident, necessity or malice. However,
instead of designing to eliminate error, we have to accept the potential for error,
and seek instead mechanisms of recovery.

All this means that the agent society will have to be open, and not just in
the trivial sense that agents may join and leave the system at any time, but
also in the sense of Artikis et al [3] (heterogeneous components, unpredictable
outcomes, and sub-ideality), and in the sense of, and following the principles of,
Popper's Open Society [22]. Popper's philosophy tried to identify the positive
aspects of democracy. These included:

- Accountability: unlike object-oriented distributed systems, which aim for
  location transparency (i.e. method invocation on a remote or local object
  is indistinguishable to the caller), in agent societies location is significant;

with corresponding requirements to represent socio-legal relationships like delegation, mandate, responsibility, liability and sanction;

- Market Economy: interactions between agents involve economic activity and profit/loss can occur as a result: for example transactions with exchange of items of value in an e-commerce system, contractual access control to (limited) resources in an ad hoc network, and so on. An essential aspect of such interaction is trust;
- The Rule of Law: for Popper, this was taken as a theoretical limit on the power of government; we are concerned with the performance of designated acts by empowered individuals which establish conventional facts related to norms (permissions, obligations, and indeed powers);
- No universal truth: the idea that 'today can be different from tomorrow', in other words, that knowledge and laws are not immutable, and so it is possible for 'truth' to be relative (a matter of opinion) and for the laws to be adapted (by the action of empowered agents performing designated acts, as above).

These observations provide the motivation for our research programme, outlined in the next section.

## 2.2   Motivation: Research Programme

We therefore propose to study the logical and computational foundations of the open agent society: socially-organised, norm-governed, distributed multi-agent systems.

An Open Agent Society is a distributed computer system or network where the relationships and dependencies between components is a microcosm of a human society, and therefore includes aspects of communication, conventional rules, memory, self-determination, and self-organisation. An Open Agent Society is therefore an appropriate concept for designing and running a group of networked nodes where the links between the nodes are, conceptually, representative of social relations, communicative acts performed by nodes have conventional (rather than physical) significance, and, in the absence of any hierarchy, a timely and appropriate response to prevailing operational conditions requires collective action which might only be partially successful. Such networks have potentially many applications, in, for example, ad hoc networks, vehicular networks, sensor networks, enterprise networks and virtual organisations.

Our approach to specifying and implementing *participatory adaptation* in open agent societies is based on developing a logical framework for parameterising adaptation, based on:

- Rules of Social Exchange. $\mathcal{M}$, being open, will require agents to gain knowledge over time by exchanging information with each other. Each agent must therefore be capable of reliable opinion formation, based on the opinions gathered from the contacts in their own social networks. Processes of belief revision, belief merging, judgement aggregation and truth tracking are therefore important [13, 24];

- Rules of Social Choice. $\mathcal{M}$ consists of heterogeneous, self-interested agents that can have conflicting preferences in decision-making situations; these agents' preferences can be aggregated by taking votes over potential outcomes. In practice, an election is held, and the winning candidate is declared to be the agreed choice [6, 21];
- Rules of Social Order. $\mathcal{M}$ consists of agents whose actions have a conventional significance (according to the social rules of an institution); actions are therefore norm-governed. This requires characterising the permissions, obligations and (institutional) powers of each agent to determine which actions are valid, meaningful, legal, and so on [3, 4, 21].

We then propose to investigate algorithms for adaptation within this formal framework, which may be based on case-based reasoning, machine learning, etc. In the next section, we describe a framework as a first step in realising this programme of work; prior to that we review some aspects of related research.

### 2.3   Related Research

The investigation into adaptive, agent-based systems is not, of course, new. However, the approach taken in this paper is in the 'tradition' of norm-governed multi-agent systems [3, 4, 21], where the emphasis is on features such as institutional power and conventional rules, and our concern here is the adaption of the conventional rules. Since most other adaptive agent systems don't have this concept, what actually gets adapted is rather different in nature.

One approach to adaptation is to adapt the agents themselves. [10], for example, present what they call a tuning machine which allows BDI-agents to 'tune' their plans according to individual, collective or social commitments. However, this is adaptation of agent *internals* (albeit with respect to an 'external' commitment), and what we are concerned with is the adaptation of the *external* rules.

In contrast, then, [12], [14], and [9] all concentrate on the adaptation of organisational models. In [12] the adaptation is of the inter-dependence graph between agents according to load and importance to support fault-tolerance; while in [14] and [9], the adaptation is of (depending on the organisational theory) the assignment of agents to groups, roles and goals. In [14] the adaptation is a function of a mapping of the organisation model into a max flow network and solving for the max flow; and in [9] the adaptation is of the assignment, of agent and roles to goals, according to an evaluation function which assesses the 'quality' of the current assignment. In all these cases, though, the emphasis is on adaptation of the functional assignment, and not of the process (or rules) by which that assignment is achieved.

In [7] and [18], the object of adaptation is the communication protocol. [7] presents a way of adapting protocols according to context, or the preferences of agents in a given context. Their mechanism is based on transformers, which encode a generic way of converting one protocol in another form to handle this requirement. [18] uses Coloured-Petri Nets to give a formal semantics to open protocols, a flexible method of inter-agent communication lying somewhere between structured message exchange and free message passing. This is closer to the kind of adaptation with which we are concerned, interpreting individual and sequences of messages as following some rules, and being dynamically able to change those rules.

The work most closely related to our concerns here is in Electronic Institutions (EIs). An EI specifies rules (norms) determining what agents are permitted or forbidden to do, in which contexts, and so on. Bou et al [5], for example, have noted that there is a requirement for EIs (or rather the members of EIs) to be able to alter the rules and regulations to adapt to the changing needs and goals of the constituent agents. The basic mechanism proposed by Bou et al to modify norms is a normative transition function. Such a transition function maps a set of norms (and goals) into a new set of norms: changing a norm requires changing its parameters, or its effect, or both. However, in EI there is is a separate organisational agent that is watching the behaviours and changing the norms accordingly. For us, the institution does not exist at all: it is a convention agreed upon by the participating or constituent members, by which certain individuals are empowered to change, rather than learn, the norms.

## 3  Scenario and Experimental Set-Up

We will consider the following scenario for some simple initial experiments in organised adaptation exploiting aspects of this framework.

Let $\mathcal{M}$ be a multi-agent system consisting of a set of agents $A$. The system operates on a possibly infinite sequence of time slices $t_0, t_1, \ldots, t_n, \ldots$ At each time slice, an agent may be present or absent, and the set of agents present at any $t$ is denoted by $A'_t$, $A'_t \subseteq A$. To satisfy each of their individual goals, each agent $a \in A'$ offers, at each time slice, an allocation of resources $O^a_t$, and requests, at each time, an allocation of resources $R^a_t$. We stipulate that, for all $a \in A'$, $R^a_t > O^a_t$: in other words, they can only satisfy each of their individual goals by mutual sharing of their collective resources.

It follows that not all of the individual requests can be satisfied without 'bankrupting' the system. Therefore, at each $t$, the set of present agents $A'_t$ take a vote on who should have their resource request satisfied. If an agent $a$ receives a number of votes greater than a threshold $\tau_t$ then its request is granted. The problem then is that:

- if $\tau_t$ is too low and there are many agents present, too many resources will be allocated and the system is over-subscribed; and
- if $\tau_t$ is too high and there are too few agents present, too few resources will be allocated and the individual agents will be increasingly dissatisfied.

The implicit, unwritten system objective is to ensure that the available resources oscillates around some positive value and the agents are in some sense pareto optimal, rather than either of the two extremes: firstly, satisfied agents but bankrupt system (tragedy of the commons), so the system dies anyway; and secondly excess resources but dissatisfied agents which consequently leave the system, also causing the system to die.

The challenge then is for the agents to agree – again by a vote – a new value for $\tau$ in time slice $t + 1$ based on their prediction of how many agents will be present, available resources, and so on. In other words, they are adapting the rule (informally, for a formal expression of the normative rule, see [2, 21]):

*the resource controller is obliged to grant access to the resource to a requester, if the number of votes for the requester is greater than or equal to $\tau$*

by manipulating the value of $\tau$.

Formally, then (dropping the subscript $t$ where it is implicit from context), the external state of multi-agent system $\mathcal{M}$ is specified, at a time slice $t$, by:

$$\mathcal{M}_t = \langle A_t, \rho_t, B, \mathbf{f}_t, \tau_t \rangle$$

where:

$$A = \text{the set of agents}$$
$$\rho : A \rightarrow \{0, 1\}$$
$$B : \mathbb{Z}$$
$$\mathbf{f} : A \rightarrow \mathbb{N}_0$$
$$\tau : \mathbb{N}$$

Intuitively, $\rho$ is the presence function, i.e. if $\rho(a) = 1 \leftrightarrow a \in A'$; $B$ is the 'bank', indicating the overall system resources available; and $\mathbf{f}$ is the allocation function, which gives the number of resources allocated to each $a$ in this time slice. Obviously, if $\rho(a) = 0$ then $\mathbf{f}(a) = 0$; otherwise the value is given by the vote over allocation of resources. This vote depends on $\tau$, the threshold, i.e. if an agent gets a number of votes equal to or greater than $\tau$ then the agent is entitled to its resource request, otherwise $\rho(a) = 0$.

The system operation is given by the following cycle. We assume, through some role assignment protocol, that some agent has been elected to the role of resource controller. Then, at each time slice $t$:

$A'_t = \{a | a \in A \wedge \rho_t(a) = 1\}$
each agent $a \in A'_t$ offers resources $O^a_t$
each agent $a \in A'_t$ requests resources $R^a_t$
each agent $a \in A'_t$ votes for one other agent in $A'_t$
$\mathbf{f}_t$ is computed from the votes cast and $\tau$
$B$ is updated according to the resources allocated
each agent updates its satisfaction rating (see below)
the resource controller proposes a value for $\tau_{t+1}$
each agent $a \in A'_t$ votes for/against this proposal

The idea is that each agent makes a prediction of the number of agents likely to be present in the next time slice, if they agree with the resource controller they vote in favour, otherwise against. In practice we expect this version of the voting protocol may have several rounds before a majority of the agents accepts it, with a maximum number of rounds to ensure termination.

To participate in this system, each agent then requires the following data and functions (we drop the superscript $a$ since it is implicit from context):

$\langle$ Name           $a$,

| | |
|---|---|
| Presence | $p : t \rightarrow \{0, 1\}$, |
| Resources offered | $O : t \rightarrow \mathbb{N}$, |
| Resources required | $R : t \rightarrow \mathbb{N}$, |
| Satisfaction | $\sigma \in [0..1]$, |
| Satisfaction Increase Rate | $\alpha \in [0..1]$, |
| Satisfaction Decrease Rate | $\beta \in [0..1]$, |
| v | voting function which maps a list of agent/resource requests to a member of $A'$ |
| $\pi$ | a set of predictor functions which compute $\lvert A'_{t+1} \rvert$ |

$\rangle$

Each agent uses **v** to compute its preferred candidate for receiving resources in this time slice, and the set of predictor functions $\pi$ to compute how many agents it thinks will be present in the next time slice, which will be used to inform which way it will vote on the recommended value $\tau$ in the next time slice.

$$\pi = \{\pi_1, \pi_2, \pi_3 \cdots \pi_n\}$$

$$prediction = \sum_{i=1}^{n} w_i \pi_i$$

Where $w_i$ is a weight corresponding to the past success an agent has had using $\pi_i$. We take $\Pi$ to be an infinite set of predictors as specified in section 4, and assign the finite subset $\pi$ to each agent similar to the solution proposed in [1] regarding the the El Farol Bar problem.

'Satisfaction' can be modelled based on election outcomes. Here, $\alpha$ corresponds to the satisfaction rate, $\beta$ to the dissatisfaction rate, and $0 < \sigma_0 < 1, 0 < \alpha < 1, 0 < \beta < 1$, where $\sigma_0$ is the initial satisfaction. Satisfaction in a time slice is dependent on whether resources are allocated, in which case overall satisfaction is increased according to:

$$\sigma_{t+1} = \sigma_t + (1 - \sigma_t) \cdot \alpha$$

or not, in which case overall satisfaction is decreased according to:

$$\sigma_{t+1} = \sigma_t - \sigma_t \cdot \beta$$

The core voting protocol has been described in [21]. However, that work was primarily focused on characterising the concept of 'enfranchisement' in normative terms, with formalising rules of order [25], and its animation in the Event Calculus [15]. The object of the protocol was to reach a 'yes/no' decision in a committee meeting for example. We note that we have *two* variants of this basic protocol to instantiate in this scenario. The first variant is the vote is taken on which other agent should receive resources. We have chosen initially to count just the single expressed preference, although more sophisticated alternatives are possible; for example, single transferable vote, multiple rounds (with the 'winner' of each round removed for the next). Whichever option we chose has to take into account the resource allocation threshold, though. The second variant is, as mentioned above, is the vote to fix this threshold. This is a multi-round vote designed to converge on a preferred value for $\tau$ in the next time slice.

One issue that could be considered in a programme of experiments with this scenario is the possibility of manipulation of the outcome. Manipulation of elections has been the subject of study for a long time, and particularly in the domain of computational social choice, with a number of results that can be taken into consideration when designing a voting protocol, e.g. [8, 23, 26]. This is one aspect of rules of social choice that the formal framework will have to take into account; another is the rules of social exchange that are required which might inform or influence agents for whom to cast their votes.

## 4 Experimental Testbed

### 4.1 PreSage

PreSage is a simulator and animator for agent societies [19] based on discrete time in which simulations can be designed by creating subclasses of abstract objects provided by the programming environment. Agents act and interact by creating and implementing intentions, and communicating through the messaging system. These tools facilitate the construction of a volatile, decentralised system of heterogeneous agents.

PreSage operates based on simulation cycles as opposed to an analogue-time event-driven system. Event-driven agents save processor time by sleeping until they are scheduled to execute an intention, but it is only then that they are able to change their perception of the environment. Discrete-time systems such as PreSage give agents the opportunity to act and respond to changing conditions every cycle. This makes the platform well-suited for the implementation of the time-sliced operation of the multi-agent system specified in the previous section.

### 4.2 Agent Architecture

As agents must be able to guess future system values, each will contain a set of predictors. However, modelling a society of agents who have access to the same information can be problematic when they are all given the same reasoning capacities. With identical inputs, agents will inevitably draw the same conclusions and behave as a homogeneous population. We instead employ a set of predictors $\Pi$, constructed using a randomly weighted average of historical values.

Each voter also contains a personalised activity profile which represents whether it wishes to participate in an election. The profile is only queried at the beginning of a timeslice and without loss of generality we can assume that an agent does not leave or fail during a timeslice. The profile of an agent has been defined according to the satisfaction of an agent, and whether or not the agent was active in the previous cycle. This introduces an incomplete knowledge of the system, and avoids the issue of identical inputs.

A bias has been enforced such that if an agent was active in a previous cycle it is less likely to switch states than an agent who wasn't; this is further influenced by how successful an agent has been in the system. The activity profile is formed in real-time using three variables, the probability $p$ that an agent will change from inactive to active, the probability $q$ that an agent will switch from active to inactive, and the satisfaction $\sigma$. If we take $x$ to be uniformly distributed between 0 and 1, then if an agent is active in the current timeslice it will switch to inactive if $x.\sigma < q$; and if it is inactive it will switch to active if $x.\sigma < p$.

The outcome of this is that we cannot accurately predict the presence function; but over time some agents' predictors will perform better and will in turn be active more often and for longer. In future work we might experiment with reputation effects based on accuracy and continuity metrics.

### 4.3   Voting Protocol

Robert's Rules of Order [25] defines an election in terms of a chair, a proposer, a seconder and a voter. This is a standard foundation for a flexible election, but superfluous to the needs of this experiment. In our case, an election is initiated by the chair but the motion itself is implicit in the context of the system, therefore requiring neither a proposer nor a seconder.

In order to accommodate a society of voting agents we implemented a structure based on a simplified plurality voting protocol. From the standby state, the protocol moves to the subscribing state in which agents can sign up to vote. If the election is attended by an insufficient number of voters, the chair can cancel the election; otherwise, the ballot is opened and voting begins. The protocol concludes by closing the ballot and declaring the result.

### 4.4   Simulation Timeslice

We have designed the simulator to hold consecutive elections, as a parallel system significantly hampers an agent's ability to make predictions. Each timeslice is initiated once the chair sends a start-election message to the entire population. To save processor time, these messages are also sent to neighbouring agents, so everyone has a list of participants for the current timeslice. The chair then asks the voters to make public the amount of resources the voter is offering and how many they are requesting should they win the election. Participants require this information to improve their predictions with regards to the next time-slice.

Once all information has been made available, agents can check how well their predictors are working and re-rank them accordingly. The chair will then open the ballot and agents can start to cast their votes. Voting information can be used to ascertain whether malevolent parties are trying to manipulate the system to distribute too many resources for short term benefit. Our experiments will involve a set of agents who are either responsible, selfish or overly cautious and whose aim it will be to change the system rules to maximise their respective perceptions of utility.

Responsible agents have a duty to vote for a value of $\tau$ which will result in a stockpile level as close to zero as possible. This requires predictions of the amounts of available resources in the system. This can be broken down using three sets of predictors which keep track of the average amount of resources requested by an agent $R$, the average amount of resources offered by an agent $O$, and the active population $|A'_t|$.

If we have predictions for each of these values and know the current level of resources stockpiled by the system $S$, a reasonable value of $\tau$ might be calculated in the following way, where $L$ the number of agents to whom the system can afford to give resources based on current predictions:

$$L = \frac{S + O.\,|A'_t|}{R}$$

We can take this further to express a desired probability that any one active agent receives resources

$$p = \frac{S + O.\,|A'_t|}{|A'_t|\,.R}$$

The question is how do we ensure that $\tau$ provides us with this probability. As $\tau$ is discrete, we can only get as close as possible by modelling the election using a binomial distribution, where $X$ corresponds to the number of votes received by an agent, and we assume the probability of receiving a vote is uniformly distributed over the population.

$$X \sim Bin\left(|A'_t|, \frac{1}{|A'_t|}\right)$$

$$P(X \geq \tau) = p$$
$$P(X < \tau) = 1 - p$$

$$\Pr(X \leq \tau) = \sum_{j=0}^{\tau-1} \binom{|A'_t|}{j} \left(\frac{1}{|A'_t|}\right)^j \left(1 - \left(\frac{1}{|A'_t|}\right)\right)^{|A'_t|-j}.$$

To find the value of $\tau$ necessary for a given probability, we can approximate this binomial model with the normal distribution and then invert the cumulative distribution function.

$$\Phi^{-1}_{\mu,\sigma^2}(p) = \mu + \sigma\sqrt{2}.\mathrm{erf}^{-1}\left(2\left(\frac{1}{|A'_t|}\right) - 1\right)$$
$$= \tau$$

where

$$\mathrm{erf}(x) = \frac{2}{\sqrt{\pi}} \int_0^x e^{-t^2}\,dt.$$

However, the inversion of this function must be done numerically and has not yet been implemented in the simulation. As such, we have settled for a simpler decision where agents vote for an incremented $\tau$ value if the prediction indicates that the pool of resources will be positive after the agents have completed their offers, otherwise the vote will be for a decremented $\tau$. This should result in an stockpile of resources oscillating about a value just below zero.

Once the $\tau$-votes have been collected agents can then vote for one another to receive resources, voting is then closed and subsequent submissions are ignored. Messages are then sent to the active population including a list of the winners according to the value of $\tau$ decided in the previous timeslice. The chair must check at this point whether the resource debt is too great and the system is 'broken'. It is in this way that we enforce the tragedy of the commons. The value of $\tau$ for the next timeslice is then calculated by taking the average of the votes while bounding candidate values sensibly to prevent outlier manipulation.

Finally, as the agents receive the list of winners, they update their satisfaction values. Currently, we increase satisfaction if an agent wins, and decrease otherwise. This is somewhat blunt, and can later be improved by having agents take a more philosophical approach by taking into account how well the system is performing globally as well as at the agent's local level.

## 5   Results

### 5.1   Analytic Results

In order to check that the system was stable we performed a number of analyses, the most important of which regarded the activity profiles of the agents. As specified in section 4 the population of $N$ agents enter and leave the system with probabilities of $p$ and $q$ respectively. This can be shown to reduce to a Markov chain where $Active_t$ and $Inactive_t$ refer to the active and inactive populations at time $t$

$$\begin{bmatrix} Inactive_t(1-q) + Active_t p \\ Inactive_t q + Active_t(1-p) \end{bmatrix} = \begin{bmatrix} Inactive_{t+1} \\ Active_{t+1} \end{bmatrix}$$

$$\begin{bmatrix} (1-q) & p \\ q & (1-p) \end{bmatrix} \begin{bmatrix} Inactive_t \\ Active_t \end{bmatrix} = \begin{bmatrix} Inactive_{t+1} \\ Active_{t+1} \end{bmatrix}$$

By finding the eigenvector corresponding to the unity eigenvalue we can get the steady state population of the active population

$$Active_\infty = N \frac{p}{p+q}$$

We then ran repeated simulations to demonstrate the population of the system tended towards this steady state value in PreSage. One such representation is shown in Figure 1. It is from this foundation that we can run our main experiments to investigate if the combination of agent type and their adaptation of $\tau$ disrupt or reinforce the convergence to a steady state. Because the agent population is initialised randomly, each run is based on an essentially different starting population, but a similar pattern was observed for each run.

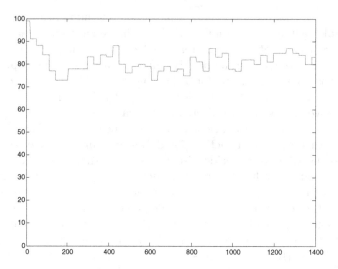

**Fig. 1.** Active agents in a satisfied population of 100 agents, with $p = 0.08$, and $q = 0.02$

## 5.2   Overly Cautious and Selfish Agents

Overly cautious agents vote for a value of $\tau$ that is too high, resulting in very few agents receiving resources from the system. This results in a fall in satisfaction, and reduction per election of resources being offered by agents. This dynamic can be observed in figure 2, where we note that the irregularity at time 800 can be matched on the curve of the active population.

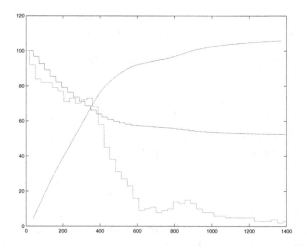

**Fig. 2.** Results of an overly cautious population of 100 agents, where resources increase to a limit ($\approx 110$), and satisfaction steadily decreases causing an attendance of almost zero by the end of the simulation

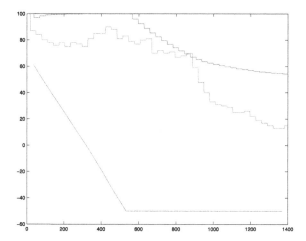

**Fig. 3.** Results of a selfish population of 100 agents, where resources are squandered linearly to the point where the system breaks, resulting in an initially high satisfaction ($\approx 100$), but an inevitable fall in satisfaction and participation when no more resources are given

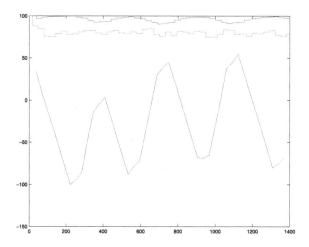

**Fig. 4.** Results of a responsible population of 100 agents, where the resources oscillate slowly about about a value just below zero, and the attendance ($\approx 80$) and satisfaction ($\approx 95$) remain high

Selfish agents vote for a low value of $\tau$ resulting in a distribution of resources to whoever requests them. This yields a highly satisfied population, until of course the system breaks, and no resources are distributed at all. Figure 3 clearly illustrates the point at which the system breaks. The knock on effect can be seen

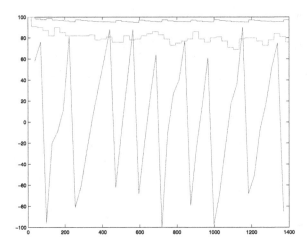

**Fig. 5.** Results of a population of 100 agents under a dictatorship, where the resources oscillate about zero, and the attendance ($\approx 80$) and satisfaction ($\approx 95$) remain high

on the other two curves, where the satisfaction takes a dramatic fall, and the agents begin to withdraw from the system, until only a handful remain.

### 5.3   Responsible Agents Versus a Dictatorship

Responsible agents use the more sophisticated method of prediction described in section 4. Figure 4 shows an oscillating stockpile limit. Looking at the other curves, we see that satisfaction is negatively proportional to the amount of resources in stock, which was what we expected.

We use Figure 5 to put Figure 4 in context by demonstrating how a system with complete knowledge would operate. Although the resources curves have been scaled to fit the graphs, we note that the satisfaction and active population curves are largely the same. The dictatorship is only superior in providing an smaller oscillation frequency and amplitude of the stockpiled resources.

## 6   Summary and Conclusions

In this paper, we have described:

- a proposed framework for defining participatory adaptation in open agent societies, based on rules of social order, social choice, and social exchange;
- a scenario, common to several multi-agent system applications (for example, in mobile ad hoc networks, vehicular networks, and virtual organisations) of collective access to a limited common resource, and given a formal model of this scenario;
- progress towards the implementation of an experimental testbed for this scenario, based on the multi-agent animation platform PreSage.

Preliminary results indicate that with overly cautious agents or selfish agents, the system 'self-destructs', but co-operative agents can achieve a 'steady-state' equilibrium using an altruistic adaptation of the voting rules.

In conclusion, we have started to converge three areas of study:

- norm-governed systems: a norm-governed multi-agent system is to any set of interacting agents whose behaviour is (intended to be) regulated by norms, where a norm is a rule which prescribes organisational concepts like permission, obligation, sanction, and so on;
- mechanism design: the mapping of a set of expressed preferences into an outcome; in particular we note that one way of effecting this is to take a vote;
- ad hoc networks: the principles behind self-creation, self-maintenance and self-regulation of a set of mobile nodes into an ad hoc network, which have many of the features discussed above.

To fully realise the logical framework proposed, there is a fourth area of study to be introduced, based on the rules of social exchange. These are the rules which allow opinions to be exchanged as part of the function of deciding for whom to vote. We believe that the properties of PreSage, which allow considerable re-use and re-configuration, and facilitate introduction of an opinion exchange protocol.

Finally, we note that there are interesting possibilities offered by this scenario for the exploration of a limited form of "law making". For example, the EU FP6 project ALIS is investigating the development of an intelligent legal system which applies principles of game theory and computational logic to four levels of jurisprudence: regulatory compliance, conflict prevention, alternative dispute resolution, and law making. This latter is intrinsically difficult, requiring a significant number of procedural steps, the involvement of several institutions, and a degree of knowledge representation and reasoning that presents a considerable challenge to the current state-of-the-art in Artificial Intelligence and computational logic. However, a scenario and testbed such as this does offer the opportunity to constrain the complexity and explore some aspects of the process of making law – as we have done here, by defining an institution and enabling the institution's members to adapt the rules.

## Acknowledgements

The first author is supported by a UK EPSRC studentship. The second author is supported by the EU FP6 Project ALIS 027958. Some of this work has emerged from discussions with colleagues: grateful thanks for this is acknowledged. Thanks for support is also due to Alexander Artikis, Lloyd Kamara, Brendan Neville, and Daniel Ramirez-Cano. Thanks also for the useful comments from the anonymous reviewers.

# References

1. Arthur, W.: Inductive reasoning and bounded rationality. American Economic Review 84, 406–411 (1994)
2. Artikis, A., Kamara, L., Pitt, J., Sergot, M.: A protocol for resource sharing in norm-governed ad hoc networks. In: Leite, J., Omicini, A., Torroni, P., Yolum, P. (eds.) DALT 2004. LNCS, vol. 3476, pp. 221–238. Springer, Heidelberg (2005)
3. Artikis, A., Pitt, J., Sergot, M.: Animated specifications of computational societies. In: Castelfranchi, C., Johnson, L. (eds.) Proceedings of the First International Conference on Autonomous Agents and Multi-Agent Systems (AAMAS), pp. 1053–1062. ACM Press, New York (2002)
4. Artikis, A., Sergot, M., Pitt, J.: An executable specification of a formal argumentation protocol. Artificial Intelligence 171(10-15), 776–804 (2007)
5. Bou, E., López-Sánchez, M., Rodríguez-Aguilar, J.-A.: Using case-based reasoning in autonomic electronic institutions. In: Sichman, J.S., Padget, J., Ossowski, S., Noriega, P. (eds.) COIN 2007. LNCS, vol. 4870, pp. 125–138. Springer, Heidelberg (2008)
6. Chevaleyre, Y., Endriss, U., Lang, J., Maudet, N.: A short introduction to computational social choice. In: van Leeuwen, J., Italiano, G.F., van der Hoek, W., Meinel, C., Sack, H., Plášil, F. (eds.) SOFSEM 2007. LNCS, vol. 4362, pp. 51–69. Springer, Heidelberg (2007)
7. Chopra, A., Singh, M.: Contextualizing commitment protocols. In: Proceedings of the Fifth International Conference on Autonomous Agents and Multi-Agent Systems (AAMAS), pp. 1345–1352 (2006)
8. Conitzer, V., Sandholm, T., Lang, J.: When are elections with few candidates hard to manipulate? Journal of the Association for Computing Machinery (JACM) 54(3), 14 (2007)
9. DeLoach, S., Oyenan, W., Matson, E.: A capabilities-based model for adaptive organizations. Autonomous Agents and Multi-Agent Systems 16(1), 13–56 (2008)
10. Dunin-Keplicz, B., Verbrugge, R.: A tuning machine for cooperative problem solving. Fundamenta Informaticae 63(2-3), 283–307 (2004)
11. Ferber, J., Gutknecht, O.: A meta-model for the analysis and design of organizations in multi-agent systems. In: Proceedings of the First International Conference on Multi-Agent Systems (ICMAS), pp. 128–135 (1998)
12. Guessoum, Z., Ziane, M., Faci, N.: Monitoring and organizational-level adaptation of multi-agent systems. In: Proceedings of the Third International Conference on Autonomous Agents and Multi-Agent Systems (AAMAS), pp. 514–521 (2004)
13. Hartmann, S., Pigozzi, G.: Aggregation in multi-agent systems and the problem of truth-tracking. In: Proceedings of the Sixth International Conference on Autonomous Agents and Multi-Agent Systems (AAMAS), pp. 674–676 (2007)
14. Hoogendoorn, M.: Adaptation of organizational models for multi-agent systems based on max flow networks. In: Proceedings of the Twentieth International Joint Conference on Artificial Intelligence (IJCAI), pp. 1321–1326. AAAI Press, Menlo Park (2007)
15. Kowalski, R., Sergot, M.: A logic-based calculus of events. New Generation Computing 4(1), 67–96 (1986)
16. Lamport, L.: The part-time parliament. ACM Trans. Comput. Syst. 16(2), 133–169 (1998)
17. Lamport, L.: Paxos made simple. ACM SIGACT News (Distributed Computing Column) 32(4), 51–58 (2001)

18. Mazouzi, H., El Fallah-Seghrouchni, A., Haddad, S.: Open protocol design for complex interactions in multi-agent systems. In: Castelfranchi, C., Johnson, L. (eds.) Proceedings of the First International Conference on Autonomous Agents and Multi-Agent Systems (AAMAS), pp. 517–526 (2002)
19. Neville, B., Pitt, J.: A programming environment for the animation and simulation of agent societies (2007)
20. Ostrom, E.: Governing The Commons: The Evolution of Institutions for Collective Action. Cambridge University Press, Cambridge (1990)
21. Pitt, J., Kamara, L., Sergot, M., Artikis, A.: Voting in multi-agent systems. Computer Journal 49(2), 156–170 (2006)
22. Popper, K.: The Open Society and its Enemies, 5th edn. The Spell of Plato, vol. 1. Routledge (1962)
23. Procaccia, A., Rosenschein, J., Zohar, A.: Multi-winner elections: Complexity of manipulation, control and winner-determination. In: Veloso, M. (ed.) Proceedings of the 20th International Joint Conference on Artificial Intelligence (IJCAI), pp. 1476–1481 (2007)
24. Ramirez-Cano, D., Pitt, J.: Follow the leader: Profiling agents in an opinion formation model of dynamic confidence and individual mind-sets. In: Proceedings of the 2006 IEEE/WIC/ACM International Conference on Intelligent Agent Technology, pp. 660–667 (2006)
25. Robert, H., Evans, W., Honemann, D., Balch, T.: Roberts Rules of Order Newly Revised (RONR), 10th edn. Perseus Publishing (2000)
26. Rosenschein, J.S., Procaccia, A.D.: Voting in cooperative information agent scenarios: Use and abuse. In: Klusch, M., Rovatsos, M., Payne, T.R. (eds.) CIA 2006. LNCS, vol. 4149, pp. 33–50. Springer, Heidelberg (2006)
27. Sierra, C., Rodríguez-Aguilar, J., Noriega, P., Esteva, M., Arcos, J.: Engineering multi-agent systems as electronic institutions. European Journal for the Informatics Professional V(4), 33–39 (2004)

# Decentralised Structural Adaptation in Agent Organisations

Ramachandra Kota, Nicholas Gibbins, and Nicholas R. Jennings

School of Electronics and Computer Science
University of Southampton
Southampton SO17 1BJ, UK
{rck05r,nmg,nrj}@ecs.soton.ac.uk

**Abstract.** Autonomic computing is being advocated as a tool for maintaining and managing large, complex computing systems. Self-organising multi-agent systems provide a suitable paradigm for developing such autonomic systems. Towards this goal, we demonstrate a robust, decentralised approach for structural adaptation in explicitly modelled problem solving agent organisations. Our method is based on self-organisation principles and enables the agents to modify the organisational structure to achieve a better allocation of tasks across the organisation in a simulated task-solving environment. The agents forge and dissolve relations with other agents using their history of interactions as guidance. We empirically show that the efficiency of organisations using our approach is close to that of organisations having an omniscient central allocator and considerably better than static organisations or those changing the structure randomly.

## 1 Introduction

Autonomic systems, capable of self-management, are being advocated as a solution to the problem of maintaining modern, large, complex computing systems. We also contend that self-organising multi-agent systems provide a suitable paradigm to develop these autonomic systems [16], because such self-organising systems can arrange and re-arrange their structure autonomously, without any external control, in order to adapt to changing requirements and environmental conditions. Furthermore, such systems need to be decentralised, so that they are robust against failures; again, a characteristic that fits with the multi-agent paradigm. With this motivation, this paper explores the area of self-organisation in agent systems, and particularly focuses on the decentralised structural adaptation of agent organisations.

In more detail, self-organisation is viewed as *the mechanism or the process enabling the system to change its organisation without explicit external command during its execution time* [4]. Thus, self-organisation can consist of either forming an organisation from disordered entities, or arranging an existing organisation, similar to maintaining computing systems. Self-organisation can be generated in multi-agent systems in several ways [5, 1]. For example, self-organisation may emerge from stigmergic or reinforcement mechanisms in agents [14] or can arise

G. Vouros et al. (Eds.): OAMAS 2008, LNAI 5368, pp. 54–71, 2009.

from the locally cooperative actions of the agents [3]. However, most of the work on self-organisation in agents deals with multi-agent systems that do not have any organisation defined explicitly; the social interactions of the agents are not guided by definite regulations.

However, we require our design of agent systems to be able to be mapped onto computing systems that perform tasks so that our research on self-organising agents is useful for the development of autonomic systems which are composed of such computing systems. For this purpose, we focus on developing self-organisation techniques for multi agent systems that act as problem solving organisations (organisations that receive inputs, perform tasks and return results)[1]. A study of the various self-organisation mechanisms reveals that most of them are not applicable to an explicitly modelled agent organisation because they cannot be incorporated into agents that are working towards organisational goals. The few self-organisation mechanisms that do consider agent organisations [11, 2, 9] are centralised in nature, thereby not addressing the requirement for decentralisation. Though [10] suggest a somewhat distributed method (using a central blackboard), it involves a diagnostic subsystem for detecting faults in the organisation that, in turn, map to some fixed pre-designed reorganisation steps. Such a method is not applicable when all the states of the system cannot be anticipated by the designer. Furthermore, some mechanisms, like organisation self-design [13], achieve self-organisation by dynamically spawning and merging agents according to the changing requirements. However, since agent based development of autonomic systems involves modelling the individual components as agents, changing the characteristics of these components may not be possible on all occasions due physical and accessibility limitations.

Against this background, we seek to develop a decentralised reorganisation method that can be employed by the agents in an organisation to either maintain or improve the performance of the organisation. Following the self-organisation principles, the method should be a continuous process that is followed by all agents utilising only local information for the benefit of the organisation as a whole. Furthermore, we attempt to develop reorganisation techniques that can be applied to organisations in which the agents and their internal characteristics cannot be changed. Hence, we are primarily interested in reorganisation based on the structural adaptation of the organisation. Thus, our reorganisation mechanism will serve as a self-management tool similar to those visualised in autonomic systems. However, before undertaking this task, we need to have an explicit model of a problem solving agent organisation that can act as the platform on which to found our reorganisation mechanism (section 2). Then in section 3, we describe the framework that forms the basis for our reorganisation method. Section 4 shows our empirical evaluation of its effectiveness and we conclude with a summary and a short discussion about future work in section 5.

---

[1] This is in contrast to organisations which just provide guidelines to be obeyed by agents participating in the organisation to achieve their individual goals [15]. These organisations do not have any specific goals to achieve, but only act as regulating authorities and so are not relevant in this context.

## 2   The Organisation Model

Organisation modelling involves modelling the agents comprising the organisation, the organisational characteristics, and the task environment. There are several existing frameworks for such modelling in the existing literature [6, 17, 15]. However, we mainly build on the ideas presented by [12], [7] and [8] as we found these suitable and sufficient for designing a problem solving organisation matching our requirements. In this context, it should be noted that our main contribution is the reorganisation method and not the organisation model per se. Furthermore, though our reorganisation method is demonstrated using this particular organisation model, it can be equally applied to any organisation model if desired.

In our model, the agent organisation comprises a group of problem solving, cooperative agents situated in a task environment. By problem solving agents, we mean agents that receive certain input (task), perform some actions on the basis of this input (processing or execution) and return a result. Correspondingly, the task environment presents a continuous dynamic stream of tasks that have to be performed. This environment also has other parameters, independent of the task stream, which have a bearing on the organisation. These can be considered to be the costs associated with the environment (e.g communication cost, reorganisation cost and so on).

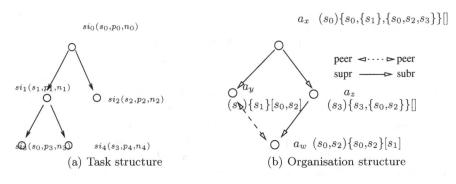

(a) Task structure        (b) Organisation structure

**Fig. 1.** Representation of an example task and organisation

In more detail, the tasks are composed of a series of service instances (SI), each of which specifies the particular service, the amount of computation per time-step (the computational rate; this amount cannot be broken up or spread across agents or time-steps) and the number of time-steps required. The SIs of a task need to be executed following a precedence order which is specified in the form of dependency links between the SIs. The precedence order is in the form of a tree structure in which the SIs that form the child nodes of a particular SI need to be executed first before that SI (parent node) can be executed. As this is followed recursively, any node can be executed only after all the SIs in the sub-tree rooted at that node have been executed. Figure 1 shows an example task which is composed of five SIs ($si_0$, $si_1$, $si_2$, $si_3$ and $si_4$) each requiring services $s_0$, $s_1$, $s_2$, $s_0$ and $s_3$ respectively. Furthermore, these services instances require their respective services at the specified computational rate (denoted by $p_0$, $p_1$ and so on) for the specified time duration (denoted by $n_0$, $n_1$ and so on). The SIs also have dependencies among them as shown (an arrow indicates that the SI at the source node can only be executed once the SI at the end node is completed).

The organisation consists of agents that provide these services. Every agent is capable of a fixed set of services and possesses a fixed computational capacity. Thus, an agent is of the form $a_x = \langle S_x, L_x \rangle$ where $S_x \subseteq S$ ($S$ is the complete set of services provided by the organisation) and $L_x$ is the agent's capacity defined in terms of available computational units in a time step (these are consumed by the SIs as they are executed)[2]. Tasks enter the system at random time-steps and their processing should start immediately. The processing of a task begins with the assignment of the final SI (root node) to a randomly selected agent. An agent who is ready to execute a particular SI is also responsible for the allocation of the SIs on which it is dependent (as specified by the dependency links of the task) to agents capable of those services. Thus, the agents have to perform two kinds of actions: (i) allocation of service instances and (ii) execution of service instances. So, if the SI allocated to an agent is dependent on two other SIs, then that agent needs to find and allocate appropriate agents to execute those two SIs, obtain the results of the executions, then execute its own SI and finally send back its result. Moreover, every action has a load associated with it. The load incurred for the execution of a SI is equal to the computational rate specified in its description (the number of computational units it consumes in a time-step) while the load due to allocation (management load) depends on the relations of that agent (will be explained later). As every agent has a limited computational capacity, an agent will perform the required actions on a first-came first-served basis, in a single time-step as long as the cumulative load on the agent is less than its capacity. If the load exceeds the capacity and there are actions still to be performed, these remaining actions will be deferred to the next time-step and so on.

As described earlier, agents need to interact with one another for the allocation of the SIs. The interactions between the agents are regulated by the structure of the organisation. This structure of the organisation is based on the relationships between the agents. The three levels of the agent relationship are: (i) acquaintance (knowing about the presence of, but no interaction), (ii) peer (low frequency of interaction) and (iii) superior-subordinate (high frequency of interaction). The type of relation present between two agents determines the information that they hold about each other and the interactions possible between them. We can distinguish between the various relations as follows:

– An agent possesses information about the services that it provides, the services provided directly by its peers and the accumulated service sets of its

---

[2] To keep the model simple, we limit the resource type to just computational resources and ignore resources based on memory etc.

subordinates. The accumulated service set of an agent is the union of its own service set and the accumulated service sets of its subordinates recursively. Thus, the agent is aware of the services that can be obtained from the sub-graphs of agents rooted at each of its subordinates, though it might not know exactly which agent (the subordinate itself or a subordinate of its subordinate, and so on) is capable of the service.

– During the process of allocation of a SI, an agent will always try to perform the SI by itself if it is capable of the service and has available computational capacity. Otherwise, it will delegate it to one of its subordinates (which contains the service in its accumulated service set). Only if it finds no suitable subordinate (no subordinate or their subordinates are capable of that service), will it try to delegate the SI to its peers. In case it is unable to do so either (no peer is capable of the service) it will pass it back to one of its superiors (who will have to find some other subordinate or peer for delegation).

Therefore, an agent mostly delegates SIs to its subordinates and seldom to its peers. Thus, the structure of the organisation influences the allocation of SIs among the agents. Moreover, the relations of an agent also determine the management load incurred by it for its allocation actions. That is, an agent with many relations will incur more management load per allocation action when compared to an agent with fewer relations. Also, a subordinate will tend to cause more management load than a peer because an agent will search its peers only after searching through its subordinates and not finding a capable agent (mathematically explained in the following subsection). As mentioned earlier, all the agents in the organisation are cooperative and work selflessly for the organisation. Therefore, an agent willingly accepts all SIs delegated to it by its superiors or peers. Note that to avoid an infinite loop of delegation, the superior-subordinate relations are not permitted to have cycles. In summary, the superior-subordinate (also called authority) relations impose the hierarchical structure in the organisation while the peer relations enable the otherwise disconnected agents to interact closely. Using this model, we abstract away the complex interaction problems relating to issues like service negotiation, trust and coordination. We do so to focus on the essence of self-organisation and to isolate its impact on system performance. Figure 1 shows an example organisation structure. Acquaintance relations are not explicitly depicted because we assume that all agents are acquaintances of each other. Furthermore, the information possessed by the agents about the services provided by their relations is shown beside them. The parenthesis denote the services provided by the agent itself, the curly braces contain the accumulated service set of the agent and the square brackets contain the services provided by the peers. For example, the accumulated service set of agent $a_x$, in turn, contains three sets representing its own service ($s_0$), the accumulated service set of its subordinate $a_y$ ($s_1$) and the accumulated service set of its other subordinate $a_z$ ($s_0, s_2, s_3$). Next, we describe the evaluation method that is required to measure the effectiveness of an organisation structure.

## 2.1 Organisation Performance Evaluation

Before designing any kind of reorganisation techniques, there needs to be a mechanism that can evaluate the performance of an organisation for some given stream of tasks. Towards this end, we introduce the concept of load, cost and benefit of an agent and thus also of the organisation in total [12]. The total cost and benefit of the organisation are considered to be the two parameters measuring the efficiency of the organisation. We calculate the cost and benefit of the organisation at every time-step and hence the overall cost and benefit is an average over all these values obtained for all the time-steps of a simulation run.

The cost of the organisation is based on the amount of resources being consumed by the agents. In this case, we consider the cost of an agent to be equal to the network resources utilised to transmit its messages. Therefore, cost to the organisation due an agent $a_x$, for a time-step, is $cost_x = C.c_x$ where $c_x$ is the number of messages sent by that agent in that time-step and $C$ is the communication cost coefficient. Moreover, the cost of the organisation is the sum of the costs of all the messages being transmitted in that time-step:

$$cost_{ORG} = C.\sum_{x=0}^{|A|} c_x \qquad (1)$$

where $A$ is the set of agents in the organisation. As stated earlier, agents have limited capacities and their computational load cannot increase beyond this capacity. The load on $a_x$ in a time-step is calculated as:

$$l_x = \sum_{i=0}^{|T_{x_E}|} e_{i,x} + M \sum_{i=0}^{|T_{x_F}|} m_{i,x} \qquad (2)$$

- $e_{i,x}$ is the amount of execution computation of $a_x$ required by task $t_i$
- $m_{i,x}$ is the amount of management computation done by $a_x$ for task $t_i$
- $T_{x_E}$ is the set of tasks being executed by $a_x$
- $T_{x_F}$ is the set of tasks being allocated by $a_x$
- $M$ is the management load coefficient

More specifically, $e_{i,x}$ represents the sum of the computational units of all the SIs of task $t_i$ that are being executed by $a_x$ in that time-step. Similarly, $m_{i,x}$ represents the total number of other agents that $a_x$ had to consider to allocate any of the required SIs of task $t_i$ in that time-step.

This load $l_x$ on $a_x$ cannot exceed its capacity $L_x$. Any excess tasks will be waiting for their turn in the set $T_{x_W}$ and will adversely affect the benefit of the agent. Therefore, the benefit value reflects the speed of completion of the tasks. Hence, the benefit of an agent at a time-step is equal to the total amount of computation of the SIs being executed by that agent subtracted by the amount of computation required by the SIs that are waiting to be executed or allocated by the agent. Therefore,

$$benefit_x = \sum_{i=0}^{|T_{x_E}|} e_{ix} - \sum_{i=0}^{|T_{x_W}|} e_{ix} \qquad (3)$$

In more detail, $T_{x_W}$ represents the set of tasks that have SIs waiting to be either executed by $a_x$ or assigned by $a_x$ to appropriate agents. Therefore, to obtain the maximum possible benefit, the agent should never have any waiting tasks (it should never be overloaded) and the assignment of the dependent SIs should occur in the same time-step that they are discovered as dependencies. Finally, the total benefit of the organisation ($benefit_{ORG}$) is simply the sum of the individual agent benefits:

$$benefit_{ORG} = \sum_{x=0}^{|A|} benefit_x \qquad (4)$$

In conclusion, the performance of the organisation is measured by its efficiency:

$$efficieny_{ORG} = benefit_{ORG} - cost_{ORG} \qquad (5)$$

The benefit should be maximised while the cost needs to be minimised. It is important to note that while the agents have their own individual benefit values, trying to selfishly increase their own benefit needn't necessarily lead to an increase in the overall benefit of the organisation because an agent's actions affect the other agents. For example, an agent can perform allocations quickly by having just one subordinate and delegating most SIs to that agent (thus not causing any loss to its own benefit), but that subordinate agent may be overloaded as a result, leading to a significant decrease in its benefit and that of the organisation. Therefore, the agents, being cooperative, need to maximise the organisation benefit, but they do not possess the complete information about the load and benefits of the other agents that contribute to it.

## 3   Decentralised Reorganisation

The aim of our reorganisation method is to determine and effect changes in the organisation structure to increase its efficiency (Eqn. 5). Our method is based on the past interactions of the agents. We use only the past information of the individual agents because we assume the agents do not possess any information about the tasks that will come in the future. Specifically, agents use the information about all their past allocations to evaluate their relations with their subordinates, peers and acquaintances. This evaluation is based on the possible increase or decrease of the overall load and cost in case a subordinate or peer relation had previously existed (an acquaintance had been a subordinate or a peer), the relation had been different (had a peer been a subordinate or vice versa) or the relation hadn't existed (a peer or a subordinate had only been an acquaintance). For example, an agent $a_x$ evaluates its relation with its subordinate $a_y$ on the basis of the number of its service instance dependencies that have been executed by $a_y$. More specifically, $a_x$ assumes that had $a_y$ not been its subordinate, then all its delegations to $a_y$ would have gone indirectly via some intermediary agents. Therefore, $a_x$ will check whether the possible reduction in its own load had $a_y$ not been a subordinate (because one less subordinate will lead to a lower management load during allocations) is more than the possible increase in the load and cost across the organisation (due to the resultant longer assignment chains).

We formulate our reorganisation method using a decision theoretic approach since it provides us with a simple and suitable methodology for representing our method in terms of actions and utilities. Decision theory specifies that the agent chooses the action that maximises the expected utility. We denote the actions of an agent as establishing or dissolving relations with other agents. Considering our model, there are two possible relations between any two agents— peer or authority (assuming that the agents are always acquaintances of each other). Therefore, four atomic actions are possible:- $E = \langle$ form_peer, rem_peer, form_subr, rem_subr $\rangle$. The actions are mutually exclusive and can be performed if the relation between the agents is in the requisite state (explained later). Moreover, each of these actions has to be jointly performed by the two agents involved in forming/removing the relationship link. Furthermore, the actions are deterministic (there is no uncertainty regarding the outcome of an action which is the formation or deletion of a link; only the utility of the outcome is not pre-determined). Therefore, the agents have a value function (also called an ordinal utility function) which they attempt to maximise.

Since our environment is characterised by various factors like the communication costs, the load on the agents and so on, the value function will have multiple attributes to represent these different factors. In terms of two agents $a_x$ and $a_y$ jointly deliberating an action, we list the five attributes that will constitute the value function:

1. change to the load on $a_x$
2. change to the load on $a_y$
3. change to the load on other agents
4. change in the communication cost of the organisation
5. reorganisation cost

Moreover, this set of attributes exhibits mutual preferential independence (MPI). That is, while every attribute is important, it does not affect the way the rest of the attributes are compared. Therefore, the value function can be represented as simply a sum of the functions pertaining to the individual attributes. That is, it is an additive value function of the form:

$$V = \Delta load_x + \Delta load_y + \Delta load_{OA} + \Delta cost_{comm} + \Delta cost_{reorg} \qquad (6)$$

Against this background, we discuss the actions and states of the agents. For every pair of agents, the relation between them has to be in one of the states— no relation (just acquaintances), peer relation or superior-subordinate relation. For each of these states, the possible choices of action available to the agents are:

1. **$a_y$ is only an acquaintance of $a_x$:** (i) $form\_peer_{x,y}$; (ii) $form\_subr_{x,y}$; (iii) $no\_action$.
2. **$a_y$ is a subordinate of $a_x$:** (i) $rem\_subr_{x,y}$; (ii) $rem\_subr_{x,y} + form\_peer_{x,y}$ (to change to a peer relation); (iii) $no\_action$.

3. $a_y$ **is a peer of** $a_x$: (i) $rem\_peer_{x,y}$; (ii) $rem\_peer_{x,y} + form\_subr_{x,y}$ (to change to a subordinate relation); (iii) $no\_action$.
4. $a_y$ **is a superior of** $a_x$: (i) $rem\_subr_{y,x} + form\_subr_{x,y}$; (ii) $rem\_subr_{y,x} + form\_subr_{x,z}$ (where $a_z$ is a (indirect) superior[3] of $a_y$); (iii) $no\_action$.

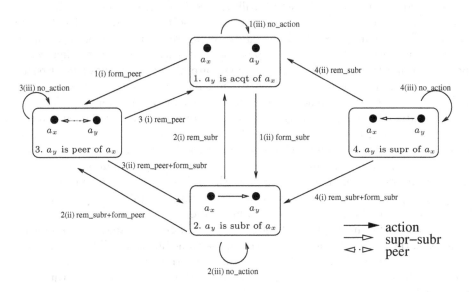

**Fig. 2.** State transition diagram

The possible actions for transitions between the various states are further illustrated by Fig 2. Thus, three actions are possible in any state. For example, the $form\_subr_{x,y}$ action denotes that $a_x$ and $a_y$ take the action of making $a_y$ a subordinate of $a_x$. We do not need a transition from state 2 to 4 because it is equivalent to the transition from 4 to 2, by interchanging $a_x$ and $a_y$. Similarly, we do not need a transition from 1 to 4 or between 3 and 4. In this way, depending on the state, the agents jointly calculate the expected utilities for the possible actions based on the value function and choose the action giving the maximum expected utility in accordance with standard decision theory. The evaluation for $no\_action$ will always be 0 as it does not result in any change to the expected load or cost of the organisation. The evaluation for the rest of the actions is obtained from the value function (Eqn. 6). The evaluation for the composite actions ($rem\_subr + form\_peer$, $rem\_peer + form\_subr$ or $rem\_subr + form\_subr$) for transition between two relations will simply be the sum of the individual evaluations of the comprising actions. Moreover, since any action will be taken jointly by the two agents involved, even the evaluation of the value function

---

[3] When $a_z$ is an indirect superior of $a_x$ via $a_y$, it is not possible for $a_x$ to have $a_z$ as its subordinate (since cycles are not permitted), hence it dissolves its relation with its immediate superior in the authority chain which is $a_y$.

**Table 1.** Showing the attribute calculations for $form\_subr_{x,y}$ with $a_x$ as superior

| Attribute | Function | Agent |
|---|---|---|
| $\Delta load_x$ | $-Asg_{x,total} * M * filled_x(n_x^{total})/n_x^{total}$ | $a_x$ |
| This represents the management load that will be added on to $a_x$ due to an additional subordinate (the negative sign denotes that this value represents an increase in the load). However, the increase in the load is detrimental to the efficiency only in the cases when the capacity is filled and tasks are kept waiting. Therefore, it is multiplied by a factor which represents how often this increased load will affect the benefit. This factor is the amount of time-steps that $a_x$ had waiting tasks divided by the total time. | | |
| $\Delta load_y$ | $-Asg_{x,y}^{LOAD} * filled_y(n_{x,y}^{subr}) * n_x^{total}/(n_{x,y}^{subr})^2$ or 0 if $n_{x,y}^{subr} = 0$ | $a_y$ |
| This represents the management load that will be added on $a_y$ due to possible assignments from $a_x$. It is estimated by considering the load on $a_y$ due to $a_x$ when it was the subordinate of $a_x$ previously and multiplying it with the fraction of time $a_y$ had waiting tasks while in that relation and dividing it by the fraction of total time that the relation existed. Thus, the load values are normalised to correspond to the total time and not just the relation time. Note that if $a_y$ had never been a subordinate of $a_x$, then this value is assumed to be 0 | | |
| $\Delta load_{OA}$ | $IA_{x,y}^{LOAD}$ | $a_x$ |
| This represents the reduction in the management load on the intermediate agents that had been involved in the delegations to $a_y$ by $a_x$. As this load value is sent by an intermediate agent only if it has waiting tasks, no time factor, unlike above, is required. | | |
| $\Delta cost_{comm}$ | $IA_{x,y}^{COST}$ | $a_x$ |
| This represents the reduction in communication cost that was associated with the delegations to $a_y$ by $a_x$. | | |
| $\Delta cost_{reorg}$ | $-D$ | constant |
| This is the reorganisation cost associated with forming or dissolving a relation. Though, it is a one time cost, it's affect is spread over the same time window as the rest of the attributes' evaluations. | | |

is jointly conducted by the agents with each of them supplying those attribute values that are accessible to them. To understand further, we shall look at an example of calculating the result of the value function for the $form\_subr_{x,y}$ action. The agent's value function is an additive of the function of the attributes as shown in Eqn 6. To represent the performance condition of the organisation ($efficiency_{ORG}$ should be maximised), reduction in cost or load (excess load adversely affects the benefit) is considered to add positively to the value and vice versa. Table 1 lists out how the five attributes of the value function are measured for this sample action $form\_subr_{x,y}$. The last column in the table denotes which agent will be performing the calculation for that particular attribute. The notation useful to understand the table is given below:

1. **Assignments** $Asg_{x,y}$: The number of SIs assigned by $a_x$ to $a_y$. Assignment of a SI $si_i$ by $a_x$ to $a_y$ means that $a_x$ had to allocate $si_i$ (it was either assigned to $a_x$ or forms a dependency of a SI being executed by $a_x$) and it assigned $si_i$ to $a_y$. Thus, $a_y$ will have to be a subordinate, peer or a superior of $a_x$. Also, $a_y$ need not necessarily execute $si_i$ itself, it may reassign it to one of its own subordinates, peers, or superiors, forming an assignment chain.

2. **Delegations** $Del_{x,y}$: The number of SIs delegated by agent $a_x$ to $a_y$. Delegation of a SI $si_i$ by $a_x$ to $a_y$ means that $a_x$ had to allocate $si_i$ (as it formed a dependency of a SI being executed by $a_x$) and $a_y$ is the agent that finally executed $si_i$ (i.e $a_y$ is the delegated agent). Note that $a_y$ may just have an acquaintance relationship with $a_x$. The delegation is achieved through one or more assignments. The last agent in the assignment chain is always the delegated agent.

3. **C**: Communication cost coefficient. This denotes the cost incurred by the organisation for passing a single message between two agents.

4. **M**: Management load coefficient. This represents the amount of computational capacity used up by an agent when it checks whether another agent is capable of being assigned a SI.

5. **D**: Reorganisation cost coefficient. This denotes the cost incurred by the organisation to either form or dissolve a relation between two agents.

6. $n_x^{total}$: The total number of time-steps that have passed since $a_x$ came into existence.

7. $n_{x,y}^{subr}$: The number of time-steps that $a_x$ and $a_y$ had a superior-subordinate relation.

8. $filled_x(n)$: The number of time-steps out of the time denoted by $n$ that $a_x$ had waiting tasks (capacity completely filled by load).

9. $Asg_{x,total}$: The number of SIs that have been assigned by $a_x$ to all the other agents.

10. $Asg_{x,y}^{LOAD}$: The management load that is added onto $a_y$ because of assignments from $a_x$ (which are $Asg_{x,y}$).

11. $IA_{x,y}$: The total number of times other agents (intermediate agents) were involved in the delegations of SIs ($Del_{x,y}$) by $a_x$ to $a_y$.

12. $IA_{x,y}^{LOAD}$: The overall management load put on all the intermediate agents involved in the assignment of the SIs in $Del_{x,y}$. The load values are reported back to $a_x$ along with the assignment information. If an intermediate agent has available capacity (no waiting tasks), it will report a 0 load value for the assignment. Otherwise, the agent will report the actual management load that was put on it due to that SI assignment.

13. $IA_{x,y}^{COST}$: The communication cost due to the SIs in $Del_{x,y}$. For every agent in $IA_{x,y}$, a cost of $2C$ is added because a message is sent once forward and once back. Therefore, $IA_{x,y}^{COST} = IA_{x,y} * 2 * C$.

Similar to the example in Table 1, every pair of agents jointly evaluate the utility for taking any of the possible actions (depending on their relation) towards changing their relation, at every time-step (though, newly formed relations are allowed to stabilise and are re-evaluated only after some time has elapsed. We set this interval to 15 time-steps). Here, joint evaluation means that each agent supplies some of the attribute values only (as denoted by the last column in the table), but the resultant value for the action is applicable to both the agents. Therefore, the agents do not have conflicts as the value corresponds to the utility of the relation to the organisation and not to the individual agents. Thus, this continuous adaptation in the relations helps in the better allocation of SIs amongst the agents as they will maintain relations with only those agents with whom they require frequent interactions.

Additionally, when an agent has two or more SIs of a particular service waiting for execution (because of filled capacity), it will search among its acquaintances for agents capable of performing that highly demanded service and will specifically calculate the utility of performing a $form\_subr$ with these agents. While calculating the value as above, it will also include the possible gain from the decrease to its own load resulting from the delegation of its waiting load (when the relation is formed) to the new subordinate. Thereby, overloaded agents can form subordinate relations with other similarly capable agents leading to a more equitable load distribution across the organisation.

In summary, our reorganisation method guides the agent to form, change or dissolve relations with other agents in the organisation on the basis of their history of interactions. Thus, it will result in changes to the organisation structure in an attempt towards improving the efficiency of the organisation. Clearly, our method is agent-based and completely decentralised as it will be used by all the agents in the organisation. Moreover, it is used by the agents throughout their existence, thus making the adaptation a continuous process. Therefore, our method satisfies the properties of self-organisation that we outlined in section 1.

## 4   Experimental Evaluation

We conducted a number of experiments in order to evaluate the effectiveness of our reorganisation method. For comparison, we also implemented four other strategies for modifying the organisation structure. These are:

1. **Static:** A non-reorganising approach, the structure of the organisation is not modified during the simulation run.
2. **Random:** The agents randomly choose some of their relations for modification every time-step. The rate of change was adjusted so that the overall number of changes in relations in a simulation run is roughly equal to that of our approach on an average so that the performance is not affected due to the aggregation of reorganisation cost.
3. **Central:** A central agent, which is external to the organisation, is responsible for the allocation of SIs. This agent has complete information about the organisation including the services, capacities and current load on the agents.

When any agent needs to find another agent for allocating a SI, it will assign it to the central agent, who will then delegate it to the most suitable agent (capable of the service and having the maximum free capacity). Thus, every delegation is a fixed two step process with the central agent acting as an intermediary. Also, the organisation can be viewed as having a star structure in which all the agents are connected solely to this external central agent.

4. **Oracle:** Instead of a single, central external agent as above, we assume that every agent has complete information about the organisation and so performs the best allocation of SIs possible. However in this case, the agents are assumed to not incur any load for their allocation actions. Thus, as all the delegations are a one-step process without causing any management load, this approach acts as an upper bound for our evaluation.

We evaluate the effectiveness of the different strategies on the basis of the efficiency of the organisations which is determined by the average cost and benefit of the organisation for a simulation run. Thus, the organisation cost and benefit are the two experimental data variables of interest. On the other hand, we focus on two independent variables for the experiments— (i) distribution of services across agents (ii) similarity between tasks. They are described below:

– **Distribution of services across agents:** After deciding the number of agents and services for a particular simulation, the next step is to distribute these services among the agents. The two extreme possibilities are: (i) each agent capable of a unique set of services and (ii) all agents are capable of all services. The services capabilities are allocated to agents on the basis of a probability called service probability (SP). That is, an agent $a_x$ is allocated a service $s_i$ with a probability SP. Thus, when SP is 0, every agent is capable of a unique service only (as every agent should offer at least one service and every service should be offered by at least one agent). When it is 1, every agent is capable of every service. Since, the services are allocated on basis of a probability, there is always randomness in the way the services are allocated to the agents. In our experiments, we vary SP from 0 to 0.5 only (since we found that beyond 0.5, when the agents are quite homogeneous, the organisation structures did not influence the performance significantly).

– **Similarity between tasks:** The tasks presented to the organisation over the period of a simulation run may be completely unrelated to each other or they may have some common SIs and dependency links. We control the similarity between the tasks belonging to the same simulation run on the basis of what we call *patterns*; stereotypical task components used to represent frequently occurring combinations of SIs and dependency links. Therefore, they are also composed of SIs, like tasks, but are generally smaller in size. So, instead of creating tasks by randomly creating dependency links between the SIs, tasks can be constituted by connecting some patterns by creating dependency links between the SIs belonging to the patterns. In this way, the dependencies between the SIs may follow some frequent orderings (resulting from the dependencies internal to a pattern as the pattern may occur in several tasks) and some random dependencies (due to the dependencies created between the patterns). Thus, this method of generation enables us to control the similarity between the tasks using the number of patterns (NoP) as the parameter. In our experiments, we vary the NoP from 1 (all tasks are composed of the same pattern repeated multiple times leading to a high degree of similarity) to 10 (several different patterns interlinked leading to low similarity across tasks). We also conducted a set of experiments with NoP set to 0 (tasks are completely dissimilar). We consider that the similarity between the tasks is an interesting parameter to vary because it provides us insights into how well our adaptation method performs in different kinds of task environments. This is an important factor for evaluation because our method is based on the past interactions between the agents which are, in turn, related to their past task allocations and executions. Moreover, the presence of similarities between tasks is an existing phenomenon in the real world. When tasks of several kinds are received by a system, often the tasks comprise of parts that are common across the different tasks. For example if the tasks are about constructing different cars, they will have some common sub-tasks like making a wheel, a windshield etc.

We conducted the experiments by running 1000 simulations runs for every data point to achieve statistically significant results. All results are shown with 95% confidence intervals obtained by multiplying the standard error by 1.96 (z-test). For every simulation, the set of agents and services is first generated and then the services are assigned to the agents on basis of the service probability SP. Next, the set of tasks is generated using number of patterns (NoP) as the parameter. In our experiments, we used a maximum of 20 agents in the organisation which, in turn, faces 100 tasks over 1000 time-steps to constitute one simulation run. Also, we set the total number of services equal to the number of agents (though the distribution will vary according to SP) and the maximum number of SIs in a task to 20. Furthermore, we set a value of 0.5 to $M$. This means that any allocation process will take up at least half a computational unit. Also, the computation rate required for the SIs is ranged between 1-10 units per time-step and the value of $D$ (the reorganisation cost coefficient) is set to 0 so that the reorganisation process is not inhibited due to high costs. Finally, the maximum size of a pattern is limited to 6 so that, on average, three patterns are required to compose a task (which has a maximum of 20 SIs).

We present our results in the form of graphs plotting the cost and benefit values averaged for one time-step for all the 5 strategies. A better performance is reflected in a high benefit and a low cost result. Note that, for convenience, we refer to our method as 'smart'. In Fig 3, the service probability increases along the x-axis from 0 (when all agents have a unique service set) to 0.5 (when every agent is capable of approximately half the services). In more detail, Fig 3(a) and 3(b) display the cost and benefit when the tasks are highly similar (made up of 5 patterns only), while in Fig 3(c) and 3(d) the tasks are completely dissimilar (not made of patterns). We find that the oracle outperforms all other methods significantly, as expected. Also, the static and random methods perform worse

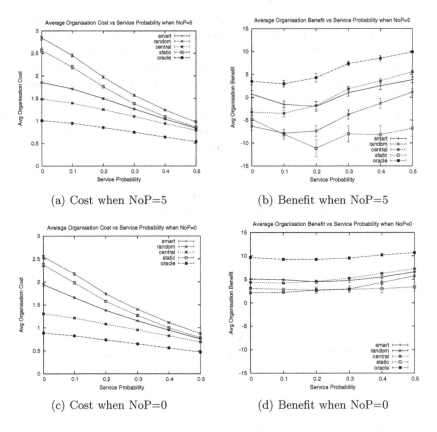

(a) Cost when NoP=5          (b) Benefit when NoP=5

(c) Cost when NoP=0          (d) Benefit when NoP=0

**Fig. 3.** Average cost and benefit as similarity between agents increases

than the rest. More importantly, we see that the performance of our method is very close to the central strategy on both the occasions, thus showing that our method, which is decentralised in nature, succeeds in generating organisation structures that lead to efficient allocation of tasks. Another interesting result is that the difference in the results between the methods is more apparent when the tasks are highly similar (when NoP=5). This is because the organisation structure has more influence over the performance when the tasks are similar as a good structure leads to an efficient task allocation and vice versa.

Similar trends are also observed (see Fig 4) when the the dissimilarity between tasks is increased along the x-axis. The huge drop in benefit for all methods seen in Fig 4(b)(the range has been limited to -40 for better readability) when the tasks are highly similar occurs because the tasks are made up of only one pattern, leading to a high demand for a few services. However, since the agents are unique, each of those services will be provided by one agent only, resulting in the overloading of those agents. This drop in benefit is less pronounced in Fig 4(d) because, here the agents have overlapping service sets and therefore a better distribution of load takes places. It is also interesting to note that

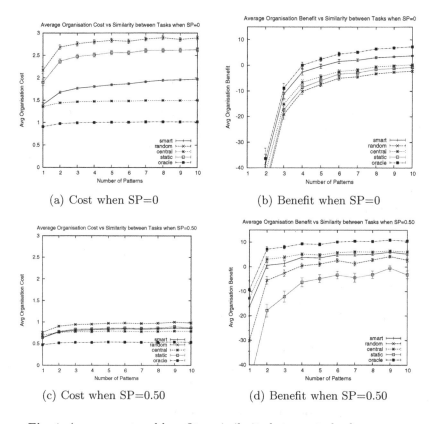

(a) Cost when SP=0                    (b) Benefit when SP=0

(c) Cost when SP=0.50                 (d) Benefit when SP=0.50

**Fig. 4.** Average cost and benefit as similarity between tasks decreases

our method performs significantly better than central when the agents have unique service sets. This is because, the extra information possessed by the central agent about the load on agents is not really useful because only one agent is capable of any service and has to be allocated those corresponding SIs irrespective of the load on it. At the same time, one step delegations are possible in our method while the central method always requires a two-step delegation (with the central allocator as the intermediary), thus leading to a better performance of our method. However, as the heterogeneity of the agents decreases with an increase in SP, the central method outperforms our method as it is able to better distribute the load across the agents. This is because it has access to the information about the loads and capacities of all the agents.

In summary, we find that our reorganisation method always performs better than a random reorganisation or a non-reorganising approach. Furthermore, our method performs similar to the approach based on an external omniscient central agent performing the allocations. We have also experimented by increasing the workload on the organisation by supplying it with 200 tasks over 1000 time-steps and found the resultant trends to be similar to those discussed here.

## 5    Conclusions and Future Work

This paper addresses the problem of developing decentralised adaptation methods for problem solving agent organisations based on the paradigm of self organisation. More specifically, we formulated a simple organisation model to serve as a framework for developing adaptation methods. We then developed a structural adaptation method using a decision theoretic approach that can be applied individually by the agents in order to improve the organisation performance. According to the method, the agents consider all their past allocations of tasks to other agents, particularly the resultant cost and load due to these interactions, and restructure their organisational relations with the other agents on the basis of this information. A useful feature of our adaptation method is that it works purely by redirecting agent interactions (via the organisation structure) and does not entail any modifications to the agents themselves or their internal characteristics. Thus, the work documented in this paper demonstrates a simple and robust, decentralised approach for improving the efficiency of problem solving agent organisations, thereby providing an important accessory for the development of autonomic systems.

At present, our method requires the agents to re-evaluate all their relations at every time-step. Now, this might not be suitable if the deliberation and calculation of utilities requires the agents to expend significant computing resources that could otherwise be used for task completion. Therefore, the initial part of future work will involve making our adaptation method more computationally efficient. Specifically, we plan to improve it by developing a method that will enable the agent to just consider a small subset of its relations, at a time, for reorganisation. Second, it is evident that in our current settings, the set of agents and their characteristics are invariant. We acknowledge that this might not always be the case in many of our target applications. Thus, we intend to investigate the usability of our method in more dynamic scenarios where agents might join, change or leave the organisation. Therefore, the next step of future work will be to extend our work for such dynamic organisations. A final stream of future work will focus on methods of structural adaptation that involve three or more agents at the same time, thereby requiring multi-step actions and planning.

## References

[1] Bernon, C., Chevrier, V., Hilaire, V., Marrow, P.: Applications of self-organising multi-agents systems: An initial framework of comparison. Informatica (2006)
[2] Bou, E., Lopez-Sanchez, M., Rodriguez-Aguilar, J.A.: Self-configuration in autonomic electronic institutions. In: Coordination, Organization, Institutions and Norms in Agent Systems Workshop at ECAI Conference, Italy, pp. 1–9 (2006)
[3] Capera, D., George, J.-P., Gleizes, M.-P., Glize, P.: The amas theory for complex problem solving based on self-organizing cooperative agents. In: Proceedings of the 12th International Workshop on Enabling Technologies (WETICE 2003), Washington, DC, USA, p. 383. IEEE Computer Society Press, Los Alamitos (2003)
[4] Di Marzo Serugendo, G., Gleizes, M.-P., Karageorgos, A.: Self-organization in multi-agent systems. The Knowledge Engineering Review 20(2), 165–189 (2005)

[5] Di Marzo Serugendo, G., Gleizes, M.-P., Karageorgos, A.: Self-Organisation and Emergence in Multi-Agent Systems: An Overview. Informatica 30(1), 45–54 (2006)

[6] Dignum, V.: A model for organizational interaction: based on agents, founded in logic. PhD thesis, Proefschrift Universiteit Utrecht (2003)

[7] Ferber, J., Gutknecht, O.: A meta-model for the analysis and design of organizations in multi-agent systems. In: Proceedings of the 3rd International Conference on Multi Agent Systems (ICMAS 1998), Washington, USA, pp. 128–135 (1998)

[8] Hannoun, M., Boissier, O., Sichman, J.S., Sayettat, C.: Moise: An organizational model for multi-agent systems. In: Proceedings of the International Joint Conference, 7th Ibero-American Conference on AI (IBERAMIA-SBIA 2000), London, UK, pp. 156–165. Springer, Heidelberg (2000)

[9] Hoogendoorn, M.: Adaptation of organizational models for multi-agent systems based on max flow networks. In: Proceedings of the 20th International Joint Conference on Artificial Intelligence (IJCAI 2007). AAAI Press, Menlo Park (2007)

[10] Horling, B., Benyo, B., Lesser, V.: Using self-diagnosis to adapt organizational structures. In: Proceedings of the Fifth International Conference on Autonomous Agents (AGENTS 2001), pp. 529–536. ACM Press, New York (2001)

[11] Hubner, J.F., Sichman, J.S., Boissier, O.: Using the MOISE+ for a cooperative framework of MAS reorganisation. In: Bazzan, A.L.C., Labidi, S. (eds.) SBIA 2004. LNCS, vol. 3171, pp. 506–515. Springer, Heidelberg (2004)

[12] Jin, Y., Levitt, R.E.: The virtual design team: A computational model of project organizations. Computational & Mathematical Organization Theory (1996)

[13] Kamboj, S., Decker, K.S.: Organizational self-design in semi-dynamic environments. In: Proc. of the 6th AAMAS, Honolulu, USA, pp. 1220–1227 (2007)

[14] Mano, J.-P., Bourjot, C., Lopardo, G., Glize, P.: Bio-inspired mechanisms for artificial self-organised systems. Informatica 30(1), 55–62 (2006)

[15] Sierra, C., Rodrguez-Aguilar, J.A., Noriega, P., Esteva, M., Arcos, J.L.: Engineering multi-agent systems as electronic institutions. UPGRADE The European Journal for the Informatics Professional 4, 33–39 (2004)

[16] Tesauro, G., Chess, D.M., Walsh, W.E., Das, R., Segal, A., Whalley, I., Kephart, J.O., White, S.R.: A multi-agent systems approach to autonomic computing. In: Proceedings of the 3rd International Joint Conference on Autonomous Agents and Multiagent Systems (AAMAS 2004), pp. 464–471. IEEE Computer Society, Los Alamitos (2004)

[17] Vazquez-Salceda, J., Dignum, V., Dignum, F.: Organizing multiagent systems. Autonomous Agents and Multi-Agent Systems 11(3), 307–360 (2005)

# Modeling Feedback within MAS: A Systemic Approach to Organizational Dynamics

Wolfgang Renz and Jan Sudeikat*

Multimedia Systems Laboratory,
Hamburg University of Applied Sciences,
Berliner Tor 7, 20099 Hamburg, Germany
Tel.: +49-40-42875-8304
{wr,sudeikat}@informatik.haw-hamburg.de

**Abstract.** Organization–oriented modeling approaches are established tools for Agent–Oriented Software Engineering (AOSE) efforts. *Role* and *Group* concepts are prevalent concepts in the design of agent–based applications. These allow the definition and partition of static organizational structures and facilitate the description of agent behaviors in terms of role/group changing activities. Due to a growing interest in the construction of *adaptive* and *self–organizing* dynamics within MAS – i.e. applications that adjust their organizational structure at runtime – developers require tools for expressing the *dynamics* of MAS organizations, that result from individual agent activity and adaptiveness.

In this paper we discuss how the macroscopic behavior of organizational structures can be modeled by relating systemic modeling techniques to MAS designs. Particularly the notions of *causal loop diagrams*, composed of *system properties* connected by *causal links* are applied to express the timely behavior of role and group occupations. Corresponding modeling activities are facilitated by a graphical notation that highlights feedback loops. Since simulations are indispensable to examine complex, non–linear behaviors, we discuss how the systemic semantics can be translated into systems of *stochastic process algebra* terms, therefore enabling model simulation.

## 1 Introduction

Conceiving complicated distributed applications as *Multi–Agent Systems* (MAS), composed of autonomous, pro–active agents, is a prominent development approach [1]. As the intended system functionality results from agent interplay, developers face the challenge to revise agent models to ensure both the correct individual functions as well as the effective coordination of agent activities.

---

* Jan Sudeikat is doctoral candidate at the Distributed Systems and Information Systems (VSIS) group, Department of Informatics, Faculty of Mathematics, Informatics and Natural Sciences, University of Hamburg, Vogt–Kölln–Str. 30, 22527 Hamburg, Germany, jan.sudeikat@informatik.uni-hamburg.de

G. Vouros et al. (Eds.): OAMAS 2008, LNAI 5368, pp. 72–89, 2009.

A number of *Agent Oriented Software Engineering* (AOSE) methodologies [2] address the top–down development of agent–based applications. These are typically tailored to fit specific agent architectures [3] and guide top–down refinement procedures. *Organization–centric* modeling notions supplement AOSE methodologies by providing agent architecture independent descriptions of organizational structures [4,5]. MAS are typically described in terms of *roles* and *groups*. Roles provide abstractions of agent behaviors. These can be used to characterize agent activities and normative behaviors within organizational contexts. A prominent concept to describe these contexts are groups, which partition MAS organizations into sets of individuals that share characteristics.

A major benefit of MAS–based application designs is that they allow for the *decentralized coordination* of individual agents, therefore enabling *self–organizing* systems dynamics [6]. Self–organization, as observed in physical, biological and social systems, takes place when global structures arise from the local activities of decentral coordinated agents, i.e. in absence of distinguished elements that coordinate explicitly [7]. Decentralized coordination schemes particularly facilitate the development of *adaptive* applications, since the the rise, maintenance and change of macroscopic system structures can be steered in a decentralized, fault–tolerant way. While development practices and methodologies focus on the revision of microscopic agent implementations, is it an ongoing research challenge how to guide the revision of microscopic agent models to enforce the rise of macroscopic properties.

The establishment of self–organizing properties can be traced back to the presence of feedback loops [8,9] and *systemic* modeling notions [10] (cf. section 3.1) have been successfully applied to analyze [11] and design [12] complex MAS behaviors. Mathematical and formal modeling approaches to self–organizing dynamics typically address macroscopic description levels by modeling the timely development of system properties. However, deriving these models from MAS designs and implementations is a considerable modeling effort, that is hindered by the generic nature of systemic modeling notions (see e.g. [13]).

Developers of self–organizing MAS rely on established agent architectures and implementation platforms but intend system properties that elude from top–down design but are observable on a quantitative, macroscopic description level. For this community it is desirable to reuse existing development support [2] but combine it with appropriate description levels. In order to enable examinations of organizational dynamics and facilitate the usage of feedback loops as design and analysis concepts in MAS development, we discuss how to supplement organizational MAS models with systemic descriptions of feedback structures. A tailored modeling notation and its semantics are presented, which allow to express the stochastic, time dependent behavior of role and group occupation numbers, i.e. the role changing behaviors of agents. Since the dynamic behavior of an organization structure – particularly under the influence of self-regulatory feedback loops – can not be trivially inferred from graphical notations or algebraic expressions, we outline how simulation models can be inferred and exemplify how to express the modeling semantics in stochastic process algebra.

This paper is structured as follows. The next section summarizes current best practices to the construction of adaptive, self-organizing MAS. The following section 3 introduces a systemic supplement to MAS organizational modeling. Utilization of this modeling and simulation approach is exemplified in section 4. After discussing related work (section 5) we conclude and give prospects for future work.

## 2    Engineering Adaptivity via Self–organization

The utilization of self–organizing processes in MAS enables system wide adaptivity, due to collectively coordinated behavior adjustments of individuals. Applications have the ability to self–organize when the coordination of agent activities is handled by decentralized mechanisms that rule out the need for centralized elements to explicitly coordinate. Instead, the coordination effort is shared among a community of continuously adapting individuals.

*Feedback cycles* can be instrumental in steering self–organizing applications [8]. In [9], the currently available means to the construction of feedback in MAS have been reviewed. One prominent strategy to the development of self–adaptive applications is the *bionic* utilization of well-known, nature-inspired dynamics (e.g. reviewed in [11]). Directly referring to nature–inspired design metaphors is a successful strategy to approach computational challenges [14]. However, intensive manual effort and considerable expertise is required to identify appropriate problem solving strategies and tune system implementations as well as parameters, leading to highly specialized algorithms. Natural self-organizing systems serve as *design metaphors* [15], or have been studied to a level of detail that allowed the extraction of reusable *decentralized coordination mechanisms* (DCM) [16,17]. The utilization of these tools provides means for non–linear agent interactions and addresses the establishment of global system phenomena. The system wide effects of agent coaction can not be entirely anticipated from the designs of individual agents. Therefore, simulation–based development procedures have been proposed [18].

DCMs provide reusable patterns of coordination distribution. These have been classified and discussed according to (1) their underlying computational techniques [6], (2) the properties of the resulting macroscopic phenomena [19], (3) their sources of inspiration (e.g. social & economic: [20]) and (4) their ability to exhibit distributed feedback loops [9]. Development efforts that apply decentralized coordination mechanisms to steer application adaptiveness have to solve the dilemma of how to design and revise *microscopic* agent models and their interactions in order to ensure the rise of *macroscopic* system behaviors and properties [21]. MAS developers that aim to apply decentralized coordination mechanisms have to (1) select appropriate mechanisms, (2) map their constituent parts (behavior selection and interaction modes) to the addressed application domain, (3) implement them in an agent architecture of their choice and finally (4) tune system / agent parameters to allow for the intended behavioral regimes (cf. [22]).

In [12], a catalog of environment mediated design metaphors (from [15]) has been extended with dynamic models (cf. section 3.1) of the inherently present macroscopic feedback loops. These models have been applied to design applications as combinations of metaphors [12] and to enable the elicitation of the requirements on the MAS to be [11].

The available *decentralized coordination mechanisms* (DCMs) and design metaphors provide field–tested coordination schemes that can be used to establish self–organizing dynamics. Therefore, it is desirable to support their utilization in software engineering practices. Since development teams intend the system to exhibit specific dynamics, it is essential to their successful utilization to support the concept of feedback structures in MAS and validating the behaviors that are to result from agent coordination.

# 3   A Systemic Approach to Modeling Organizational Dynamics

In order to facilitate the use of feedback cycles as design concepts for MAS development, we present an adjustment of systemic modeling notions to describe MAS behaviors. In the following, we briefly summarize system dynamics concepts, outline a tailored notation and discuss how simulation models of the role/group changing semantics can be derived.

## 3.1   System Dynamics

*System dynamics* research [10] addresses the examination of complex system behaviors by modeling the macroscopic *causal* relationships between system states. Systems are understood as collections of system state variables that are causally linked. These links denote the mutual influences of states, i.e. how state changes influence the rates of change of linked system states.

A prominent graphical notation is the *causal loop diagram* (CLD) [10]. In CLDs, macroscopic variables (nodes) are connected by arcs that indicate *positive* and *negative* causal links. Positive links (+) indicate that changes in originating state variables lead to equally directed changes (increase causes increase and decrease causes decrease, respectively). Negative links (-) cause reactions in opposite directions. Circular link sequences form either *reinforcing* (R) or *balancing* (B) feedback loops. The type of feedback is defined by the number of negative links. Odd numbers influence negatively, i.e. balancing, while even numbers rule out and indicate increases, i.e. reinforcing dynamics [10]. Therefore, reinforcing feedback loops indicate the system properties tend to increase as positive influences traverse the system. Balancing feedback loops regulate system properties. These generic properties allow to examine system behaviors qualitatively [10].

The simulation of these models typically relies on the derivation of differential equations that describe the rates of system state changes and allows to animate system behaviors. Inferring these rate equations is typically composed of two steps. First, the accumulative values and their input as well as output are identified. This is facilitated by *stock and flow* diagrams [10], which denote the inflow and outflow of from/to accumulations. Secondly, rates and the relation of these on other system properties need to be identified.

The major modeling efforts are (1) to derive meaningful system states and (2) identify appropriate links to characterize system operations. A general discussion of system dynamics tools can be found in [10], and their application in MAS contexts are exemplified in [11,12].

## 3.2   Organizational Modeling MAS

Organizational modeling approaches (e.g. reviewed in [5,4]) supplement agent-oriented development methodologies. Methodologies are typically biased toward implementation architectures [3] and support top–down development. Organizational approaches provide architecture independent abstractions. Modeling approaches typically refer to *roles* and *groups* as abstractions to characterize agent activity [23,24]. Roles describe commitments to normative agent behaviors and allow the denotation of agent activities and normative behaviors within organizational contexts. The adoption of roles may include commitments. Here, we use the role concept to classify agent behaviors. Groups partition MAS organizations into sets of individuals that share characteristics, therefore providing the contexts of roles. Both notions are typically applied within AOSE practices to describe the static semantics of MAS organizations in terms of role allocations and group formations. A prominent example is the Agent–Group–Role (AGR) model that provides a graphical notation and uses *AUML* sequence diagrams [25] to express the role/group changing behavior of individuals [26]. The provided concepts and notations address the design of organizational settings as well as the definition of role behaviors. Predicting the organizational dynamics arising from agent coaction is not supported and a demand for expressing organizational dynamics has been recognized (e.g. in [5]).

## 3.3   MAS Dynamics

Designed as a general purpose tool, the generic nature of CLDs complicates their usage and refinements have been proposed to remove possible sources of ambiguities and facilitate transfers of graphs to equations (e.g. discussed in [13]). In order to allow for unambiguous semantics in modeling MAS organizations, a tailored graphical representation of the causal structures of MAS organizations is given.

Models consist of directed graphs $G = (V, E)$. $V$ denotes the set of nodes, which represent accumulative values of the four node types that are shown in figure 1 (left). These are *role types*, *group membership*, *group count* and *environment property* ($V = R \cup GM \cup GC \cup E$). *Role* nodes describe the amount of agents executing specific roles. *Group memberships* comparably denote the counts of agents that are members of specific groups. When groups are dynamically created, developers may also want to track the number of groups of a specific type, indicated by the *group count* nodes. Finally, agents will sense and act on an environment and therefore react upon and influence *environment properties*. Node types can be stacked in order to merge nodes, i.e. combine nodes that

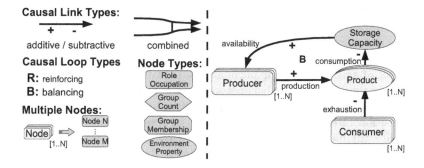

**Fig. 1.** MAS Dynamics node / link types (left) and modeling example (right)

are subject to common causalities. An optional annotation below nodes allows to denote the different node types. Edges between these nodes describe additive (+) and subtractive (-) contributions to the accumulative values of nodes. Causalities do not need to be between two nodes only, and *combined* links denote when causalities only take place mutually, i.e. in combination. Cyclic node sequences can be documented and exhibit either balancing (B) or reinforcing (R) feedback dynamics. Figure 1 (right) exemplifies the notation. Agents in a hypothetical setting can play *producer* and *consumer* roles. The stacked nodes indicate that different types of producers, products and consumers exist. These share a common storage capacity. This capacity is limiting the production of products, i.e. causes a balancing feedback loop.

### 3.4 Examination of Organizational Dynamics

The utilization of static descriptions of organizational structures is established in AOSE (cf. section 3.2). The adjustment of CLDs presented here aims at supplementing these models by facilitating the examination of their macroscopic, quantitative dynamics. The systemic models (CLDs) provide descriptions of the time dependent, causal behavior of the entities given in an organizational MAS model. The commonly used concepts of roles and groups can be mapped directly between both description levels (cf. figure 2, A).

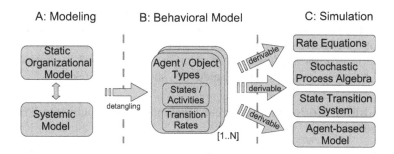

**Fig. 2.** Transforming CLDs into simulation models

In order to enable simulations, it is required to *detangle* role behaviors, i.e. the possible behaviors of *individual* roles and groups need to be refined, allowing one to express the role/group changing activities of individuals. Figure (cf. figure 2) denotes this process. Static and systemic models describe a MAS design, i.e. a common set of agent role /group occupations. In order to enable the qualitative simulation of the MAS design, it is necessary to *detangle* the role /group changing behavior of agents. The agents are broken up into sets of state /activities and their transition rates. Several representations of these intermediate, behavioral models are available, e.g. system dynamics research established stock–and–flow diagrams for this purpose. These explicitly define the rates of in– and out–flow from system states [10]. However, their derivation from CLDs is non-trivial and demands precise mathematical modeling effort to ensure correct mappings. On the other hand, software engineering teams can (re)use other means for describing of role/group changing activities (e.g. expressed in AUML sequence diagrams; see [24,26], cf. 3.5). Mapping the previously defined macroscopic system states (as defined in CLDs) to the detailed designs of individual roles/group members allows to infer the observable role changing activities, while hiding mathematical details. After the possible transitions have been defined, their rates need to be quantified. These intermediate behavioral models can be transferred into different formalisms that support system simulations.

Several means are available to simulate and observe the behavior of the detangled models (cf. figure 2, C). First, averaged state transitions can be expressed by differential equations, this technique is typically applied to analyse self–organizing dynamics in general and has been applied to MAS [27]. Since the behavior of agent–based systems is subject to stochastics that result from the non–determinism of agent reasoning as well as environmental dynamics it is inherently difficult to show the equivalence of mathematical models and MAS implementations (e.g. [28,29]). Due to these difficulties, simulation models are typically applied. Detangled state/role models can be understood as Continuous Time Markov Chains (CTMCs) which can be expressed in stochastic process algebra. Recently, these have been applied to examine self–organizing dynamics in MAS [30]. CTMCs can also be expressed in state transition systems, e.g. to enable model checking of macroscopic properties [31]. As an alternative approach, it has been discussed how state–based agent models can be derived from stock–and–flow diagrams [32].

In order to enable the simulation of MAS dynamics as well as to clarify the semantics of the above presented modeling approach we discuss in the following section how the macroscopic behavior of MAS organizations can be described by stochastic process algebra. This derivation is exemplified in section 4 and compared to a purely mathematical model to show equivalence.

## 3.5   Enabling Model Simulations: Derivation of Stochastic Process Algebra

In the following, we detail the previously given procedure to derive simulation models from sets of corresponding AOSE / CLD models. Stochastic process algebra models can be constructed by detangling the role /group changing behavior of agent models (cf. figure 2). At any given time the state of a MAS is given by its configuration, i.e. the states of its nodes (V; cf. section 3.3). Following the systemic modeling approach, node states are given as property occupation numbers, e.g. the number of agents that exhibit a specific role, and changes take place by adding and removing elements. Process types represent system properties and process counts denote property occupation numbers (cf. section 3.3). Process terms are derived from models of the role / group changing behavior of agents as well as their influences on the number of environment elements.

**The Stochastic $\pi$ Calculus.** *Stochastic Process Algebra* (SPA) are established tools for the quantitative analysis of concurrent systems. They allow to describe system as sets of independently executing *processes* that communicate via *channels*. A prominent example is the Stochastic $\pi$ calculus (S$\pi$) [33] that extends the original $\pi$ calculus [34], with stochastic delays and channel rates. This extension transfers the underlying transition systems to Markov transition systems by annotating *activity rates* $(r_i)$ to channel definitions $S \overset{r_i:a}{\rightarrow} S'$ and *delays* $(\tau_\delta)$ to process activities. Activity rates define how the transition probability between $S$ and $S'$ increases in time via an exponential distribution. In the following we use a subset of the S$\pi$ language. The available actions comprise sending ($!c$) and and receiving ($?c$) values via channels $(c)$ as well as delays $(\tau_\delta)$. Dots (.) separate states. P+Q denotes the choice between two courses of action and P|Q denotes the parallel execution of processes. Channels can be created on the fly via (new c) and Processes can be parametrized (P(c)). details on the language and its syntax can be found in [35,36]. Interpreters for the simulation of S$\pi$ models are freely available.[1]

SPAs are particularly attractive to model quantitative aspects of systems dynamics and have been applied to biological and chemical processes [35,36] as well as to self–organizing MAS dynamics [30]. They facilitate the description of concurrency while enabling the compositionality of models. These properties distinguish them from other formalisms (e.g. state automaton and petrinets; discussed in [37]). Here, we use SPA to express the occupation numbers of role/group models.

The key element in phenomenologic descriptions of agent behaviors are roles. These allow to classify the macroscopic observable agent behaviors independently from the applied agent architecture (e.g. cf. [5]). First, we show how roles are interact with each other. Then we discuss how roles interact with groups and how roles as well as group members interact with environment properties. These operations allow to represent the additive and subtractive links between CLD node types. In addition, the presented operations guide the derivation of stochastic simulation models from MAS organizational designs.

**Role / Role Interactions.** Operations on roles in generic organizational models have been discussed in [24,23]. In the following we assume that agents

---

[1] E.g. the Stochastic Pi Machine (SPiM): http://research.microsoft.com/~aphillip/spim/

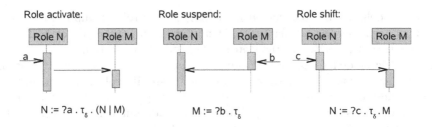

**Fig. 3.** Role interactions in (A)UML and $S\pi$ calculus

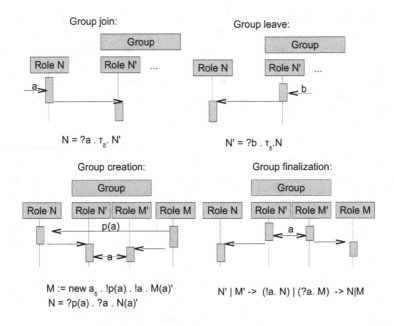

**Fig. 4.** Group interactions in (A)UML and $S\pi$ calculus

exhibit a static settings of roles that they can play. The considered operations are denoted in figure 3. AUML sequence diagrams visualize the *activation* and *suspension* of roles as well as *shifts* between roles [24]. The associated $S\pi$ fragments mimic these operations. Individual roles are represented by processes and interprocess communication is used to trigger process creations and suspension. A delay ($\tau_\delta$) without a subsequent activity terminates processes.

**Group Interactions.** Groups are structured in roles, i.e. group members play roles that are associated to certain groups. Therefore, *join* and *leave* operations can be expressed as role shifts (cf. figure 4). An alternative to representing group membership by role activity is the representation of the number of groups by the number of (private) channels that are established for group internal communication. This scheme has been applied to mimic complexations of molecules [36,38] and can be used to express *creation* and *finalization* of groups. The

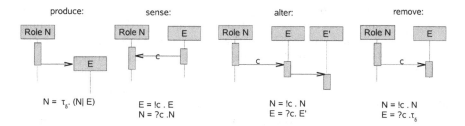

**Fig. 5.** Environment element interactions in (A)UML and S$\pi$ calculus

possibility of group formations is represented by a public channel $(p)$, where agents can interact to form groups by role changes. For each group a private channel is separately created on the fly $(new\ a_\delta)$. Communication via this private channel can be used to subsequently break up the group. Reception of values can trigger agents to leave the group, i.e. shift roles [36].

**Environment interactions.** Environment interactions comprise the creation, sensing, altering and removing of environment properties (cf figure 5). These elements are also represented processes and interactions take place via public channels. Sensing is enabled by reception of messages and alternation as well as removal of elements can be described as sending operations.

The resulting S$\pi$ models can be described by rate equations as well (cf. figure 2). The derivation of rate equations from the S$\pi$ calculus is done in two steps. As we have already argued, our S$\pi$ representation describes a system with reaction equations for system variables. In the second step, the corresponding rate equations that determine the dynamic behavior of frequencies of system state variables can be obtained from the reaction equations in a straight forward manner like in chemical reaction systems [39]). This is exemplified in the following section.

## 4 Case Study: Modeling an Agent–Based Resource Allocation Application

Prominent examples of nature–inspired application designs are resource allocation algorithms. The here presented modeling approach is exemplified by modeling a *dynamic allocation* strategy that is inspired by the foraging behavior in *honey bee* societies [40]. We examine an application setting that follows [40], where a cluster of servers that host web services are to be coordinated. Since the usage of services (as websites, etc.) varies, it is desirable to avoid static allocations and enable the dynamic allocation of services to be offered to adjust to changing demands on the fly. Besides, when the capability to host individual services (as websites, etc.) is charged on a *pay–per–use* basis, the effective coordination of resources (servers) is crucial for economic success. Dynamic co-hosting involves enabling each server to select independently which customers service to host [40].

We assume a cluster of independent servers that are either *unbound* or are *associated* to a specific service, i.e. are prepared to answer requests. The incoming *jobs* (requests) vary and are issued by various *requesters*. The macroscopic system dynamics are denoted in figure 6 (I), i.e. the two balancing feedback loops are expected to be exhibited. Requests should be handled (i.e.: satisfied; negative link) and their presence should enforce the number of team members that are available to handle requests (positive link). Team formations are to be balanced, by releasing under-worked servers (negative link) and the allocation of unused resources (positive link).

The utilization of *honey bee foraging* strategies has been proposed in [40] to guide server allocations. The dynamics of this design metaphor is denoted in figure 6 (II), where two kinds of agents cooperate. *Scouts* wander an environment and encounter *resources*. These agents return to their nest and communicate the availability of resources, along with locally conceivable quality measures (distance to nest, quality of nectar, etc.) via *waggle dances*. These communication acts draw the attention of *foraging* bees that start to repeatedly exploit the communicated resources and are free to switch to more beneficial resources when communicated by scouts.

Following [12], these systemic models of pattern can be used to refine the feedback loop by mapping loop structures. Figure 6 (III) denotes the mapping of the described metaphor to the application domain from [40]. This mapping shows how the dynamics of the bee foraging strategy (cf. figure 6, II) can be applied to realize the two balancing feedback loops that were identified as system requirements (cf. figure 6, I). The *jobs* that enter the system represent the resources

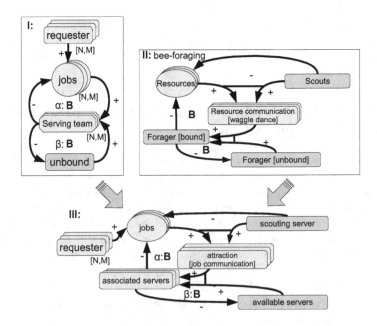

**Fig. 6.** The macroscopic dynamics of an agent–based load balancing application

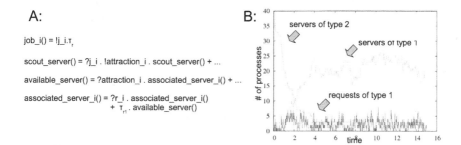

**A:**

job_i() = !j_i.τ_r

scout_server() = ?j_i . !attraction_i . scout_server() + ...

available_server() = ?attraction_i . associated_server_i() + ...

associated_server_i() = ?r_i . associated_server_i()
                       + τ_rt . available_server()

**Fig. 7.** A: Sπ–calculus model; B: Simulation of a responsive behavioral regime

that are to be foraged. Servers are either *associated* to specific job types and represent bound bee *foragers* or are *available*, i.e. not bound to a specific job type. A third server type (*scouting server*) is introduced. These scouts randomly change their service allocation and communicate high service demands (*attraction*). It represents the supplement to an organizational design that addresses role dependencies (e.g. in GAIA [41], AGR [26], etc.) and AOSE models that detail the agent architecture specific designs of role (changing) activities.

Figure 7 denotes a sπ model that resembles the dynamics of the previously given MAS design (cf. figure 6 (left)), by representing the behavior of the passive job items as well as the agent roles as independent processes. *Jobs* ($j\_i$) that enter the system to be satisfied are represented as passive processes that can only be consumed ($?j\_i$). The index i (1..K) indicates the different job types. Two kinds of agent types are distinguished, each exhibiting two behaviors. Servers can act as *scouting server* (scout_server) randomly reconfigure and perform tasks ($!j\_i$). Successful performances and their quality are communicated ($!attraction\_i$). Servers that mimic foragers are initially *available* servers (*available_server*), listen to communications from scouts ($?attraction\_i$) and are free to shift roles and allocate to *associated* servers (*associated_server*) to answer corresponding request types. With a low rate, they are returning to unbound state to allow perturbations, i.e. (re–)allocation to different request types.

The system requirements (cf. figure 6, I) and the detailed system model (cf. figure 6, III) describe that the allocation of servers is to be steered by a balancing feedback loop ($\alpha$). This loop ensures that increases of jobs increase the allocation of associated servers (positive link). In addition, a second feedback loop ($\beta$) ensures that associated servers can be freed to allow their allocation to more demanded services. Figure 6 (right) shows simulation results of the derived sπ model that validate the presence of these causalities. The system is initialized with a low number of agents to satisfy requests of type 1 and a high number of agents to satisfy requests of type 2. When subsequently only requests of type 1 enter, the coordination scheme responds with server (re–)allocations to satisfy the increased demand.

It remains to show that the derived stochastic model actually resembles the dynamics that are described by the CLD-based notation. CLDs are typically examined by inferring rate equations that describe their dynamic behavior [10]. The translation of rate equations from $S\pi$ calculus has been discussed in [39]. The agreement of the models is shown by comparing the rate equations that describe the design and the derived $s\pi$ model.

Derivation of rate equations from CLD require to identify the accumulative values and the rates of increase and decay. For the CLD (cf. figure 6: C) the dynamics are given in the following, where $job_i$ denotes the number of requests of a certain type $i$, $gen_i$ denotes their generators, $attr_i$ denotes their attraction, $ss$ denotes the amount of scouting servers, $as_i$ denotes the amount of servers associated to a job type $i$, $av$ denotes the amount of available servers and $\alpha$, $\beta$, $\gamma$, $\delta$, $\epsilon$ denote transition rates.

$$\frac{d\,job_i}{dt} = \alpha\,gen - \beta\,ss\,job_i - \delta\,as_i\,job_i \tag{1}$$

$$\frac{d\,attr_i}{dt} = \beta\,ss\,job_i \tag{2}$$

$$\frac{d\,as_i}{dt} = -\epsilon\,as_i + \gamma\,av\,attr_i \tag{3}$$

$$\text{with} \quad gen, ss = const \tag{4}$$

$$\text{and} \quad av + \sum_i as_i = const \tag{5}$$

$$\text{with} \quad i = 1, \ldots, K \tag{6}$$

In [39] the derivation of rate equations from simple $S\pi$ models has been approached by deriving intermediate reaction equations that quantify how process instances interact. The defined mappings use the same calculus operations and therefore the here derived simulation model can be treated in the same way. The reaction equations are:

$$gen_i \xrightarrow{\alpha} job_i + gen_i \tag{7}$$

$$job_i + ss \xrightarrow{\beta} attr_i + ss \tag{8}$$

$$av + attr_i \xrightarrow{\gamma} as_i \tag{9}$$

$$as_i + job_i \xrightarrow{\delta} as_i \tag{10}$$

$$as_i \xrightarrow{\epsilon} av \tag{11}$$

With this case study we have exemplified the equivalence of the simulation model ($S\pi$–calculus) and the differential equations which resemble the dynamics that are described by the CLD–based model. The correctness of equation (4) and (2) is a direct consequence of equations (7) and (8), whereas equation (10) is needed in addition to obtain the correctness of equation (1). Similarly, Equations (3) and (5) follow from equations (9) and (11), again according to the rules for chemical reaction kinetics (cf. [39]). The general proof of equivalence of both modeling approaches remains future work.

# 5   Related Work

Conceiving MAS applications in organizations of roles and groups is facilitated by few general purpose AOSE methodologies. E.g. *GAIA* [41] proposes the design of MAS by inferring static organizational settings from the requirements on the MAS to be. Organizational modes provide an abstract implementations independent view–point on MAS designs. Therefore, platform independent modeling approaches such as *MOISE+* [42] and *AGR* [26] are revised and supplement methodologies that focus on certain agent architectures or implementation platforms [3]. Particularly the well–known *Agent–Group–Role* (AGR) model [26] has been subject to improvements. E.g. to address the inclusion of MAS environments [43]. However, established approaches address static organizational settings and are not appropriate to analyse dynamic properties of organizational activities. The need for the expression of organizational dynamics has been identified (e.g. in [5]), and is addressed in this paper by adjusting macroscopic modeling tools from system dynamics research. The system behavior is described in terms of averaged influences / reactions. We expect this approach to be generally applicable as it describes the effects of agent interactions in contrast to their realization. Therefore, the effects of social behaviors can be described. E.g. authority dependencies would establish causal relations between authorities and the enforced behaviors of subordinates.

Purely mathematical approaches [27,44] have been proposed to model decentralized reorganizations that focus the the derivation of rate equations from state–based agent models. The derived equations result from Master Equations that describe underlying Markov processes. System states are reflected by the sum of the microscopic agent behaviors. Agents are assumed to have a fixed number of executable behaviors (i.e. states) and system states are described by the fraction of agents executing them. These approaches address homogeneous MAS designs and are extended by the here presented transfer of organizational models to mathematical and algebraic simulation models.

A graph–based approach has been applied to model organizational performance in [45]. Directed graphs are used to denote the rates of changes of the *workload* on fixed sets of roles in non–changing organizational settings. The notion of feedback structures has yet found minor attention in MAS development. The indication of *information flows* within microscopic, i.e. UML–based, designs has been proposed [46]. However, assessing and validating the changes of organizations themselves require simulation efforts. E.g. a *Temporal Trace Language* has been applied in [47] to specify and simulate the activities of role executing agents. Algebraic modeling techniques have been successfully applied to calculate and simulate dynamic system properties. An algebraic approach to MAS organizational changes has been given in [48], particularly addressing environment mediated interactions. Mathematical results on self–organizing dynamics have been obtained from process algebraic models [49] and stochastic process algebras have been successfully applied to directly simulate decentralized coordination in MAS [30]. In this paper, a systemic, graph–based notation is proposed and its usefulness demands tools to execute and simulate the derived models. Process algebraic simulation tools have been applied to bridge this gab by combining both research directions and facilitating model validation.

# 6   Conclusions

In this paper, the utilization of *systemic* modeling concepts and notations has been proposed to express the behavior of MAS in terms of causal relations between organizational modeling concepts. The presented modeling notions and the tailored notation supplement current AOSE practices by facilitating phenomenological description of the dynamic behavior of MAS organizations. This description level can be used analytically, by deriving simulations from implemented agent designs, as well as predictively in order to simulate the macroscopic dynamics of conceived designs.

The proposed modeling approach addresses macroscopic dynamics in terms of causes and influences. The causes for these influences can be described on more detailed description levels that address social and/or authority dependence relationships. Derivation of systemic models from these descriptions has not been examined and is left for future work. The here presented modeling approach remains to be formalized as a method fragment [50] to tailor development procedures. The simulation of MAS designs by iterating stochastic transition systems requires considerable manual effort for both model derivation and parameter (transition rate) adjustment. Future work will examine guidelines to these activities as well as the utilization of other simulation tools besides SPAs to animate *detangled* systemic models of MAS. E.g. the the application of model checking techniques to self–regulatory behaviors has been approached in [31]).

## Acknowledgments

One of us (J.S.) would like to thank the *Distributed Systems and information Systems* (VSIS) group at Hamburg University, particularly Winfried Lamersdorf, Lars Braubach and Alexander Pokahr for inspiring discussion and encouragement.

## References

1. Jennings, N.R.: Building complex, distributed systems: the case for an agent-based approach. Comms. of the ACM 44(4), 35–41 (2001)
2. Henderson-Sellers, B., Giorgini, P. (eds.): Agent-oriented Methodologies. Idea Group Publishing (2005) ISBN: 1591405815
3. Sudeikat, J., Braubach, L., Pokahr, A., Lamersdorf, W.: Evaluation of agent–oriented software methodologies - examination of the gap between modeling and platform. In: Odell, J.J., Giorgini, P., Müller, J.P. (eds.) AOSE 2004. LNCS, vol. 3382, pp. 126–141. Springer, Heidelberg (2005)
4. Coutinho, L.R., Sichman, J.S., Boissier, O.: Modeling organization in mas: a comparison of models. In: Proc. of the 1st. Workshop on Software Engineering for Agent-Oriented Systems (SEAS 2005) (2005)

5. Mao, X., Yu, E.: Organizational and social concepts in agent oriented software engineering. In: Odell, J.J., Giorgini, P., Müller, J.P. (eds.) AOSE 2004. LNCS, vol. 3382, pp. 1–15. Springer, Heidelberg (2005)

6. Serugendo, G.D.M., Gleizes, M.P., Karageorgos, A.: Self–organisation and emergence in mas: An overview. Informatica 30, 45–54 (2006)

7. Mühl, G., Werner, M., Jaeger, M.A., Herrmann, K., Parzyjegla, H.: On the definition of self-managing and self-organizing systems. In: Braun, T., Carle, G., Stiller, B. (eds.) KIVS 2007 Kommunikation in Verteilten Systemen – Industriebeiträge, Kurzbeiträge und Workshops, VDE–Verlag (2007)

8. Parunak, H.V.D., Brueckner, S.: Engineering swarming systems. In: Methodologies and Software Engineering for Agent Systems, pp. 341–376. Kluwer Academic Publishers, Dordrecht (2004)

9. Sudeikat, J., Renz, W.: Building Complex Adaptive Systems: On Engineering Self–Organizing Multi–Agent Systems. In: Applications of Complex Adaptive Systems, pp. 229–256. IGI Global (2008)

10. Sterman, J.D.: Business Dynamics - Systems Thinking an Modeling for a Complex World. McGraw-Hill, New York (2000)

11. Sudeikat, J., Renz, W.: On expressing and validating requirements for the adaptivity of self–organizing multi–agent systems. System and Information Sciences Notes 2, 14–19 (2007)

12. Sudeikat, J., Renz, W.: Toward systemic mas development: Enforcing decentralized self–organization by composition and refinement of archetype dynamics. In: Proc. of Engineering Environment–Mediated Multiagent Systems. LNCS. Springer, Heidelberg (2007)

13. Richardson, G.P.: Problems with causal–loop diagrams. System Dynamics Review 2, 158–170 (1986)

14. Bonabeau, E., Dorigo, M., Theraulaz, G.: Swarm Intelligence: From Natural to Artificial Systems. Santa Fe Institute Studies on the Sciences of Complexity. Oxford University Press, Oxford (1999)

15. Mamei, M., Menezes, R., Tolksdorf, R., Zambonelli, F.: Case studies for self-organization in computer science. J. Syst. Archit. 52, 443–460 (2006)

16. DeWolf, T., Holvoet, T.: Decentralised coordination mechanisms as design patterns for self-organising emergent applications. In: Proceedings of the Fourth International Workshop on Engineering Self-Organising Applications, pp. 40–61 (2006)

17. Gardelli, L., Viroli, M., Omicini, A.: Design patterns for self–organizing systems. In: Burkhard, H.-D., Lindemann, G., Verbrugge, R., Varga, L.Z. (eds.) CEEMAS 2007. LNCS (LNAI), vol. 4696, pp. 123–132. Springer, Heidelberg (2007)

18. Edmonds, B.: Using the experimental method to produce reliable self-organised systems. In: Brueckner, S.A., Di Marzo Serugendo, G., Karageorgos, A., Nagpal, R. (eds.) ESOA 2005. LNCS (LNAI), vol. 3464, pp. 84–99. Springer, Heidelberg (2005)

19. DeWolf, T., Holvoet, T.: A taxonomy for self-* properties in decentralised autonomic computing. In: Chapter in Autonomic Computing: Concepts, Infrastructure, and Applications (2006)

20. Hassas, S., Marzo-Serugendo, G.D., Karageorgos, A., Castelfranchi, C.: On self–organized mechanisms from social, business and economic domains. Informatica 30, 62–71 (2006)

21. Renz, W., Sudeikat, J.: Emergence in software. KI – Künstliche Intelligenz 02/07, 48–49 (2007)

22. DeWolf, T., Holvoet, T.: Towards a methodolgy for engineering self-organising emergent systems. In: Proceedings of the International Conference on Self-Organization and Adaptation of Multi-agent and Grid Systems (2005)

23. Odell, J., Van Dyke Parunak, H., Brueckner, S., Sauter, J.: Changing roles: Dynamic role assignment. Jounal of Object Technology 2, 77–86 (2003)

24. Odell, J.J., Van Dyke Parunak, H., Brueckner, S.A., Sauter, J.: Temporal aspects of dynamic role assignment. In: Giorgini, P., Müller, J.P., Odell, J.J. (eds.) AOSE 2003. LNCS, vol. 2935, pp. 201–213. Springer, Heidelberg (2004)

25. Odell, J., Parunak, H.V.D., Bauer, B.: Extending UML for agents. In: Proceedings of the Agent-Oriented Information Systems Workshop at the 17th National conference on Artificial Intelligence (2000)

26. Ferber, J., Gutknecht, O., Michel, F.: From agents to organizations: An organizational view of multi-agent systems. In: Giorgini, P., Müller, J.P., Odell, J.J. (eds.) AOSE 2003. LNCS, vol. 2935, pp. 214–230. Springer, Heidelberg (2004)

27. Lerman, K., Galstyan, A.: A general methodology for mathematical analysis of multiagent systems. USC Inf. Sciences Tech.l Report ISI-TR-529 (2001)

28. Axtell, R., Axelrod, R., Epstein, J.M., Cohen, M.D.: Aligning simulation models: A case study and results. Computational & Mathematical Organization Theory 1, 123–141 (1996)

29. Wilson, W.: Resolving discrepancies between deterministic population models and individual–based simulations. The American Naturalist 151, 116–134 (1998)

30. Gardelli, L., Viroli, M., Omicini, A.: On the role of simulations in engineering self-organising mas: The case of an intrusion detection system in tucson. In: Brueckner, S.A., Di Marzo Serugendo, G., Hales, D., Zambonelli, F. (eds.) ESOA 2005. LNCS, vol. 3910, pp. 153–166. Springer, Heidelberg (2006)

31. Winfield, F.T., Sa, J., Fernandez-Gago, M.C., Dixon, C., Fisher, M.: On formal specification of emergent behaviours in swarm robotic systems. International Journal of Advanced Robotic Systems 2, 363–370 (2005)

32. Borshev, A., Filippov, A.: From system dynamics and discrete event to practical agent based modeling: Reasong, techniques, tools. In: Proceedings of the 22nd International Conference of the System Dnymics Society (2004)

33. Priami, C.: Stochastic $\pi$–calculus. Computer Journal 6, 578–589 (1995)

34. Milner, R., Parrow, J., Walker, D.: A calculus of mobile processes (i and ii). Information and Computation 100, 1–77 (1992)

35. Phillips, A., Cardelli, L.: A correct abstract machine for the stochastic pi-calculus. In: Bioconcur 2004. ENTCS (2004)

36. Blossey, R., Cardelli, L., Phillips, A.: Compositionality, stochasticity and cooperativity in dynamic models of gene regulation. HFSP Journal (2007)

37. Gardelli, L., Viroli, M., Omicini, A.: On the role of simulation in the engineering of self-organising systems: Detecting abnormal behaviour in MAS. In: AI*IA/TABOO Joint Workshop (WOA 2005), pp. 85–90 (2005)

38. Regev, A.: Computational Systems Biology: A Calculus for Biomolecular knowledge. PhD thesis, Tel Aviv University (2002)

39. Cardelli, L.: On process rate semantics. Theoretical Computer Science (2008), http://lucacardelli.name/Papers/OnProcessRateSemantics.pdf

40. Nakrani, S., Tovey, C.: On honey bees and dynamic server allocation in internet hosting centers. Adaptive Behavior 12, 223–240 (2004)

41. Zambonelli, F., Jennings, N., Wooldridge, M.: Developing multiagent systems: the gaia methodology. ACM Trans. on Software Engineering and Methodology 12, 317–370 (2003)

42. Hübner, J.F., Sichman, J.S., Boissier, O.: Moise+: Towards a structural, functional, and deontic model for MAS organization. In: Proc. of the First Int. Joint Conf. on Autonomous Agents and Multi-Agent Systems (AAMAS 2002), pp. 501–502 (2002)

43. Ferber, J., Michel, F., Baez, J.: Agre: Integrating environments with organizations. In: Weyns, D., Van Dyke Parunak, H., Michel, F. (eds.) E4MAS 2004. LNCS, vol. 3374, pp. 48–56. Springer, Heidelberg (2005)

44. Lerman, K., Galstyan, A.: Automatically modeling group behavior of simple agents. In: Agent Modeling Workshop, AAMAS 2004, New York, NY (2004)

45. Hoogendoorn, M., Treur, J., Yolum, P.: A labeled graph approach to analyze organizational performance. In: Proceeding of the 2006 IEEE/WIC/ACM International Conference on Intelligent Agent Technology (IAT 2006), pp. 482–489. IEEE Computer Society Press, Los Alamitos (2006)

46. DeWolf, T., Holvoet, T.: Using UML 2 activity diagrams to design information flows and feedback-loops in self-organising emergent systems. In: Proc. of the Sec. Int. Workshop on Engineering Emergence in Decentralised Autonomic Systems (EEDAS 2007) (2007)

47. Hoogendoorn, M., Schut, M.C., Treur, J.: Modeling decentralized organizational change in honeybee societies. In: Proceedings of the Sixth International Conference on Complex Systems, NECSI (2006)

48. Viroli, M., Omicini, A.: Process-algebraic approaches for multi-agent systems: an overview. Applicable Algebra in Engineering, Communication and Computing 16, 69–75 (2005)

49. Tofts, C.: Describing social insect behavior using process algebra. Transactions of the society for Computer Simulation, 227–383 (1991)

50. Cossentino, M., Gaglio, S., Garro, A., Seidita, V.: Method fragments for agent design methodologies: from standardisation to research. Int. J. Agent-Oriented Software Engineering 1, 91–121 (2007)

# Coordination in Adaptive Organisations: Extending Shared Plans with Knowledge Cultivation

Kathleen Keogh[1,2], Liz Sonenberg[2], and Wally Smith[2]

[1] School of Information Technology and Mathematical Sciences
University of Ballarat, Mt Helen, VIC 3353, Australia
`k.keogh@ballarat.edu.au`
[2] Department of Information Systems, University of Melbourne, Parkville, VIC 3052

**Abstract.** Agent-based simulation can be used to investigate behavioural requirements, capabilities and strategies that might be helpful in complex, dynamic and adaptive situations, and can be used in training scenarios. In this paper, we study the requirements of coordination in complex unfolding scenarios in which agents may come and go and where there is a dynamic organisational structure. This is a step on the way to developing a simulation framework that can be part of a training system in the domain of emergency management. We argue the need for an extension to the SharedPlans formalism required to support the sharing of knowledge about a dynamically unfolding situation, specifically: who is in the team? and who holds relevant knowledge? Our rationale for such an extension is presented based on a prior case study of a railway accident and a further analysis of the coordination and communication activities amongst the disaster management team during its recovery. We conclude that in addition to the obligations imposed by the standard SharedPlans framework, agents in complex unfolding scenarios also need *knowledge cultivation* processes to reason about the dynamic organisational structure and the changing world state. We briefly express the requirements of knowledge cultivation as obligations that could be imposed on agents. We argue that in order to facilitate appropriate knowledge cultivation, agents need access to explicit models of organisational knowledge. This knowledge encapsulates the relational structure of the team, along with shared beliefs, goals and plans. We briefly present a formal representation of this model in order to clearly identify the rich information needed in an adaptive organisation.

## 1   Introduction

We are motivated to develop believable artificial agents to work with humans in simulations of complex situations such as Disaster Management (DM). Such agents could replace human team members and enable research into team coordination using simulations. Using synthetic agents to provide expert feedback and guided practice in training has also been shown to be helpful [7,22] but the skills

G. Vouros et al. (Eds.): OAMAS 2008, LNAI 5368, pp. 90–107, 2009.

required to coordinate an expert team need to be developed in a realistic and suitably complex simulation environment [2,22]. Teaming agents with humans requires a model for collaboration and coordination.

Team coordination in dynamic situations can be very complex as dependencies between tasks must be managed and priorities can change as the situation changes. Additional complexities are introduced if the team organisational structure is allowed to evolve during the collaboration. So, when people and agents engage in joint activity, agents need to be sensitive to the needs and knowledge of the people. There needs to be an interpredictability of behaviour so that each team player can predict the behaviour of others in order to coordinate their own plans [11].

In the real world domain of DM, the team is distributed across different locations and communication may be limited by radio bandwidth and accessibility. It is usual for multiple service agencies to be involved. The organisational structure is dynamic, people may leave and join the recovery team during the management of the disaster and roles may change. Due to the emergent nature of the situation and the uniqueness of each emergency, team members mutually adjust their behaviour to work with and support others in the team, to achieve a goal. There are shared goals, default plans and some agreed protocols (e.g., the disaster site must be secured by the Fire agency before the Ambulance officers can enter), but the overall coordination is adaptive and flexible.

This coordination is not explicitly controlled by fixed norms. There are significant subtleties evident in an analysis of real-world behaviour that point to a richness of awareness and communication. It could be dangerous to attempt to simplify such to a mere list of requirements, however in an attempt to move closer to a form that might be computationally achievable, we analyse these requirements based on a real world case study in section 2.

The SharedPlans framework [8,9] offers a form of adaptive dynamic team planning needed in DM. Team Situation Awareness and Shared Mental Models of the task and team are not made explicit in SharedPlans, although they are important in enabling adaption in human teams [2]. The SharedPlans formalism focuses on knowledge related to decision making, and although intentions-that in SharedPlans could be employed to address a group's commitment to maintaining accurate and up-to-date shared beliefs about the environment, this has not been explicitly addressed to date. In this paper, we seek to describe the essential requirements and hence capabilities to be enabled in artificial teams for adaptive strategic and coordinated collaboration. We extend SharedPlans to accommodate commitments concerning beliefs about the unfolding situation - including the state of the environment which is only partly observable by any individual, and information about the organisation of individuals involved in resolving the problem.

DM involves the establishment and maintenance of a management system as well as directing and controlling operational tasks. The management system is the dynamic group of agents and resources engaged with sharing the goal of resolving the disaster. Following Smith and Dowell [15], we define DM coordination as "the resolution of interdependencies between the activities of the disparate resources of the incident organization". An organisation is a set of actors, with a social order and working toward a common goal. The organisational structure defines roles and enables coordination[3]. Coordination requires adaptivity that occurs within 'coordination loops' or collections of groups that form to achieve a goal. Such groups require synchronisation and mutual adjustment of tasks[20]. Within the DM system, sub-teams or groups form to plan and act together to resolve subgoals (e.g., secure site, attend to injured). These sub-teams may involve people from different agencies working together, who form a team to collaborate on a shared goal. When such a (sub)-team emerges during DM, without a need for explicit negotiation, there must be assumed obligations and responsibilities taken on regarding the need to communicate and share related knowledge - knowledge of the situation and regarding planning for action, as well as knowledge regarding who is involved in the team [2]. In our abstract architecture, we attempt to explicitly describe the processes and artefacts needed to enact these obligations. The next step is to formalise these proposed extensions.

When teams of people are working to resolve a situation, as the following case analysis will highlight, communication to share vital information regarding the accident situation can be crucial to a coordinated response. When artificial agents become part of teams collaborating in such domains, we suggest it is important to provide a mechanism for awareness and knowledge sharing in agents to avoid problems derived from decision making based on incorrect knowledge. Teams need to establish common ground - sharing pertinent knowledge, beliefs and assumptions [11]. For effective team coordination and collaboration, beliefs need to be shared and to some degree beliefs need to be held as mutual. In order to facilitate appropriate knowledge sharing, there needs to be awareness of who is 'in the team', 'who knows what' and 'who might need to know'.

Agent technology has been shown to be useful in aiding human teams in response to emergency situations (e.g. [1,4,13]). Tate and colleagues relied on human initiative and intuition to control information availability to other humans in the team [1], others have used adjustable autonomy allowing agents to defer to humans for complex decisions [13]. Using an information system to deliver filtered, context based situational knowledge to appropriate people in the DM team could help human performance[19]. Our architecture is aimed at naming explicit obligations that the artificial agents need to have to compel the appropriate automated sharing of knowledge. Having shared dynamic artefacts available to enable human collaboration has been shown to be effective [1]. Sharing mental models and agents having a representation to enable the identification of relevant knowledge to share has been demonstrated to improve human behaviour in human-agent teams [4]. Sharing mental models including shared situation awareness is important to the functioning of adaptive human teams [2,12,19]. Our interest is in the design of realistic (believable), autonomous, adaptive, artificial team agents.

In the remainder of this paper, we outline requirements of adaptive coordinating teams in DM by analysis of an existing real world case study. We then suggest the capabilities needed for adaptive team agents. We formalise the requirements in terms of obligations on each team member and suggest an extension to the SharedPlans framework to address these issues. We have chosen SharedPlans as it provides an intention driven formalism based on adaptive human behaviour. We hope it would result in believeable and predictable agent behaviour. We present a model of the components that comprise an adaptive organisation and express these using an extension to an existing formalism. This formal organisational model provides a language for describing the adaptive organisations in our case study.

# 2    Case Study – Ais Gill Train Accident

In this section, we describe the scenario of a train accident based on previous work by Smith and Dowell [15]. Our analysis is focusing on identifying beliefs and knowledge emerging about the situation and the associated communication to share this. We highlight the need for appropriate sharing of beliefs across a distributed team in order to successfully coordinate a response. This case study motivates our proposal in section 4.

## 2.1    Overview of Accident Scenario

At 18:49, 31st January, 1995, UK Emergency Services were notified that a train had become derailed somewhere between Kirkby Steven and Blea Moor in the county of Cumbria. Six minutes later, a second train crashed into the derailed train resulting in escalation of the incident. A train conductor was killed, 6 passengers and a train driver were seriously injured. A significant period of time elapsed (about an hour) during which the exact location of the train crash was not clear. Initially, the emergency services were unaware that the second train had crashed into the derailed train and the number of injured was thought only to be 2. A number of agencies were involved in the response: Ambulance, Fire, Police, Volunteer Mountain Rescue, and Railtrack. The accident site was not easily accessed by road and the first to arrive on the scene were fire crews 30 minutes after the accident. When ambulance crew from Brough arrived (55 minutes after the initial accident) it became known that there were closer to 30 injured people and one deceased. It took a further hour after the location and number of injured was known, before decisions regarding how to transport the injured to hospital were finally settled.

The seriously injured driver was carried along the train track to meet an ambulance at a road bridge. It was raining and this proved hazardous. Earlier, a request was made inquiring about the possibility of sending a rescue train to transport the injured via rail to Carlisle train station, to be met by ambulances. This emerged into a reality, and so other injured people were kept dry in the train waiting for the rescue train. Communication difficulties occurred with the inappropriate dissemination of this decision: ambulances were not informed in a timely way and continued en-route to the disaster site rather than being redirected to Carlisle railway station. There was also confusion regarding the eventual destination of the injured, so one hospital remained on standby longer than necessary.

## 2.2 Development of Situational Knowledge Regarding the Incident

As with many disaster situations, the knowledge regarding details of the incident was not clear initially and were established with difficulty over an extended period. In a DM team, the people involved need to share obligations to pass on relevant information to others in the team. As the actual situation changed at Ais Gill, beliefs were shared and revised. This is 'fill in the blanks' type of coordination - establishing uncertain facts such as location and number of injured. During this first phase, the team focus is information gathering and situation awareness[2]. Information is shared according to protocols and obligations to keep others in the disaster recovery system informed and up to date. Some incorrect conjectures were made whilst details were uncertain. It was assumed that there wouldn't have been many passengers on the train, so the number of injured passengers was (incorrectly) assumed to be small.

Communication was significantly constrained. Firstly, in the hilly terrain there was disruption to radio. Second, ambiguity and uncertainty about the situation made it difficult to know what to communicate. Third, while many agencies are in the process of building up their response, each individual agent knows little about who to communicate with. The difficulties and errors in communication highlight these challenges in such a dynamic situation. But, passing on relevant information to others in the system is crucial. The fire crew, arriving at 19:25 passed on accurate location information "1 mile north of Ais Gill" to the fire control, who passed it to railtrack, who passed it to ambulance control centre in Carlisle, who then passed it to the Brough ambulance crew with instructions to change course en route to the site. Examining this communication with the eyes of a potential designer of a response system including artificial agents, we conclude that agents engaged in such a scenario need obligations to follow similar protocols to humans: to pass on new or revised situational information such as the accident location and number of injured.

*Observation 1. The agents in an adaptive team need obligations defined to pass on new or revised information about the disaster situation to relevant others in the system. This implies that agents need to have a mechanism to judge the relevance of information to pass on. This is complicated by the continuous nature of change in the task and that relevance is relative to the recipients' context - knowledge and experience that the sender doesn't necessarily possess.*

## 2.3 Coordinating Interdependent Dynamic Goals

It could be said that the people involved were all motivated by the high level goal to resolve the disaster, enacting a sub-goal to mobilize resources to the site. Control centres off site have responsibility for strategic and planning goals.

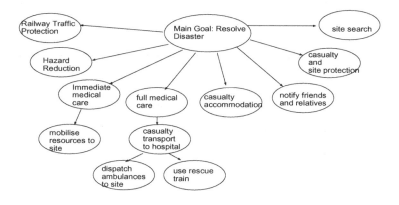

**Fig. 1.** Initial goal decomposition

Recipe for **GOAL**: Save Lives and Relieve Suffering
**SUBGOALS**: (listed in order of priority)

| subgoal | group allocated to enact this goal |
|---|---|
| 1.Railway Traffic Protection | Railtrack |
| 2.Hazard Reduction: Fire, instability | Fire and Regional Railway Company |
| 3.Immediate Medical Care | Fire and Ambulance |
| 4.Casualty Transport (to hospital) | Fire, Ambulance, Volunteers, RailTrack, Regional Railway Company |
| 5.Full medical care | Hospital H |
| 6.Casualty Accommodation | Regional Railway Company |
| 7.Notification of friends and relatives | Police |
| 8.Casualty and Site Protection | Fire and Police |
| 9.Site search | Police |

**Fig. 2.** Generic High level Incident Plan

Unknown parameters such as exact location and number of injured need to be established. Based on an analysis of this incident [15], we can suggest a potential partial hierarchy of goals (Figure 1) that represent the system early in the response . This is based on the high level incident plan - a default allocation of roles and responsibilities in any incident (Figure 2). Each agency would likely operate following generic recipes that are initially partial and then elaborated and verified as the situation unfolds. In this case of DM at least, there was the need to maintain multiple possible goals and to make (and enact) multiple, possible alternative (partial) plans based on available information. It is not practical to wait and establish facts in isolation before any action is taken, so it is better to enact multiple options until it becomes clear which will be fully enacted. Plans are revised or dropped as more details are established as will be discussed in the next section.

The high level incident plan for the disaster response in Figure 2 shows the broad allocation of responsibilities to each agency [16]. Sometimes these goals

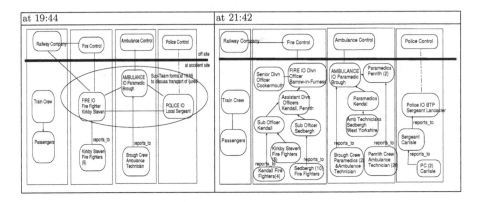

**Fig. 3.** Organisation Structures at Ais Gill

might be enacted autonomously, though in most cases, interdependencies require collaboration and communication between agencies for coordination.

At 21:42 when the rescue train arrived at the accident site, for example, collaboration and coordination of interdependencies occurred between many agencies: fire, police, ambulance, railtrack and the railway company.

### 2.4   Evolution of the Organisational Structure

The system which manages a disaster - agents, resources and technologies - is not only distributed over space but its structure evolves over time.

We can picture the disaster recovery system that includes each of the response agencies: police, fire, ambulance, plus organizations such as railtrack, volunteers and emergency services. A simplified organisational network focusing on the 3 main agencies: Fire, Ambulance and Police depicting how system might look early in the response and then about 2 hours later, is shown in Figure 3.

The command structure develops organically. Roles of individuals are adjusted flexibly responding to the disaster with resources available [16]. Organic role adjustment occurs with the Fire Incident Officer (IO) role reallocated to 4 different people, driven by new arrivals at the site. At 19:20, the leading Fire Fighter from Kirkby Steven assumes the IO role. As a more senior ranking officer arrives at the scene, that person may take over as IO. At 19:35 a sub-officer from Sedbergh became IO. At 20:01 two Assistant Divisional Officers (ADOs) were present and one of these (Penrith) took over as IO, with assistance from the other (Kendal). At 20:11 the Divisional Officer from Barrow-in-Furness arrived, worked collaboratively with the 2 ADOs, then gradually took over the IO role. In some cases, the role of IO is not handed over - for example, when the Senior Divisional Officer from Cockermouth arrived at 21:00, he made it explicit that he would not be taking command from the existing IO, but would remain and observe.

As the organisational structure changes, the team needs to be aware of current team structures to enable appropriate adjustment and sharing of planning and situational knowledge. At Ais Gill, there were difficulties in maintaining a shared mental model of the organisation [15] and as will be described in the next section, this hampered communication of a change in the plan regarding transport of injured to hospital. This led to further coordination problems. Team shared mental models of resources, tasks and team members are essential for team processes [2]. A shared representation of the organisation is needed to enable knowledge transfer and task level shared mental models[15].

*Observation 2. In order for appropriate sharing of relevant information, adaptive team agents/people need to have some representation of the current DM system's organisational structure.*

*Observation 3. Adaptive Team Agents need defined obligations to explicitly* **maintain** *an appropriate shared mental model of the DM system's organisational structure.*

*Observation 4. As the organisation is dynamically adapting structurally and members may join/leave, there is a complexity beyond a simple predetermined hierarchy or pattern. This subtlety requires an awareness of relevancy linking knowledge to actors in the organisation, to enable appropriate knowledge sharing.*

## 2.5   Development (or Revision) of Plans in Response to the Incident

During an incident, decision making occurs to assign resources to operational or management tasks. These decisions are informed by the current incident plan and knowledge of the current situation. Both of these are changing with time as more details are known. The incident plan is initially based on generic predefined plans described at an organizational level; it is then developed or revised in response to the actual situation. In DM, there are typically two types of coordination: Filling in the unknown details into existing predefined default plans (e.g., location of incident, type of incident, number and type of casualties); and revising a chosen plan recipe in response to the situation, (e.g., the decision regarding the transport of injured to hospital).

Knowledge regarding the Ais Gill incident was distributed between people and the decision to use a rescue train was shared. A sub-team including the paramedic, police sergeant and leading fire fighter were partially responsible for the revised decision to use a rescue train, although it remains unclear when this proposition became an actual decision. They queried if a rescue train might be possible at 20:00. At 20:10 the reply, without further communication or collaboration was 'ETA train 60 minutes and also coach from Robinson of Appleby is mobile'.

This revised plan was not shared with ambulances off site, resulting in them continuing to travel toward the roadside near the accident where they could not be useful. The ambulance controller in Carlisle didn't know about the rescue train until 20:55. During the 45 minutes prior to 20:55, ambulances and PTS were dispatched toward the site where they weren't needed. This illustrates the importance of keeping relevant others informed of new/revised plans. The communication regarding the decision and adopting of a revised plan to transport

---

1  Establish location of accident (LA)

2a CHOICE 1: transport casualties to Hospital, H. via ROAD using ambulances with pick up at LA access point. [DEFAULT option assumed in initial plan]

2b CHOICE 2: transport casualties to Hospital, H. using a RESCUE TRAIN to railway station RS

2c CHOICE 3: transport casualties to Hospital, H. on foot along train track then via ambulance with pick up at LA - nearby road-bridge

**unknown parameters: LA, RS, H(either Carlisle or Lancaster)**

---

**Fig. 4.** Potential recipe for transporting injured to hospital

the injured to hospital using a rescue train involved a plan revision. This revised decision was not well communicated and led to coordination problems later (for example, not enough ambulances were available in the correct location at the train station when the rescue train arrived; staff at Lancaster hospital that could not have been used due to the limitations on the direction of the train were kept on standby for longer than necessary; and adequate police resources were not at Carlisle station to provide protection to the injured passengers from media).

### 2.6   Multiple Uncertain, Partial and Adaptive Plans

Typical of disaster recovery, at Ais Gill, multiple plans were concurrently considered and partially enacted, due to uncertainty and incomplete knowledge availability. A disaster team cannot afford to do nothing until all information is known. Planning and action occur in parallel. As in this case, decisions may not be made explicitly, but may emerge as the best option and the actual selection of the final decision may not be clearly distinguished. Our architecture for knowledge sharing in a human-agent team needs to account for **multiple plans** and may well need to **provide a mechanism for recognising the certainty related to knowledge** (for example: uncertain, possible, probable).

Assuming predefined recipes outlining actions toward goals, existed at least implicitly for the people involved as Ais Gill, we might imagine that there was a recipe for the goal: Transport Injured to Hospital. It could look something like the recipe shown in Figure 4. Initially, all the participants would have adopted the default plan assuming that the injured would be transported to hospital via road using ambulances. Due to particular constraints of this disaster, the plan was revised. At Ais Gill, all three choices were partially enacted, before choice 2 became the final decision. We would presume the poor communication regarding the change of plan was not due to the people concerned being unaware that others needed to know, but it could well be the case that the obligation to tell was not clearly defined. Who was responsible for telling those away from the disaster scene? It could have been presumed by the people at the scene that others away from the scene had already been told by the railway authority. During phase 2 of the team response - plan formulation [2], this example serves to indicate that when creating artificial agents to engage with people in coordination in such a domain, **obligations to share knowledge about (new or revised) plans**

**need to be clearly stated**. This is in part addressed by the SharedPlans formalisation within the decision making team, though needs extension to include explicit sharing with others in the system who may need to know. This will be discussed further in section 4.

*Observation 5. Adaptive Agents need obligations to share knowledge about changed elements of plans to relevant others in the organisational system.*

This particular incident exemplifies some general features of DM that are important to note. The changing demands of a disaster situation result in instability of the incident organisation [16]. Decision making can be highly reactive due to the novelty and instability of most disasters. Decisions can be made in part by following predefined rules and protocol but also a level of flexible adjustment of these plans is needed to deal with the developing nature of an incident.

During phase 3 - plan enactment [2], further team adaption and flexibility is needed to respond to changing plans and awareness is needed understanding uncertainty relating to multiple plans being partially enacted concurrently. At Ais Gill, the ambulance controller recalled the ambulance crews en route to site at 20:55 when he learnt of the alternative plan to use the rescue train.

# 3    Defining Components of an Adaptive Coordination Team

In order to be coordinated whilst being distributed across multiple locations and between various agencies, as our case study shows, we need to be able to share up to date, mutual knowledge regarding the situation. This mutual knowledge includes details of the situation, current and future plans, the current team organization and 'who knows what'. In order to know 'who else might be interested' in new or revised knowledge, the current system organization needs to be available to 'look up' and attached to the people/agents in the system, we need an indicator of relevancy: who is interested in particular beliefs.

In this section, we describe in abstract terms features of a team capable of the coordination described thus far. In DM, there are many teams that work as part of one overall system response team. Each sub-team that forms is linked by either sharing plans, or sharing knowledge or an interest in certain knowledge. Overall, the team is distributed and it is unlikely that all members have access to all knowledge. Such a team comprises of actors or agents in multiple organisational networks based on agents' relationships with others in terms of shared knowledge interests, hierarchy of organisational structure, and shared goals. These organisational groups are similar to the coordination loops described for adaptive and complex situations[20]. Coordination loops are defined in three classes: horizontal, vertical and projective. These different loops indicate multiple ways that individuals can be connected and inter-related. Such loops define reciprocity obligations and enable anticipatory action and describe the complexity of interdependencies between tasks. An awareness of the coordination loops/organisational networks provides knowledge about relevancy and connectedness.

The SharedPlans theory [9,8] accounts for group obligations regarding the cultivation of shared group intentions and dynamic plans, but doesn't explicitly address sharing of knowledge - regarding the team/organisational structure or the situation. In order to establish common knowledge, other architectures for coordinating agent-human teams have successfully employed mental models. RCAST [4], a system for sharing of situation awareness in teams, incorporates an explicit Shared Mental Model (SMM) of team structure and task knowledge which we would also propose in an adaptive team. The RCAST architecture is based on a recognition primed decision making process rather than the SharedPlans decision making process, however using explicit shared mental models complemented by intention based obligations to maintain these suits the adaptive nature of our case study. In RCAST, SMM components include team processes, team structure, shared domain knowledge and information-needs graphs [5]. Other generic agent team models for collaboration exist (e.g. [18]).

Situation assessment and representation of situation (e.g., mental representation, status boards, maps, reports) inform the decision making in a disaster response [16]. SMMs have been used in various multi-agent team experiments, as explicit separate artefacts and implicit in shared ontologies. Yen categorises 3 types of SMM: Blackboard based, joint mental attitudes and rule based systems [6]. The model in the RCAST architecture is more than a set of mutual beliefs, all agents share a commitment toward maintaining shared awareness and proactive sharing of relevant information[21]. This model is consistent with our proposed extension to SharedPlans. Rather than use a shared artifact to represent shared knowledge, an alternative is to have individual beliefs that are shared and kept consistent by agreed update processes. When agents work together in a coalition, it is possible to broadcast interests to other agents in the group to establish information needs and enable mutual support[14]. When the team structure is dynamic, the appropriate sharing of knowledge relies upon an ability to recognise relevancy of knowledge associated with others.

Maintaining mutual beliefs between individuals requires that each individual has beliefs about the beliefs of others in the team. In DM, due to the distributed nature of the system, one central shared artifact is not feasible, so we seek to describe *processes* to ensure sharing and maintaining of knowledge about the situation. This includes beliefs such as location of the incident, number of injured, current resources deployed etc. Knowledge cultivation as described in section 4 begins to describe the details of how we might achieve sharing of relevant knowledge in adaptive teams. Such a shared model of knowledge and team organization, is comprised of an organizational network, a belief network and a relevancy network; plus the obligations to cultivate this shared knowledge.

## 4   Knowledge Cultivation – Extending Shared Plans

Grosz and Kraus have defined obligations that must be adhered to for a group of individuals to maintain shared (individual) plans around a shared goal [9]. These *intention cultivation* obligations enable dynamic, real time planning and decision making in a team without relying on shared artefacts, but controlling the mutual knowledge by obligations regarding reasoning about intentions. Grosz and Hunsberger, [8] argue that group decision making in planning and intention updating are crucial to establishing collective intentionality for coordinating dynamically. Coordinated updates of group-related intentions are the key to modelling collective intentions.

The SharedPlans formalism satisfies two requirements in our DM system team: adaptive planning - enabling a group of agents to share decision making dynamically; and distributed team work, such that a problem can be decomposed into sub-goals that can be allocated to independent sub-teams to autonomously enact. In DM the team involved is not fixed at the start of the problem – team structures emerge as the event unfolds.

We introduce *knowledge cultivation obligations*; and *explicit models of the organizational network* - linking agents/people and knowledge.

In SharedPlans, intentions are categorised into four specific types - *intentions-to* perform an action, *intentions-that* a proposition be held true, and *potential intentions* (identified, but not yet adopted) [9]. Recipes for achieving a group activity, are defined in terms of sub-acts and parameters that can be filled dynamically. Collective group intentions are used to constrain that all participants have uniform intentions, and that any agent updates their intentions only in accordance with the group [8].

"Agents have a Shared Plan to do $\alpha$ if and only if they hold the following beliefs and intentions: 1.individual intentions that the group perform $\alpha$; 2. mutual belief of a (partial) recipe for $\alpha$; 3. individual or group plans for the sub-acts in the (partial) recipe; 4. intentions that the selected agents or subgroups succeed in doing their sub-acts (for all sub-acts that have been assigned to some agent or group); and 5. (in the case of a partial Shared Plan) subsidiary commitments to group decision-making processes aimed at completing the group's partial plan." [8]

Our extension includes three components:

- TSMM - a task level SMM including situational knowledge of the problem;
- RSMM - a Reflexive SMM representing the structural organization of the dynamic team [15]; and
- KC - knowledge cultivation obligations: intentions to establish and maintain common shared content amongst the team.

In the remainder of this section, we define Knowledge Cultivation obligations. In section 5, we describe a representation of the structural organization that can be used to formalise RSMM and TSMM.

We adopt the formalisms used in SharedPlans formalism, where possible. We have used the operators Mutual Belief ($MB(GR, \phi)$) interpreted as group GR mutually believes proposition $\phi$; $Bel(G, \phi)$ meaning Agent G believes proposition $\phi$; Intention.To ($Int.To(G, A)$) Agent G intends to do action A; and Intention.That ($Int.Th(G, \phi)$) representing agent G intends that proposition $\phi$ holds [9,10]. We introduce additional predicates to informally represent elements needed in the descriptions, described in table 1.

We define SGR, the System GRoup, to represent all the agents/people who are part of the DM system at any stage during the DM response. For now, we represent any organisational network (coordination loop) as RSMM and the state of the world at some time as TSMM (these will be more formally elaborated upon in section 5). The following obligations describe the processes that we impose on the SGR.

- SGR mutually believes that all members of SGR are committed to success of the goal to resolve the disaster;
- SGR mutually believes that all members of RSMM are committed to updating RSMM so that, at any time, the union of all RSMM (multiple organisational subteams) reflects the current management system structure;
- SGR mutually believes the need to update and maintain relevant knowledge about the state of the world (TSMM).

These obligations are imposed on any sub-team that forms. The SGR is a union of all RSMM that occur during the team disaster response.

We explain these obligations based on examples from the case study introduced in section 2.

**1. Awareness of system group goals.** The system group represents all involved - the injured passengers, the ambulance, fire and police agencies, British Rail and volunteers. The high level shared goal is to resolve the disaster. Each agency does not work in isolation, but is aware that other agencies are involved. There are dynamic sub-teams representing each agency, Fire, Ambulance, Police, Railway Company, similar to figure 3. There are also sub-teams that form between agencies such as the Incident Officers responsible for decision making considering options for transport of the injured. Even though, undoubtedly there was an awareness of others off site, there were problems with communication of their revised plans to ambulance control center in a timely fashion. To avoid this kind of error occurring with artificial agent teams, we need to be explicit in creating an awareness of the system group (distributed over time and space).

This group SGR has a mutual belief that all members have a goal to achieve $\alpha$ - the goal to resolve the incident.

$$MB(SGR, \forall g \epsilon GR_i : g \epsilon SGR \wedge Int.th(g, \alpha))$$

**Table 1.** Predicate definitions

| RM(gr,t) | Reflexive Model for group gr at time t. This represents the organisational structure of group gr and identifies relationships between agents. |
|---|---|
| A Rel.to B | Agent A is Related to agent B. A and B are both linked in an existing organisational hierarchy or coordination loop - a reflexive model(RM). |
| Add(x,gr) | Add agent x to group gr. |
| Update(x,RM) | Update RM to include agent x. |
| Relevant(b, BS) | belief b is relevant to a set of beliefs BS. |
| Focus(b,GR) | Belief b is in the relevant focus of interest to an agent in group GR. This may be established by a goal that is related to this belief or a role allocated to an agent in GR that is associated with this belief |

**2. Obligation to update RSMM as needed.** As figure 3 indicates, the organisational network, thus RSMM representing this is very dynamic. The communications during initial phase of establishing the details of the situation relied on appropriate notification to others in the DM system. This could only occur because there was knowledge of who else was involved. At Ais Gill, the decision-making team on the ground needed to know to share their decision regarding how to transport the injured with the ambulance controller to enable plan revision and strategic response to reallocate resources (the hospital on standby and the ambulances en route). We capture this as:

The group mutually believes that all members are committed to updating the RSMM to include new members as they join the system, where the current RSMM at time, t is represented by (RM(SGR,t).

$$MB(SGR, (\forall g_j \epsilon SGR, Int.th(\exists g_k, \exists g_i : \neg g_k \epsilon SGR \wedge g_i \epsilon SGR : g_k Rel.to(g_i))$$
$$\Rightarrow Int.to(g_j, add(g_k, SGR) \wedge update(g_k, RM(SGR, t))))$$

**3. Knowledge cultivation - obligations to share relevant knowledge.** The group has a mutual belief regarding need to update shared situational task knowledge TSMM with new relevant beliefs that are not already shared. Relevant beliefs need to be identified as such by a relationship to existing beliefs or tags to show relevancy in the belief knowledge set, BS. Updates can also be motivated by recognising that some agents have an existing focus (interest) in this knowledge.

$$MB(SGR, \exists g \epsilon GR : Bel(g, b) \wedge \neg b \epsilon BS \wedge$$
$$(Relevant(b, BS) \vee Focus(b, GR)) \Rightarrow Int.to(g, add(b, BS)))$$

As in R-CAST[5], when information is distributed, and proactive sharing required, there is a need to represent information relevancy so that it is possible to ascertain if a particular piece of information is relevant to another agent. Creating an associated obligation and commitment to agreed knowledge updates would enable agent responsibility regarding communication of knowledge to other agents to be formally represented. To recognise relevance, an agent needs a representation of their own and others' focus [17]. In R-CAST, information needs graphs are used to associate information with context, enabling matching of knowledge to previous experiences and providing a mechanism for identifying when information might be of future relevance to another team-member [5]. In the DM case, shared focus may be identified by relational links between agents within a sub-team or organisation, or identifying the coordination loops[20] that are present. In the next section, we begin to represent the structure of knowledge representing the disaster management organisation more explicitly.

## 5    Representing the Organisational Knowledge at Ais Gill

In this section, we formally represent the shared mental models in the organisations involved in our case study. We identify elements that define an organisation and give some examples of the RSMM organisations that exist based on the Ais Gill case study. This analysis takes a step closer to expressing an adaptive organisational system in a computational tractable way. Knowledge cultivation obligations define intentions to maintain these models within an organisation.

To represent each organisation involved over time during the disaster scenario, we use a formal organisational model[3]: Given W, an organization $O$ is defined in a world $w \; \epsilon \; W$ as: $O^w = \{A_o^w, \leq_o^w, D_o^w, S_o^w\}$ where $A_o^w = \{a_1, ..., a_n\}$ is the set of agents, $\{A_o^w, \leq_o^w\}$ is a partial order relation on A reflecting the structure of the organization, $D_o^w \subseteq \Phi$ is a set of objectives (states to achieve), and $S_o^w \subseteq \Phi$ is the set of current states relevant to this organisation holding at a given moment. We extend this model to include two additional components in an organisation: $B_o^w$ is the set of current mutual beliefs of the organisation and $SP_o^w$ is the set of current shared plans held by the organisation.

At Ais Gill, there were multiple organisations, with some overlapping objectives and some agents belong to more than one organisation. Each organisation, at any time, can be described using the above formalism. The SGR includes all agent sets involved in each organisation during the scenario, so SGR in this case is a union of the fire, ambulance, police and incident officer teams over time The RSMM representing each organisation is the shared model of structure $(A_o^w, \leq_o^w)$. The TSMM is the union of beliefs, objectives(goals) and shared plans: $B_o^w, D_o^w \, and SP_o^w$. The set of objectives $(D_o^w)$ can be broken into two subsets - action based objectives and information needs objectives. In the case of the DM system, as discussed, it is necessary for the organisation to access networks of relevancy. Expressing our organisational model using this formalism imposes a structure through which relevance can be identified.

Agents in our DM system include Fire Fighters (ff), Ambulance Paramedic (ap), Control (fc), Fire Incident Officer (fio), Ambulance Incident Officer (aio), Police Sergeant (ps), Objectives include: Transport to site (tS), Hazard Reduction (hR), Immediate Medical Care (mC), Casualty Transport (cT), Site Protection (sPr), Assess situation (aS), Share location details (shLoc). Information needs objectives include: Establish Location of Incident (getLoc), Establish Number of Injured (noInj). Each organisation that forms has a shared objective - either strategic or practical.

The Fireteam and Ambteam organisations are hierarchically based and share generic goals as shown in Figure 1. At Time 1, 19:20, the organisational model for the fireteam could be described as follows.

$$O_{oft}^1 = \{A_{fireteam}^1, \leq_{oft}^1, D_{oft}^1, B_{oft}^1, SP_{oft}^1, S_{oft}^1\} where$$
$$A_{fireteam}^1 = \{fc, fio, ff1, ff2, ff3, ff4, ff5\}.$$

$\{A_{fireteam}^1, \leq_{oft}^1\}$is a hierarchical structure:
$fc \leq_{oft}^1 fio, fio \leq_{oft}^1 ff1, fio \leq_{oft}^1 ff2, fio \leq_{oft}^1 ff3, fio \leq_{oft}^1 ff4, fio \leq_{oft}^1 ff5$ .
$D_{oft}^1 = (hR, mC, cT, sPr)$.
$B_{oft}^1 = (traincrash, loc : 1mileNthAisGill, 2injured)$.
$SP_{oft}^1 = (shLoc, aS)$.
$S_{oft}^1 = (traincrash, loc : 1milenthAisGill, 30injured, 1DOA)$.

Information was shared from the fire crew from Kirkby Steven who arrived at 19:25 to fire control to give accurate details on the location (originally thought to be Birkett Tunnel). Fire control then passed this information to Railtrack who passed it to Ambulance control and the Brough ambulance crew en route to Birkett Tunnel changed route to take B6259 to the accident site. The presence of the RSMM $\{A^1_{fireteam}, \leq^1_{oft}\}$ provides the awareness that enables this information sharing within the fireteam organisation.

At time 2, 19:55, the ambulance crew from Brough had arrived on scene. The more senior ambulance paramedic assumed the role of Ambulance IO. The ambteam organisation hadn't yet changed in structure, but TSMM begins to develop new beliefs and SharedPlans. These would be represented in new values for B and SP respectively in the model of the ambteam organisation.

The IOteam forms on site at 19:55. This comprises the Ambulance IO, Fire IO and Police Sergeant, shown circled in Figure 3. Members of the IOteam are in multiple organisations - at least one for their agency (Fire/Ambulance) and one for the IOteam. The IOteam generates SharedPlans for how to transport the injured to hospital Multiple plans were enacted with ultimately one being chosen eventually.

Knowledge Cultivation obligations would motivate the IOteam to share this eventual plan choice with *relevant* others in SGR. In this case, each IO would be obliged to share the plan with their relevant control officer who is in their other organisation RSMM - Fireteam (oft) or Ambteam (oat). The IOteam structure is not a hierarchy, so $\leq^2_{oio}$ does not contain any ordering relations. Their Shared-Plan $SP^2_{oio}$ would reflect Figure 4. The IOteam is represented as:

$$O^2_{oio} = \{A^2_{ioteam}, \leq^2_{oio}, D^2_{oio}, SP^2_{oio}, S^2_{oio}\}.A^2_{ioteam} = \{fio, aio, ps\}.D^2_{oio} = (PlancT).$$

As the above examples show, appropriate transfer of knowledge relies upon a structure for representing relevance of knowledge. Associating knowledge with relational organisational structures provides a network of linking knowledge with groups of agents and enables agents in an organisation to determine which other agents may have an interest in knowledge. As agents may belong to multiple organisations, each with a different focus, this limits the scope for broadcasting information, but enables information to be passed on to appropriate agents.

# 6    Conclusion and Future Work

We have described the complex demands of disaster management and proposed an extension to SharedPlans that offers a step toward meeting these demands. SharedPlans provides a framework for sharing and maintaining a team mental model of decision-making and intentions but does not account for changing team structures. We have used an existing formalism to represent the additional requirements for an adaptive organisational system.

The contribution in this paper is to introduce knowledge cultivation processes to complement the intention cultivation processes already in SharedPlans. Our underlying motivation is similar to that of Tambe and colleagues, e.g. [18], who argued for a generic teamwork model as a way to reduce the burden on the agent designer in the development of complex coordinative scenarios. Here we present the motivation for key new processes that must be present, and highlight new data requirements for achieving effective coordination in situations where not only the external environment changes but the organisation itself is organic. Further work is required to develop these ideas to implementable models. Our ambition is to work toward creating believable team agents that can work with humans and other artificial agents in simulations of such complex domains.

# References

1. Allsopp, D., Beautement, P., Kirton, M., Tate, A., Bradshaw, J., Suri, N., Burstein, M.: The coalition agents experiment: Network-enabled coalition operations. Journal of Defence Science, Special Issue on Network-enabled Capabilities 8(3) (September 2003)
2. Burke, C., Stagl, K., Salas, E., Pierce, L., Kendall, D.: Understanding team adaptation: A conceptual analysis and model. Journal of Applied Psychology 91(6), 1189–1207 (2006)
3. Dignum, V., Tick, C.: Agent-based analysis of organizations: Formalization and simulation. In: Proceedings of IAT 2007: The 2007 IEEEE/WIC/ACM International Conference on Intelligent Agent Technology, pp. 244–247. IEEE, Los Alamitos (2007)
4. Fan, X., Sun, B., Sun, S.: RPD-enabled agents teaming with humans for multi-context decision making. In: Proceedings of the Sixth International Joint Conference on Autonomous Agents and Multi Agent Systems, Hakodate, Japan (May 2006)
5. Fan, X., Sun, S., Sun, B., Airy, G., McNeese, M., Yen, J.: Collaborative RPD-enabled agents assisting the three-block challenge in command and control in complex and urban terrain. In: Proceedings of 2005 BRIMS Conference Behavior Representation in Modeling and Simulation, May 2005, pp. 113–123. Universal City, CA (2005)
6. Fan, X., Yen, J.: Modeling and simulating human teamwork behaviors using intelligent agents. Journal of Physics of Life Reviews 1(3), 173–201 (2004)
7. Gonzalez, C.: Decision support for real-time dynamic decision making tasks. Organizational Behavior and Human Decision Processes 96, 142–154 (2005)
8. Grosz, B., Hunsberger, L.: The dynamics of intention in collaborative activity. Cognitive Systems Research 7(2-3), 259–272 (2006)
9. Grosz, B., Kraus, S.: The evolution of shared plans. In: Foundations and Theories of Rational Agency, pp. 227–262 (1999)
10. Hunsberger, L.: Making sharedplans more concise and easier to reason about. In: Rao, A.S., Singh, M.P., Müller, J.P. (eds.) ATAL 1998. LNCS, vol. 1555, pp. 81–98. Springer, Heidelberg (1999)
11. Klein, G., Feltovich, P., Bradshaw, J., Woods, D.D.: Common ground and coordination in joint activity. In: Rouse, W., Boff, K. (eds.) Organizational simulation. New York, Wiley, Chichester (2005)
12. Lipshitz, R., Omodei, M., McLennan, J., Wearing, A.: What's burning? the RAWFS heuristic on the fire ground. In: Expertise Out of Context, pp. 97–112 (2007)

13. Schurr, N., Pratik, P., Pighin, F., Tambe, M.: Lessons learned from disaster management. In: Proceedings of First International Workshop on Agent Technology for Disaster Management (2006)
14. Siebra, C., Tate, A.: Integrating collaboration and activity-oriented planning for coalition operations support. In: Bredenfeld, A., Jacoff, A., Noda, I., Takahashi, Y. (eds.) RoboCup 2005. LNCS, vol. 4020, pp. 561–568. Springer, Heidelberg (2006)
15. Smith, W., Dowell, J.: A case study of co-ordinative decision-making in disaster management. Ergonomics 43(8), 1153–1166 (2000)
16. Smith, W., Dowell, J.: Inter-agency coordination in disaster management: A cognitive engineering framework
17. So, R., Sonenberg, L.: Situation awareness as a form of meta-level control. In: Proceedings of the First International Workshop on Metareasoning in Agent-Based Systems at the Sixth International Joint Conference on Autonomous Agents and Multiagent Systems, Honolulu, Hawaii (2007)
18. Tambe, M.: Towards flexible teamwork. Journal of Artificial Intelligence Research 7, 83–124 (1997)
19. van der Lee, M.D.E., van Vugt, M.: Imi - an information system for effective multidisciplinary incident management. In: Proceedings of ISCRAM 2004, Brussels (May 2004)
20. Voshell, M., Woods, D., Prue, B., Fern, L.: Coordination Loops: A New Unit of Analysis for Distributed Work. Erlbaum, Mahwah (2007)
21. Yen, J., Fan, X., Sun, S., Hanratty, T., Dumer, J.: Agents with shared mental models for enhancing team decision-makings. Journal of Decision Support Systems: Special issue on Intelligence and Security Informatics 41(2) (2005)
22. Zachary, W., Weiland, W., Scolaro, D., Scolaro, J., Santarelli, T.: Instructorless team training using synthetic teammates and instructors. In: Proceedings of the Human Factors & Ergonomics Society 46th Annual Meeting, pp. 2035–2038. Human Factors & Ergonomics Society (2002)

# An Incremental Adaptive Organization for a Satellite Constellation

Grégory Bonnet and Catherine Tessier

ONERA-DCSD, 2 avenue Edouard Belin BP 74025 31055 Toulouse Cedex 4, France
gregory.bonnet@onera.fr, catherine.tessier@onera.fr

**Abstract.** Physical agents, such as robots, are generally constrained in their communication capabilities. In a multi-agent system composed of physical agents, these constraints have a strong influence on the organization and the coordination mechanisms. Our multi-agent system is a satellite constellation for which we propose a collaboration method based on incremental coalition formation in order to optimize individual plans so as to satisfy collective objectives. This involves a communication protocol, common knowledge and two coordination mechanisms: (1) an incentive to join coalitions and (2) coalition minimization. Results on a simulated satellite constellation are presented and discussed.

## 1 Introduction

In the agent literature, and more precisely in a multi-agent context, most of the coordination mechanisms deal with *software agents* or *social agents* that have high communication and reasoning capabilities. Coordination based on norms [5], contracts [17] or organizations [10] are considered. As far as *physical agents* such as robots or satellites are concerned, information sharing and coordination depend on communication constraints. Indeed, on the one hand, an agent cannot always communicate with another agent or the communication possibilites are restricted to short time intervals. On the other hand, an agent cannot always wait until the coordination process terminates before acting. All these constraints are present in space applications.

In the space domain, autonomous satellite constellations (i.e. networks of satellites) allow to consider joint activities and ensure functional robustness [4]. We consider a set of 3 to 16 satellites placed in low orbit around the Earth to take pictures of the ground. Ground stations send the satellites asynchronous observation requests with various priorities. Satellites are also equipped with a detection instrument that allows areas of interest to be detected and on-board observation requests to be generated. As each satellite is equipped with a single observation instrument with use constraints, geographically close requests cannot be realized by the same satellite. Likewise each satellite has limited memory resources and can realize only a given number of requests before downloading. Notice that in the space lexicon downloading means transferring data to a ground station (i.e. the pictures taken when a request is realized). Finally the orbits of

G. Vouros et al. (Eds.): OAMAS 2008, LNAI 5368, pp. 108–125, 2009.

the satellites cross around the poles: two (or more) satellites that meet in the polar areas can communicate *via* InterSatellite Links (ISL) without any ground intervention. So the satellites can communicate from time to time in order to share information and coordinate.

Consequently the problem we focus on is a distributed task allocation problem in a multi-agent system with new tasks arriving asynchronously and intermittent communications. Each satellite (each agent) builds and revises a task plan such that the number of tasks realized by the constellation is the highest possible, they are realized as soon as possible, the number of redundancies (refer to Definition 5) is the lowest possible and the number of high priority tasks that are not realized is the lowest possible. Notice that these constraints are not necessarily compatible with each other.

Centralized planning is not considered because (1) the aim of future space applications is to avoid using ground stations as much as possible (operating a ground station is expensive); (2) the asynchronous generation of new requests by each satellite prevents us from having a centralized view of the problem and therefore a centralized resolution. In the literature, two distributed approaches are considered to control a satellite constellation:

1. the hierarchical approach [2,7,8,20] where a leading satellite plans for the others: this approach is very sensitive to local failures and to the arrival of new tasks;
2. the decentralized approach [4] but ISL are not considered to increase the quality of the local plans.

As new tasks arrive as time goes by, a decentralized approach in which ISL are taken into account must be considered. In this paper the allocation problem is addressed with an online incremental dynamic organization mechanism in three steps:

1. agents plan individually;
2. agents communicate in order to build common knowledge;
3. agents build and revise coalitions that influence their individual plans.

This paper is organized as follows. In Section 2 we will describe how agents are modelled in a multi-agent system. In Section 3 we will present how agents communicate and reason to build a trusted common knowledge. The organization model is presented in Section 4 and the formal mechanism is described in Section 5. Before concluding Section 6 will show results about performance and scalability of the approach.

# 2 The Agents

## 2.1 The Multi-agent System Structure

The satellite constellation is a multi-agent system defined as follows:

**Definition 1 (Constellation).** *The* constellation $\mathcal{S}$ *is a triplet* $\langle \mathcal{A}, \mathbb{T}, Vicinity \rangle$ *with* $\mathcal{A} = \{a_1 \ldots a_n\}$ *the set of n agents representing the n satellites,* $\mathbb{T} \subset \mathbb{N}$ *a set of dates defining a common clock and Vicinity* : $\mathcal{A} \times \mathbb{T} \mapsto 2^{\mathcal{A}}$ *a symmetric non-transitive relation specifying for a given agent and a given date the set of agents with which it can communicate at that date (acquaintance model). Vicinity represents the temporal windows when the satellites meet; it is calculated from the satellite orbits, which are periodic.*

**Definition 2 (Periodicity).** *Let* $\mathcal{S}$ *be a constellation and* $\{p_1 \ldots p_n\}$ *the set of the orbital cycle durations* $p_i \in \mathbb{T}$ *of agents* $a_i \in \mathcal{A}$. *The Vicinity period* $P \in \mathbb{T}$ *is the* lowest common multiple *of set* $\{p_1 \ldots p_n\}$.

In the remainder, we will note $\mathbb{T}_P \subset \mathbb{T}$ the time interval of duration $P$ such that $\mathbb{T}_P = [0 \ldots P]$.

The constellation (agents, clock and Vicinity) is knowledge that all the agents hold in common. Nonetheless each agent also holds private knowledge.

### 2.2 Observation Requests Modelled as Tasks

Each agent representing a satellite within the constellation knows some *tasks* to realize.

**Definition 3 (Task).** *A task t is an observation request associated with a priority prio(t)* $\in \mathbb{N}$ *and with a boolean* $b_t$ *that indicates whether t has been realized or not.*

In the space domain, 1 stands for the highest priority whereas 5 is the lowest. Consequently the lower $prio(t)$, the more important task $t$.

The tasks may be constrained in two ways: (1) *mutual exclusion* meaning that a given agent cannot realize several tasks at the same time $\tau$ ; (2) *composition* of $n$ tasks meaning that all the $n$ tasks must be realized : it is useless to realize only a strict subset of them. Formally,

**Definition 4 (Compound task).** *A* compound task *is a subset* $\mathcal{T}$ *of tasks such that* $(\exists t_i \in \mathcal{T}, t_i$ *is realized)* $\Rightarrow (\forall t_j \in \mathcal{T}, t_j \neq t_i, t_j$ *must be realized).*

Moreover when a task is realized by an agent, it is redundant if it has already been realized by another agent:

**Definition 5 (Redundancy).** *Let* $a_i$ *be an agent that realizes a task t at time* $\tau \in \mathbb{T}$. *There is a* redundancy *about t if and only if* $\exists\ a_j \in \mathcal{A}$ *and* $\exists\ \tau' \in \mathbb{T}$ $(\tau' \leq \tau)$ *such that* $a_j$ *has realized t at time* $\tau'$.

### 2.3 Agents' Attitudes Modelled as Intentions

An intention represents an agent's attitude towards a given task.

**Definition 6 (Intention).** *Let* $I_t^{a_i}$ *be the* intention *of agent* $a_i$ *towards task t.* $I_t^{a_i}$ *is a modality of proposition (*$a_i$ **realizes** *t) :*

- $\square$ (commitment): $a_i$ is committed to realize $t$ ;
- $\lozenge$ (proposal): $a_i$ proposes to realize $t$ ;
- $\square\neg$ (strong withdrawal): $a_i$ will not realize $t$ ;
- $\lozenge\neg$ (weak withdrawal): $a_i$ does not propose to realize $t$.

A realization date $rea(I_t^{a_i}) \in \mathbb{T} \cup \{\varnothing\}$ and a download date $tel(I_t^{a_i}) \in \mathbb{T} \cup \{\varnothing\}$ are associated with each intention.

## 2.4 Agents' Private Knowledge

The private knowledge of an agent within the constellation is defined as follows:

**Definition 7 (Knowledge).** A piece of knowledge $K_{a_i}^\tau$ of agent $a_i$ at time $\tau$ is a triplet $\langle D_{K_{a_i}^\tau}, A_{K_{a_i}^\tau}, \tau_{K_{a_i}^\tau} \rangle$:

- $D_{K_{a_i}^\tau}$ is a task $t$ or an intention $I_t^{a_k}$ of $a_k$ about $t$, $a_k \in \mathcal{A}$;
- $A_{K_{a_i}^\tau} \subseteq \mathcal{A}$ is the subset of agents knowing $K_{a_i}^\tau$;
- $\tau_{K_{a_i}^\tau} \in \mathbb{T}$ is the date when $D_{K_{a_i}^\tau}$ was created or updated.

Let $\mathcal{K}_{a_i}^\tau$ be the knowledge of agent $a_i$ at time $\tau$: $\mathcal{K}_{a_i}^\tau$ is the set of all the pieces of knowledge $K_{a_i}^\tau$.

From $\mathcal{K}_{a_i}^\tau$, we define $\mathcal{T}_{a_i}^\tau = \{t_1 \ldots t_m\}$ the set of tasks known by agent $a_i$ at time $\tau$ ; and $\mathcal{I}_{a_i}^\tau = (I_{t_j}^{a_k})$ the matrix of the intentions known by agent $a_i$ at time $\tau$. Each agent $a_i$ has resources available to realize only a subset of $\mathcal{T}_{a_i}^\tau$.

## 2.5 The Individual Planning Process

The set of an agent's intentions corresponds to its current plan. Each commitment or proposal means that the associated task is planned. The tasks associated with withdrawals are not planned. Notice that the individual planning process itself is beyond the scope of our work. Consequently we assume that each agent has an individual planner. Planning is a three-step process:

1. From the set of unrealized tasks known by $a_i$ at time $\tau$, $a_i$ computes an optimal local plan under two criteria:
   - maximize the number of planned tasks;
   - minimize the number of unplanned high priority tasks.
2. The intentions of agent $a_i$ about the tasks $t$ at time $(\tau - 1)$ constrain the planning process (step 1):
   - tasks associated with a commitment ($\square$) are *always* planned;
   - tasks associated with a strong withdrawal ($\square\neg$) are *never* planned.
3. Agent $a_i$'s plan at time $\tau$ modifies its intentions as follows:
   - each new planned task generates a proposal ($\lozenge$);
   - each new unplanned task generates a weak withdrawal ($\lozenge\neg$).

We can notice that commitments ($\square$) and strong withdrawals ($\square\neg$) are not generated by the planning process. We will see in Section 5 that these intentions are generated by a collaboration process between the agents.

## 3   Building a Trusted Common Knowledge

The agents have to reason on common knowledge about tasks and intentions. Consequently a communication protocol is defined to allow an agent to know what the other agents know. Communication is based on Vicinity: when two agents meet they can communicate. Consequently the Vicinity structure influences the communication capabilities.

### 3.1   Communication

We define communication within the constellation as follows:

**Definition 8 (Communication).** *Let $S$ be a constellation and $a_i$, $a_j \in \mathcal{A}$. An agent $a_i$ can communicate with an agent $a_j$ in two ways:*

- directly *iff* $\exists\, \tau_i \in \mathbb{T}_P$ *such that* $a_j \in Vicinity(a_i, \tau_i)$;
- indirectly *iff* $\exists\, l \in \mathbb{N}^*$ *such that* $\exists\, \{(a_{\tau_k}, \tau_k) \in \mathcal{A} \times \mathbb{T}, k \in [0\ldots l]\}$ *where:*
  1. $a_{\tau_0} \in Vicinity(a_i, \tau_i)$;
  2. $a_{\tau_{k+1}} \in Vicinity(a_{\tau_k}, \tau_k)$ *and* $\tau_i < \tau_k < \tau_{k+1} < \tau_j$;
  3. $a_j \in Vicinity(a_{\tau_l}, \tau_l)$.

Figure 1 illustrates direct communication between two agents whereas Figure 2 illustrates indirect communication.

In case of an indirect communication, $a_i$ and $a_j$ may communicate through several agents forming a *daisy chain*. As Vicinity is symmetric and non-transitive, direct communication is symmetric whereas indirect communication is oriented from one agent to another one. Each communication from $a_i$ to $a_j$ is associated with a couple $(\tau_i, \tau_j) \in \mathbb{T}^2$ with $\tau_i$ the emitting date of $a_i$ and $\tau_j$ the receipt date of $a_j$. We will write: $a_i$ communicates with $a_j$ at $(\tau_i, \tau_j)$. In case of a direct communication, $\tau_i = \tau_j$.

### 3.2   Unfolding the Vicinity Relation

In order to compute the next indirect communication between two agents from a given date, Vicinity is projected on a valued-directed-graph $\mathcal{V}$. Formally,

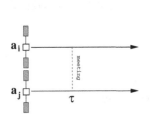

**Fig. 1.** Direct communication

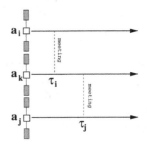

**Fig. 2.** Indirect communication

**Definition 9 (Vicinity graph).** *Let $S$ be a constellation. The Vicinity graph $V$ derived form the Vicinity relation is such that $V = (A, \{(a_i, a_j)\}, \{\{v_{ij}\}\})$ where:*

- *$A$ is the set of vertices of $V$;*
- *edge $(a_i, a_j)$ exists iff $\exists\, \tau \in \mathbb{T}_P$ such that $a_j \in Vicinity(a_i, \tau)$;*
- *each edge is labelled with set $v_{ij} = \{\tau \in \mathbb{T}_P : a_j \in Vicinity(a_i, \tau)\}$.*

The following example illustrates this definition.

**Example 1.** *Let $a_1$, $a_2$, $a_3$ be three agents. Let us suppose that Vicinity is defined as follows on period $P = 20$. The Vicinity graph is shown on Figure 1.*

$$
\begin{cases}
Vicinity(a_1, 2) = \{a_2\} \\
Vicinity(a_2, 5) = \{a_3\} \\
Vicinity(a_3, 8) = \{a_1\} \\
Vicinity(a_1, 12) = \{a_2\} \\
Vicinity(a_2, 15) = \{a_3\} \\
Vicinity(a_3, 16) = \{a_1\}
\end{cases}
$$

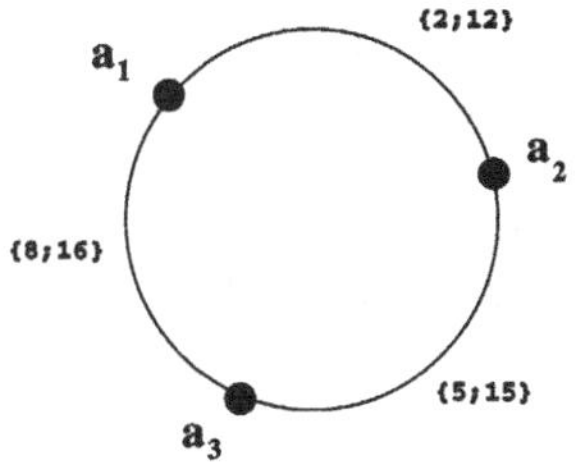

**Fig. 3.** Vicinity graph for Example 1

Intuitively an indirect communication from agent $a_i$ to agent $a_j$ is a path from vertex $a_i$ to vertex $a_j$. Thereby from this multi-valued graph, a single-valued graph with respect to the current date is unfolded and the lowest weighted path between both vertices is computed. This single-valued graph is built as it is explored. In order to do that, we propose a modified Dijkstra's algorithm where: (1) the current time $\tau_i$ is stored in vertex $a_i$ (initial time plus the weight of the current path); (2) the weight of each edge $(a_i, a_j)$ is computed online as follows: $\min v_{ij} - \tau_i \pmod{P}$.

**Example 2.** *Let us resume Example 1 and apply the algorithm in order to compute at time 1 the next indirect communication from $a_1$ to $a_3$.*

1. *Consider the edges from the vertex $a_1$, $(a_1, a_2)$ and $(a_1, a_3)$. The weights of edges $(a_1, a_2)$ and $(a_1, a_3)$ are respectively $(\min(2 - 1 \pmod{20}), 12 - 1 \pmod{20}))$, that is to say 1, and $(\min(8 - 1 \pmod{20}), 16 - 1 \pmod{20}))$, that is to say 7. The current times for vertex $a_2$ and $a_3$ are respectively 2 and 8;*
2. *As a path from $a_1$ to $a_3$ has been computed thanks to the edge $(a_1, a_3)$, a first solution has been found: a direct communication at $(8, 8)$.*
3. *Let us continue the exploration from vertex $a_2$ and consider edge $(a_2, a_3)$. Its weight is computed as $(\min(5 - 2 \pmod{20}), 15 - 2 \pmod{20})))$, that is to say 3 and the current time stored in vertex $a_3$ is 5. A new path from $a_1$ to $a_3$ has been computed through the edges $(a_1, a_2)$ and $(a_2, a_3)$. A better solution has been found: an indirect communication at $(2, 5)$.*

Because Vicinity is common knowledge within the constellation, each agent can compute all communications itself.

## 3.3  An Epidemic Protocol

An epidemic protocol based on overhearing [13] has been proposed in [3]. The agents use every communication opportunity even to communicate information that does not concern themselves:

1. each agent $a_i$ considers its own knowledge changes;
2. $a_i$ communicates the changes to $a_j \in \mathrm{Vicinity}(a_i, \tau)$;
3. $a_j$ updates its own knowledge thanks to the timestamp $\tau_{K_{a_i}^\tau}$.

It has been proved that, in a set of $n$ agents where a single agent knows a piece of information, an epidemic protocol needs $\mathcal{O}(\log n)$ communication rounds to completely propagate this information [15]. During a communication round, each agent executes a communication step that has a polynomial complexity in the number of agents and tasks [3].

The agents reason on common knowledge about intentions. Because of the communication delays, this common knowledge concerns only a subset of agents. Formally,

**Definition 10 (Common knowledge).** *At time $\tau$, agent $a_i$ knows that agent $a_j$ knows intention $I_t^{a_i}$ captured by $K_{a_i}^\tau$ iff:*

- $a_j \in A_{K_{a_i}^\tau}$ **or**
- $a_i$ communicated with $a_j$ at $(\tau_i, \tau_j)$ such that $\tau_{K_{a_i}^\tau} \leq \tau_i$, $\tau_j \leq \tau$.

## 3.4  The Trust Model

As indirect communications take time and proposals can be revised meanwhile, some agents' common knowledge may become obsolete. Therefore trust erosion has to be modelled according to the system dynamics. Our application can be viewed as an ad-hoc network, however trust literature on ad-hoc networks [14,24,28] focus on the reliability of a node itself and the way to route reliable information. In our application, as agents are trustworthy, trust erosion does not come from the nodes themselves but from interactions between nodes. Consequently we propose a trust model based on communication in order to define a trusted common knowledge.

**Last Confirmation.** When two agents communicate at time $\tau$, the agent that receives a given proposal cannot be sure that this intention will be the same at time $\tau'$ $(\tau' > \tau)$. Indeed as the environment is dynamic, an agent may receive new tasks or new intentions and modify its plan, i.e. its own intentions, accordingly. The more time between the generation of a given proposal and the realization date, the less an agent can trust this proposal. However a further confirmation transmitted by the agent that has generated this proposal increases the associated trust again.

As the agents are honest and cooperative, an indirect communication (which is a testimony) is trustworthy itself. Thereby an agent $a_i$ considers that a given proposal generated by an agent $a_j$ has been confirmed if $a_j$ communicates (directly or not) with $a_i$ without modifying its proposal. The last confirmation date is defined as follows:

**Definition 11 (Last confirmation date).** *Let $a_i$ be an agent, $I_t^{a_j}$ a proposal of an agent $a_j$ about a task $t$ known by $a_i$. The* last confirmation date *of proposal $I_t^{a_j}$ for $a_i$ at time $\tau$ is:*

$$\tau^* = \max_{\substack{\tau K_{a_i}^\tau < \tau_j \\ \tau_i < \tau}} \{\tau_j : a_j \text{ communicates } I_t^{a_j} \text{ to } a_i \text{ at } (\tau_j, \tau_i)\} \text{ and } I_t^{a_j} \text{ is unchanged}$$

**Example 3.** *Let us resume Example 1. Let us suppose that, at time 15, $a_3$ computes the trust associated with a proposal of agent $a_1$ generated at time 7. $a_1$ communicated directly with $a_3$ at time 8 then it communicated indirectly with $a_3$ at time $(12, 15)$ without modifying its proposal. Thereby the last confirmation date is 12 and $a_3$ knows that $a_1$ kept its proposal between times 7 and 12.*

**Trust.** Intuitively, the trust associated with a proposal depends on the time between its last confirmation date and its realization date. As the agents do not have a model of the environment, they cannot predict the arrival of new tasks. However as time goes by, an agent meets other agents and each meeting is an opportunity to receive new tasks and revise its intentions. Consequently an agent's trust about a given proposal is defined from the number of meetings between the last confirmation date and the realization date. This number is based on Vicinity therefore each agent can compute its own trust in the others' proposals.

**Definition 12 (Meetings).** *Let $a_i$ be an agent, $I_t^{a_j}$ a proposal known by $a_i$ and $\tau$ the current date. Let $\tau^*$ be the last confirmation date of $I_t^{a_j}$ for $a_i$ at time $\tau$. The number of agents $M_{\tau^*}^{a_i}(I_t^{a_j})$ agent $a_j$ will meet between $\tau^*$ and $rea(I_t^{a_j})$ is:*

$$M_{\tau^*}^{a_i}(I_t^{a_j}) = |\bigcup_{\tau^* < \tau' < rea(I_t^{a_j})} Vicinity(a_j, \tau')|$$

Finally, an agent trusts or does not trust a given proposal:

**Definition 13 (Trust).** *Let $a_i$ be an agent, $I_t^{a_j}$ a proposal known by $a_i$ and $\tau$ the current date. Agent $a_i$ trusts agent $a_j$ about $I_t^{a_j}$ iff $M_{\tau^*}^{a_i}(I_t^{a_j}) = 0$.*

**Example 4.** *Let $a_i$ be an agent that knows proposal $I_t^{a_j}$ at time $\tau$. Let us suppose that $M_{\tau^*}^{a_i}(I_t^{a_j}) = 5$. Agent $a_i$ does not trust $a_j$ about this proposal. Let us suppose that $a_j$ keeps its proposal for long enough to confirm it twice. At each confirmation, $a_i$ can compute $M_{\tau^*}^{a_i}(I_t^{a_j})$ again, e.g. 3 and 1, and can trust $a_j$ more.*

We can notice that the trust criterion of Definition 13 is hard: an agent is not trusted if it meets at least another agent before realizing its proposal ($M_{\tau^*}^{a_i}(I_t^{a_k}) = 0$). This pessimistic assumption can be relaxed (e.g. $M_{\tau^*}^{a_i}(I_t^{a_k}) \leq 1$).

# 4   Coalitions

## 4.1   State-of-the-Art

A coalition is an agent organization with a short life cycle. It is formed in order to realize a given goal and is destroyed when the goal is achieved. Through a coalition each agent tries to maximize its own outcome. In the literature, the methods dedicated to coalition formation are based on the exploration of the lattice of the possible coalition structures [18,25]. As the agents often have uncertain and (or) incomplete information on the other agents' costs and preferences, they need to use heuristics [12] or trust [19] to evaluate a coalition value and find the optimal structure.

Generally speaking, these methods have two limits.

On the one hand they are often centralized, assuming that all tasks are known by all agents, and they are performed off-line [6,9,16,21]; or they use an auctioneer (or other kinds of hierarchy) [1,22] that centralizes the information and organizes the negotiations.

As far as communications are concerned, methods based on the system organization structure consider constrained communications: agents can communicate through a hierarchy [1,22] or in a static vicinity [11,23]. These constraints are associated with a communication cost [27]. However in a real dynamic environment agents are not always able to exchange information and may have to decide alone. Moreover some tasks cannot wait until the complete coalition structure is computed and must be realized quickly. Consequently these methods are very sensitive to the system dynamics.

Be that as it may the coalition formation mechanisms are worthwhile for three reasons: (1) agents gather in order to realize a collective task; (2) the short life cycle of coalitions suits to dynamic environments; (3) agents search for efficient solutions under uncertain and (or) incomplete information. Moreover in our application a compound task requires that some agents should realize the subsets of tasks jointly (see Definition 4). However these joint realizations cannot be planned by the agents' individual planners as an agent does not plan for the others. In order to dynamically organize the agents, we will consider a decentralized coalition formation mechanism taking into account the features of the problem, i.e. cooperative agents and constrained communications. The mechanism is as follows:

1. Agents build maximal-size coalitions with respect to their own knowledge;
2. These coalitions are refined as the agents meet to remove useless agents.

## 4.2   Definitions

Coalitions are defined as follows:

**Definition 14 (Coalition).** *A coalition $C$ is a triplet $\langle A, O, \mathfrak{P} \rangle$:*

- *$A \subseteq \mathcal{A}$ is a subset of agents that are the members of the coalition;*
- *$O$ is the set of tasks that are the goals of the coalition;*
- *$\mathfrak{P}$ is the set of tasks that are the power of the coalition.*

*A coalition C may be:*

- complete *iff* $O \subseteq \mathfrak{P}$;
- minimal *iff C is complete and A is minimal for inclusion* $(\subseteq)$.

The next section will show how coalitions, which are built and managed *locally* by each agent, allow agents to collaborate.

## 5    Collaboration *via* Coalitions

Coalitions are built and managed locally by each agent given the knowledge it has about the other agents through communication. Indeed each agent uses the coalition notion to reason and adapt its own intentions to the others' intentions. Therefore coalitions are formed implicitly through intentions but are not explicitly built by the multi-agent system. The **collaboration steps** are such that each agent:

1. computes the current coalition structure according to its point of view;
2. checks whether it should join a coalition to increase its power;
3. checks whether it should withdraw from a coalition to minimize it;
4. modifies its intentions accordingly.

### 5.1    Computation of the Coalition Structure

Each agent $a_i$ generates the current coalition structure as follows:

I  $a_i$ organizes the set of tasks $\mathcal{T}_{a_i}^{\tau}$ as a partition $\{\mathcal{T}_1 \dots \mathcal{T}_h\}$ according to the compound tasks;

   **Example 5.** *Let $\mathcal{T}_{a_i}^{\tau}$ be $\{t_1, t_2, t_3, t_4, t_5\}$. Let us suppose that tasks $t_1$ and $t_2$ form a compound task as well as $t_4$ and $t_5$. Then $\mathcal{T}_{a_i}^{\tau}$ is organized as $\{\{t_1, t_2\}, \{t_3\}, \{t_4, t_5\}\}$.*

II  each $\mathcal{T}_i$ is the goal $O_i$ of a single potential coalition; as subsets $\mathcal{T}_i$ are disjoint[1], the number of potential coalitions generated by agent $a_i$ is given by the number of compound tasks $a_i$ knows;

III  from agent $a_i$'s point of view, the potential coalition members for subset $\mathcal{T}_i$ are defined as: $A_i = \{a_k \in \mathcal{A} : \exists t \in \mathcal{T}_i \,/\, \exists I_t^{a_k} \in \mathcal{K}_{a_i}^{\tau} \text{ such that } I_t^{a_k} \in \{\Box, \Diamond\}\}$

   **Example 6.** *Let us resume Example 5. Let us consider $t_3$ and suppose that $I_{t_3}^{a_i} = \Diamond$ and $I_{t_3}^{a_k} = \Box$. $a_i$ can build coalition $C = \langle\{a_i, a_k\}, \{t_3\}, \{t_3\}\rangle$. This coalition is complete but not minimal because $\{a_i, a_k\}$ is not minimal for inclusion. Notice that $a_i$ plans $t_3$ even if it knows that $a_k$ did the same. Indeed the others' intentions are not taken into account in the planning step: they will be taken into account in the collaboration steps (2, 3, 4).*

IV  then the power of each potential coalition is defined as: $\mathfrak{P}_i = \{t \in O_i | \exists a_k \in A_i : I_t^{a_k} \in \{\Box, \Diamond\}\}$

---

[1] The compound tasks are assumed disjoint but notice that they can overlap without modifying the collaboration process.

Notice that this framework defines the current coalition structure from agent $a_i$'s point of view. A potential coalition may be minimal (thus complete), complete and not minimal or incomplete.

## 5.2    An Incentive to Join Coalitions

An incomplete coalition means that at least one goal task is not within the coalition power. But the more tasks within the coalition power, the more goal tasks become important because a coalition must realize all its goal tasks. If the coalition remains incomplete, all its members waste their resources.

When agent $a_i$ computes the current coalition structure according to its knowledge, it can detect incomplete coalitions. As $a_i$ is cooperative it should be incited to modify its intentions and complete these coalitions when planning. In order to do that, the priorities of the goal tasks within the incomplete coalitions are increased. In the following we will note $prio(t)'$ the priority of task $t$ $a_i$ uses for its next planning step. Notice that $prio(t)'$ is a local priority only used by $a_i$ (the initial priority $prio(t)$ of task $t$ remains the same).

**Protocol 1 (Join a coalition).** *For each incomplete coalition $C = \langle A, O, \mathfrak{P} \rangle$ formed by agent $a_i$, $a_i$ computes:* $\forall\, t \in O,\ prio(t)' \leftarrow \frac{prio(t)}{1+|\mathfrak{P}|}.$

$a_i$ is incited to join a coalition if and only if the goal of the coalition is to realize a compound task that is partially planned.

As far as singletons $\{t_j\}$ are concerned, two cases may be considered. (1) If $t_j$ is not planned by $a_i$, it is because it does not satisfy the optimization criteria (Section 2.3). Therefore $a_i$ does not build any coalition concerning $t_j$ and the priority of $t_j$ remains the same. (2) If $t_j$ is planned, the coalition concerning $t_j$ is complete and its priority remains the same.

**Example 7.** *Let us resume Example 5. Let us consider $\{t_1, t_2\}$ and suppose that $I^{a_i}_{t_1} = \Diamond\neg$, $I^{a_i}_{t_2} = \Diamond\neg$, $I^{a_k}_{t_1} = \Diamond\neg$ and $I^{a_k}_{t_2} = \Box$. $a_i$ can build coalition $C = \langle \{a_k\}, \{t_1, t_2\}, \{t_2\} \rangle$. This coalition is incomplete. So $a_i$ applies Protocol 1. As $a_k$ is already a member of the coalition, the priorities of $t_1$ and $t_2$ are halved for $a_i$. Therefore at the next planning step, $a_i$ is more likely to plan $t_1$ or $t_2$ instead of other tasks.*

This mechanism is *stable*, i.e. two successive incentive steps are consistent. For instance, an agent is not incited to give up a given task in order to realize another one, then *ceteris paribus* is not incited to give up the latter to realize the former.

## 5.3    Minimizing Coalitions: Conflicts

A complete and non-minimal coalition has the power to realize its goals with useless agents, i.e. agents that have redundant intentions. Within a coalition an agent has to consider the agents that have planned the same tasks as it has, then to make a decision about modifying or not its own intentions. There is a conflict between two agents within a coalition if they have planned the same task(s). Formally:

**Definition 15 (Conflict).** *Let $a_i$, $a_j$ be two agents and $C$ a coalition $\langle A, O, \mathfrak{P} \rangle$ such that $\{a_i, a_j\} \subseteq A$. There is a* conflict *between $a_i$ and $a_j$ iff $\exists\, t \in \mathfrak{P}$ such that $I_t^{a_i} \in \{\Box, \Diamond\}$ and $I_t^{a_j} \in \{\Box, \Diamond\}$. It is a* **soft conflict** *iff either $a_i$ communicates with $a_j$ at $(\tau_i, \tau_j)$ such that $\tau_{I_t^{a_i}} < \tau_i$ and $\tau_j < \min(rea(I_t^{a_i}), rea(I_t^{a_j}))$ or $a_j$ knows agent $a_i$'s intention about $t$. Else it is a* **hard conflict**.

**Example 8.** *Let us resume Example 6. The coalition is not minimal: there is a conflict about task $t_3$ between agents $a_i$ and $a_k$. So $a_i$ has to make a decision in order to withdraw ($\Box\neg$), to keep its intention ($\Diamond$) or to commit ($\Box$).*

In the remainder, given an agent $a_i$ and a task $t$, we will denote $A^*$ the set of agents with which it is in conflict about task $t$, $A^+ \subseteq A^*$ the set of agents in soft conflict and $A^- \subseteq A^*$ the set of agents in hard conflict.

**Proposition 1 (Symmetry).** *Let $a_i$ be an agent and $A^*$ the set of agents with which it is in conflict about task $t$. $\forall\, a_j \in A^+$, the conflict is* symmetric*. $\forall\, a_j \in A^-$, the conflict is* asymmetric.

**Proof 1.** *Let $a_i$ be an agent and $A^*$ the set of agents with which it is in conflict about task $t$.*

1. *(soft conflict) $\forall\, a_j \in A^+$, $a_i$ knows $I_t^{a_j}$. Conversely either $a_j$ knows $I_t^{a_i}$, or $\exists\, \tau_i, \tau_j \in \mathbb{T}$ such that $a_i$ communicated with $a_j$ at $(\tau_i, \tau_j)$ with $\tau_{I_t^{a_i}} < \tau_i$ and $\tau_j < \min (rea(I_t^{a_i}), rea(I_t^{a_j}))$. In both cases the conflict is symmetric.*
2. *(hard conflict) $\forall\, a_j \in A^-$, $a_j$ does not know $I_t^{a_i}$ and will not know it before date $\min (rea(I_t^{a_i}), rea(I_t^{a_j}))$. So $a_j$ is not and will not be aware of the conflict.*

Both soft and hard conflicts are dealt with through protocols based on the agents' expertise for realizing the task.

## 5.4 Minimizing Coalitions: The Expertise Criterion

As we are seeking to optimize the system swiftness, it is better that the agents realize the tasks as soon as possible and use the fewest resources possible (meaning keeping the pictures in the satellite memory for the shortest time possible, i.e. downloading them as soon as possible). Let us aggregate both criteria in a single expertise criterion. Formally:

**Definition 16 (Expertise).** *Let $a_i$ be an agent and $A^* \subseteq A$ be a set of agents in conflict with $a_i$ about a task $t$. Let us note $rea^* = \min\limits_{a_k \in A^* \cup \{a_i\}} rea(I_t^{a_k})$ the earliest realization date for task $t$. The expert agent $a^*$ for $t$ is defined using the following distance:*

$$a^* = \arg\min_{a_k \in A^* \cup \{a_i\}} ||(rea(I_t^{a_k}) - rea^*, tel(I_t^{a_k}) - rea^*)||$$

Figure 4 is a representation of the expertise criterion for a task $t$ in the plan $(rea(I_t^{a_i}), tel(I_t^{a_i}))$, $a_i \in A^*$. The origin $rea^*$ is the earliest realization date for $t$ and intention $(rea^*, rea^*)$ is the ideal intention corresponding to an agent being able to realize $t$ at time $rea^*$ and download the corresponding picture immediately. $tel^*$ is the latest download date for $t$, if $t$ is realized at time $rea^*$. Obviously $tel(I_t^{a_i}) > rea(I_t^{a_i})$ therefore only the hatched part is meaningful.

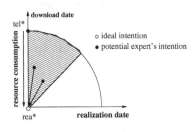

**Fig. 4.** Expertise criterion

Any point within the hatched part is a potential intention $I_t^{a_i}$ about $t$. The resource consumption, i.e. how long the picture corresponding to $t$ will remain in the memory of the satellite, is defined as a duration. The distance between a potential intention and $rea^*$ represents the projection of the time criteria on the plan $(rea(I_t^{a_i}), tel(I_t^{a_i}))$. The expert agent for $t$ is the one that minimizes this distance.

### 5.5    Minimizing Coalitions: Coordination Strategies

In order to solve a conflict, three strategies are defined. (1) With the *secure strategy* $a_i$ maintains its proposal ($\Diamond$) if it does not trust the other agents about their intentions; as these agents are likely to change their intentions, this strategy maintains redundancies to make sure that the task will be realized. (2) With the *collaboration strategy* $a_i$ commits ($\Box$) if it is the expert agent, therefore deciding on a part of the current coalition structure. (3) With the *opportunistic strategy* $a_i$ strongly withdraws ($\Box\neg$) if the expert agent is trusted, therefore minimizing the size of the coalition and saving resources for further tasks.

From the three strategies two conflict solving protocols are defined:

**Protocol 2 (Hard conflict).** *Let $A^*$ be the set of the coalition members with which agent $a_i$ is in conflict about task $t$ such that $A^- \neq \emptyset$. $a_i$ is aware of the conflict and applies:*

1. *if $\min_{a_k \in A^-} M_{\tau^*}^{a_i}(I_t^{a_k}) > 0$ then $I_t^{a_i} \leftarrow \Diamond$*
2. *else $I_t^{a_i} \leftarrow \Box\neg$*

In case of a hard conflict the agent that is aware of the conflict applies (1) the secure strategy if it does not trust the agents within the conflict; else (2) if it trusts them the aware agent applies the opportunistic strategy.

**Protocol 3 (Soft conflict).** *Let $A^*$ be the set of the coalition members with which agent $a_i$ is in conflict about task $t$ such that $A^+ \neq \emptyset$. Let $rea^*$ be $\min_{a_k \in A^+} rea(I_t^{a_k})$.*

*Then agent $a_i$ applies:*

1. *if* $a_i = \arg\min\limits_{a_k \in A_+} \|(rea(I_t^{a_k}) - rea^*, tel(I_t^{a_k}) - rea^*)\|$ *then* $I_t^{a_i} \leftarrow \square$
2. *else let* $a^*$ *be the expert agent:*
   (a) *if* $M_{\tau*}^{a_i}(I_t^{a^*}) > 0$ *then* $I_t^{a_i} \leftarrow \Diamond$
   (b) *else* $I_t^{a_i} \leftarrow \square\neg$

For soft conflicts each agent computes the expert agent. (1) If it is the expert agent, it commits. (2.a) If not, it applies the secure strategy if it does not trust the expert (2.b) If it trusts the expert it applies the opportunistic strategy.

## 6   Experiments

The different mechanisms and protocols we have described have been implemented. Two metrics are considered to compare the results: the number of realized tasks and the number of realized tasks without redundancies. The first metric corresponds to the number of distinct singletons or compound tasks realized. Experiments have been conducted on three kinds of constellations:

– *isolated*: no communication;
– *informed*: agents communicate only about tasks and coordinate *a posteriori* by withdrawing already realized tasks from their plans;
– *coordinated*: agents communicate about tasks and intentions and coordinate *a priori* thanks to coalition formation.

### 6.1   First Scenario: Dynamic Simulations

These experiments are based on a dynamic scenario with 3 agents. Every 6th hour, ground stations send 40 new compound tasks (including at least 2 singleton tasks) to the agents. The number of realized tasks is shown on Figure 5 and the number of realized tasks without redundancies is shown on Figure 6.

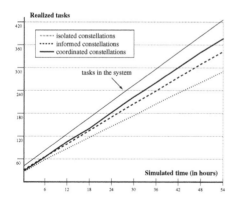

**Fig. 5.** Tasks

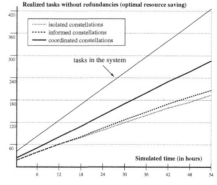

**Fig. 6.** Tasks with no redundancies

Figures 5 and 6 show that informed and coordinated constellations outperform isolated ones. However we can notice that the benefits increase as time goes by. Indeed incremental coordination allows coordinated constellations to realize more tasks than the other kinds of constellations. And as time goes by the difference between informed and coordinated constellations increases: incremental coordination allows coordinated constellations to efficiently save and reallocate resources. It is important to notice that, in this experiment, agents are not limited in terms of resources (contrary to real satellites). Consequently the number of realized tasks without redundancies is the main performance measure.

## 6.2    Second Scenario: Scalability

In order to experiment the scalability of our system we have considered a scenario with 500 atomic tasks and Walker's satellite constellations [29] of different sizes (1, 4, 6, 8, 9, 12 and 16 satellites dispatched regularly on a finite number of orbital plans). The agents must realize all the tasks and the constellation swiftness and efficiency are then compared.

**Definition 17 (Performance).** *Let $\mathbb{T}_n$ the time for $n$ agents to realize all the tasks, $K$ the set of realized observations (i.e. the realized tasks and their redundancies) and $R$ the set of realized tasks. The constellation swiftness is given by $\frac{\mathbb{T}_1}{\mathbb{T}_n}$ and the constellation efficiency is given by $\frac{|R|}{|K|}$.*

We can notice on Figure 7 that the swiftness of isolated constellations is approximated by a logarithmic function whereas the swiftness of informed and coordinated constellations are not regular. This is due to the heterogeneous structure of the satellite interactions. Indeed isolated satellites have no interactions but, for informed and coordinated constellations, interactions exist only between satellites belonging to different orbital plans (see Figure 9).

Consequently 2 satellites situated on 4 plans can have more interactions than 4 satellites situated on 3 plans: the topology of the interactions matters. More

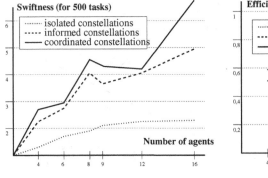

**Fig. 7.** Swiftness

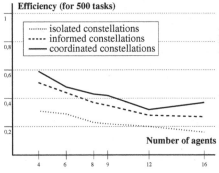

**Fig. 8.** Efficiency

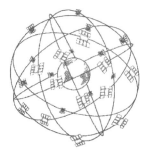

**Fig. 9.** Different orbital plans

precisely the number of satellites is not the major parameter but their orbits: few satellites may communicate often whereas many satellites may only communicate from time to time. This phenomenon can be observed between the 8- and 12-satellite constellations.

As far as efficiency is concerned, we can notice on Figure 8 that coordinated constellations are in average 5% more efficient than informed constellations. They are also 19% more efficient than isolated constellations. The constellations are scalable according to Turner [26]: a system is scalable if the resource consumption can be bounded by a polynomial function. In our application, the number of realized observations divided by the number of realized tasks $\frac{|K|}{|R|}$ represents the resource overconsumption: it is the inverse of the efficiency.

## 7   Conclusion

We have proposed a collaboration method for physical agents that communicate from time to time in a dynamic environment. This method has been applied to a constellation of satellites. A communication protocol has been proposed in order to build a trusted common knowledge (in terms of tasks and intentions) as the agents meet. As new tasks appear in the system the agents may revise their intentions. Thereby trust is defined through the communications between agents. Each time an agent communicates, it may receive new information that modifies its intentions. On the other hand the more an agent communicates, the more it can confirm its intentions and the more trust may increase.

The collaboration process is an online incremental decentralized coalition formation that proceeds through a *planning - communication - collaboration* loop within each agent. Each agent builds an initial plan. From its knowledge, each agent builds the potential coalitions that can realize the tasks it knows. Afterwards these coalitions are refined thanks both to an *incentive* mechanism and an *optimization* mechanism. As the agents communicate, they refine the coalition structure dynamically and adapt it to new knowledge.

The experimental results show that the coalition formation mechanism allows the resource consumption to be minimized. Then the saved resources are reallocated in a incremental way and the number of realized tasks is increased.

Furthermore our approach is scalable despite the non linear topology of the satellite constellations. It allows to reduce the number of involved satellites (that are highly costly) for the same swiftness. Further works will deal with the possible failures of the agents and their consequences on the collaboration process.

## Acknowledgements

We would like to thank Marie-Claire Charmeau (CNES - The French Space Agency) and Serge Rainjonneau (Thales Alenia Space) for their relevant remarks on this work.

## References

1. Abdallah, S., Lesser, V.: Organization-based cooperative coalition formation. In: Proceedings of the 4th IAT, pp. 162–168 (2004)
2. Brambilla, A., Lavagna, M., Da Costa, A., Finzi, A.E.: Distributed Planning and Scheduling for Space System Flotillas. In: Proceedings of the 8th ISAIRAS (2005)
3. Bonnet, G., Tessier, C.: Collaboration among a satellite swarm. In: Proceedings of the 6th AAMAS, pp. 275–282 (2007)
4. Damiani, S., Verfaillie, G., Charmeau, M.-C.: An Earth watching satellite constellation: how to manage a team of watching agents with limited communications. In: Proceedings of the 4th AAMAS, pp. 455–462 (2005)
5. Dignum, F.: Autonomous agents with norms. Artificial Intelligence and Law 7, 69–79 (1999)
6. Dung Dang, V., Dash, R.K., Rogers, A., Jennings, N.R.: Overlapping coalition formation for efficient data fusion in multi-sensor networks. In: Proceedings of the 21st AAAI, pp. 635–640 (2006)
7. De Florio, S., Zehetbauer, T., Neff, T.: SCOOP: Satellite Constellations Optimal Operations Planner. In: Proceedings of the Workshop on Constraint Satisfaction Techniques for Planning and Scheduling Problems at the 16th ICAPS (2006)
8. Bornschlegl, E., Guettier, C., Le Lann, G., Poncet, J.-C.: Constraint-based layered planning and distributed control for an autonomous spacecraft formation flying. In: Proceedings of the 1st ESA Workshop on Space Autonomy (2001)
9. Goradia, H.J., Vidal, J.M.: An equal excess negotiation algorithm for coalition formation. In: Proceedings of the 6th AAMAS, pp. 1052–1054 (2007)
10. Horling, B., Lesser, V.: A survey of multi-agent organizational paradigms. Knowledge Engineering Review 19, 281–316 (2004)
11. Krainin, M., An, B., Lesser, V.: An Application of Automated Negotiation to Distributed Task Allocation. In: Proceedings of the 7th IAT, pp. 138–145 (2007)
12. Kraus, S., Shehory, O., Taase, G.: Coalition formation with uncertain heterogeneous information. In: Proceedings of the 2nd AAMAS, pp. 1–8 (2003)
13. Legras, F., Tessier, C.: LOTTO: group formation by overhearing in large teams. In: Proceedings of 2nd AAMAS (2003)
14. Pirzada, A.A., McDonald, C.: Trust Establishment in Pure Ad-Hoc Networks. Wireless Personal Communications 37(1-2), 139–168 (2006)
15. Pittel, B.: On spreading a rumor. Journal of Applied Mathematics 47, 213–223 (1987)

16. Rahwan, T., Ramchurn, S.D., Dung Dang, V., Jennings, N.R.: Near-optimal any-time coalition structure generation. In: Proceedings of the 21st IJCAI, pp. 2365–2371 (2007)
17. Sandholm, T.: Contract types for satisficing task allocation. In: Proceedings of the AAAI Spring Symposium on Satisficing Models, pp. 23–25 (1998)
18. Sandholm, T., Larson, K., Andersson, M., Shehory, O., Tohmé, F.: Coalition structure generation with worst case guarantees. Artificial Intelligence 111(1-2), 209–238 (1999)
19. Sen, S., Goswami, I., Airiau, S.: Expertise and trust-based formation of effective coalitions: an evaluation of the ART testbed. In: Proceedings of the ALAMAS workshop at the 5th AAMAS (2006)
20. Schetter, T., Campbell, M., Surka, D.M.: Multiple agent-based autonomy for satellite constellation. Artificial Intelligence 145, 147–180 (2003)
21. Shehory, O., Kraus, S.: Feasible formation of coalitions among autonomous agents in non-super-additive environments. Computational Intelligence 15(3), 218–251 (1999)
22. Sims, M., Goldman, C., Lesser, V.: Self-organization through bottom-up coalition formation. In: Proceedings of the 2nd AAMAS (2003)
23. Soh, L.-K., Tsatsoulis, C.: Utility-based multiagent coalition formation with incomplete information and time constraints. In: Proceedings of the IEEE International Conference on SMC (2003)
24. Theodorakopoulos, G., Baras, J.S.: On Trust Models and Trust Evaluation Metrics for Ad-Hoc Networks. IEEE Journal on Selected Areas in Communications 24(2), 318–328 (2006)
25. Thanh-Tung, D., Frankovic, B., Sheahan, C., Bundiska, I.: Using agent coalitions for improving plan quality. Intelligent Systems at the Service of Mankind 2, 351–364 (2005)
26. Turner, P.J., Jennings, N.R.: Improving the scalability of multi-agent systems. In: Wagner, T.A., Rana, O.F. (eds.) AA-WS 2000. LNCS, vol. 1887. Springer, Heidelberg (2001)
27. Tohmé, F., Sandholm, T.: Coalition formation processes with belief revision among bounded-rational self-interested agents. Journal of Logic and Computation 9(6), 793–815 (1999)
28. Virendra, M., Jadliwala, M., Chandrasekaran, M., Upadhyaya, S.: Quantifying Trust in Mobile Ad-Hoc Networks. In: Proceedings of the IEEE KIMAS, pp. 65–71 (2004)
29. Walker, J.G.: Satellite constellations. Journal of British Interplanetary Society 37, 559–571 (1984)

# Modelling Actor Evolution
# in Agent-Based Simulations

Aristama Roesli[1], Dominik Schmitz[2], Gerhard Lakemeyer[1],
and Matthias Jarke[1,2]

[1] RWTH Aachen University, Informatik 5, Ahornstr. 55, 52056 Aachen, Germany
aristamaroesli@gmail.com, {lakemeyer,jarke}@cs.rwth-aachen.de
[2] Fraunhofer FIT, Schloss Birlinghoven, 53754 Sankt Augustin, Germany
dominik.schmitz@fit.fraunhofer.de

**Abstract.** Agent-based simulations have proven to be suitable to investigate many kinds of problems, especially in the field of social science.
But to provide useful insights, the behaviour of the involved, simulated
actors needs to reflect relevant features of the real world. In this paper, we address one particular aspect in this regard, namely the correct
reflection of an actor's evolution during a simulation. Very often some
knowledge exists about how an actor can evolve, for example, the typical
development stages of entrepreneurs when investigating entrepreneurship
networks. We propose to model this knowledge explicitly using evolution
links between roles enriched with suitable conditions and extend $i^*$, an
agent- and goal-oriented modelling framework, thereby. We provide a
mapping to the simulation environment ConGolog that serves as an intermediary approach between not providing change of behaviour at all
and very open approaches to behaviour adaptation such as learning.

**Keywords:** Evolution, $i^*$, agent-based simulation, inter-organizational
networks.

## 1  Introduction

Entrepreneurship networks [14, 20] are intended to support (potential) entrepreneurs in building up a business. Via the network, an entrepreneur gets in contact
with business angels, venture capitalists, the entrepreneurship center, etc. Each
of them has different interests and abilities to offer. But when investigating
entrepreneurship networks, it has to be taken into account that an entrepreneur
evolves over time. Several different stages of an entrepreneur with partly varying
capabilities but of course clearly varying dependencies have been identified in the
literature (see [20]). For example, while in the beginning (so called "seed stage")
the entrepreneur needs contact to a business angel with domain knowledge, in
later stages a venture capitalist that only spends sufficiently much money suffices.

Investigators of social problems via agent-based simulations very often have
knowledge on how the capabilities and dependencies of an involved actor may
change over time, i. e. how the actors within (social) simulations can evolve. This

G. Vouros et al. (Eds.): OAMAS 2008, LNAI 5368, pp. 126–144, 2009.

knowledge needs to be reflected within simulations in order to reflect real world behaviour. Current approaches to actor evolution within simulations either do not allow for it (static assignment of roles/capabilities to agents, see, for example, [16]) or follow a very generic approach in which the agents (or a central control) decide on the distribution of capabilities across the community [7] or use learning mechanisms to acquire new skills [18, 26]. While the first approach is hurting the real world requirement, the second makes it difficult to specify a particular course of evolution. The underlying concepts of distribution or learning need to be investigated in detail in order to ensure that the evolution is taken into account in the right way at the right time.

We suggest to model actor evolution explicitly by extending $i^*$ [28], a well-known agent- and goal-oriented formalism used in requirements engineering and business process reengineering. By introducing evolution links and allowing to annotate acquire and lose conditions as well as instantiation functions we enable the mapping of actor evolution to simulations. This makes it easy to consider known evolutionary paths of actors within simulations and have them respected in a way that reflects the evolution in the real world. The mapping is exemplified for the *ConGolog* [4] simulation environment that we use to model trust-based inter-organizational networks [9, 10].

The paper is organized as follows. In Sect. 2, the foundations of our proposal are introduced, i.e. the $i^*$ framework, ConGolog, and our modelling and simulation environment SNet. Section 3 presents our extensions to capture actor evolution. In Sect. 4, we describe the changes to the simulation environment and the mapping of the concrete modelling details. In Sect. 5, we consider preliminary ideas to incorporate more deliberation in the evolution process. In Sect. 6, we then discuss related work before we finally conclude (Sect. 7).

## 2    Foundations

### 2.1    The $i^*$ Framework

The $i^*$ framework [28] is a graphical language to support business process reengineering as well as requirements engineering. It includes the *strategic dependency (SD)* diagram for describing the network of relationships among actors and the *strategic rationale (SR)* diagram for capturing the internal structure of an actor in terms of tasks, goals, resources, and softgoals. In previous work [9, 10], we have extended $i^*$ to contain additional operational details such as preconditions and effects of tasks and goals, sequence links to enable the specification of an ordering on the internal structure, and a quantitative interpretation of the softgoal concept. These extensions alleviate the mapping to a simulation environment (ConGolog, see Sect. 2.2) and thereby allow for using $i^*$ to model actors in agent-based simulations.

$i^*$ knows three kinds of actors. A *role* is a generic description of a capability and covers non-agent specific details. A *position* combines several roles that are usually played together. An *agent* is a concrete actor instance that plays one or several roles or occupies one or several positions. At the strategic dependency

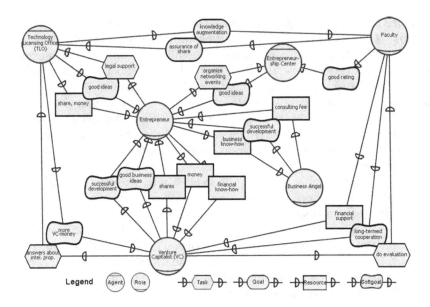

**Fig. 1.** Partial Strategic Dependency Diagram for an Entrepreneurship Network

level, four kinds of dependencies between instances of the above mentioned actor types are distinguished. A *task* dependency explicitly states the activities to be performed by the dependee. In a *goal* dependency, the depender only specifies a condition that has to be brought about but leaves the details of the how to the dependee. Similarly, a *resource* also has to be provided somehow. And finally, a *softgoal* is somehow similar to a goal, but there are no clear-cut criteria when this soft goal is fulfilled. The dependee can only contribute towards the softgoal. For example, in the entrepreneurship network (see Fig. 1), we have a *resource* dependency concerning "money" from the "entrepreneur" to a "venture capitalist". In turn, there is a *softgoal* dependency regarding "successful development" from the "venture capitalist" to the "entrepreneur".

At the strategic rationale level, the types of dependencies become modelling elements used to describe the internal rationales of an actor. This way, processes (tasks) and goals, as well as resources and softgoals can be captured. New kinds of links allow to *decompose* tasks into sub-tasks, goals etc., to describe alternatives to achieve goals (and resources) via *means-ends* links, and to model *contributions* towards softgoals of individual task or goal elements.

Figure 2 shows an excerpt of the details of the "venture capitalist" partic-ipating in the entrepreneurship network. The venture capitalist's task "choose promising entrepreneur" is decomposed into three subtasks, which are partially ordered using *sequence links*. The task "suggest business idea" is delegated to the "entrepreneur". "ask evaluation" is modelled as a goal to allow for the spec-ification of alternatives from which the modelled agent can choose at runtime. In this example, the "venture capitalist" can choose to either "do the evalua-tion" on its own or delegate this to a "faculty member". The softgoal "report quality" captures the quality of the assessment that might vary across different individuals that play the role as well as across the two basic alternatives.

## 2.2   ConGolog

ConGolog [4] is based on the situation calculus, a popular language for representing and reasoning about the preconditions and effects of actions [19]. It is a variant of first-order logic, enriched with special function and predicate symbols to describe and reason about dynamic domains. Relations and functions whose values vary from situation to situation are called *fluents*, and are denoted by predicate symbols taking a situation term as their last argument. *Successor state axioms* capture how fluents are affected by actions. Furthermore, there is also a special predicate $Poss(a, s)$ used to state that action $a$ is executable in situation $s$. ConGolog is a language for specifying complex actions (high-level plans). For this purpose, normal imperative programming constructs like sequence, procedure, *if-then-else*, but also nondeterministic (e. g. *ndet*) and concurrency (e. g. *conc*) constructs are provided. Table 1 gives an overview of the available constructs. ConGolog comes equipped with an interpreter (written in Prolog) which maps these plans into sequences of atomic actions assuming a description of the initial state of the world, the above mentioned action precondition axioms (*poss*), and successor state axioms. For details see [4].

While not providing a native construct for the representation of agents, the mapping we proposed in [9, 10] allows to represent the behaviour of agents by automatically creating a set of possibly nondeterministic procedures. Figure 3 shows a partial result of the mapping of the simple SR diagram from Fig. 2. A complex task (e. g. "choose promising entrepreneur") is transformed into a procedure whereby the body is derived from the sub-elements. The sequential relations between the sub-elements are reflected via the use of sequence and *conc*. There are primitive actions preceding and following the body, so that the preconditions to and effects of this element can be reflected in the program. For delegated subtasks (see "suggest business idea" in Fig. 2) a special procedure is generated that lists all the alternative delegation partners (not shown here).

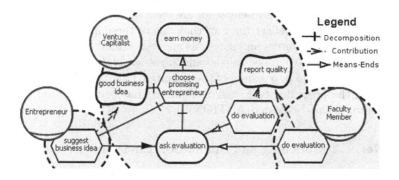

**Fig. 2.** Partial Strategic Rationale Diagram for a Venture Capitalist

**Table 1.** Overview of Available ConGolog Constructs

| | |
|---|---|
| $\alpha$ | primitive action |
| $\phi$? | test action |
| $[\sigma_1, \sigma_2, \ldots, \sigma_n]$ | sequence |
| if $\phi$ then $\sigma_1$ else $\sigma_2$ | conditional |
| while $\phi$ do $\sigma$ | loop |
| $ndet(\sigma_1, \sigma_2)$ | nondeterministic choice of actions |
| $pi(x, \sigma)$ | nondeterministic choice of arguments |
| $star(\sigma)$ | nondeterministic iteration |
| $conc(\sigma_1, \sigma_2)$ | concurrent execution |
| $pconc(\sigma_1, \sigma_2)$ | prioritized concurrent execution |
| $interrupt(x, \phi, \sigma)$ | triggers $\sigma$ whenever $\phi$ holds where $x$ is a nondeterministically chosen argument (see $pi(x, \sigma)$) |
| $proc(\beta(\overrightarrow{x}), \sigma)$ | procedure definition |

$proc(choose\_promising\_entrepreneur(Agent, venture\_capitalist),$
　　$[\, pre\_choose\_promising\_entrepreneur(Agent, venture\_capitalist),$
　　　$delegate(suggest\_business\_idea(entrepreneur)),$
　　　$ask\_evaluation(Agent, venture\_capitalist),$
　　　$decide(Agent, venture\_capitalist),$
　　　$post\_choose\_promising\_entrepreneur(Agent, venture\_capitalist)])$
$proc(ask\_evaluation(Agent, venture\_capitalist),$
　　$[\, pre\_ask\_evaluation(Agent, venture\_capitalist),$
　　　$ndet(delegate(do\_evaluation(faculty\_member)),$
　　　　$do\_evaluation(Agent, venture\_capitalist)),$
　　　$post\_ask\_evaluation(Agent, venture\_capitalist)])$
$poss(decide(Agent, venture\_capitalist), s) \equiv$
　　$executed(post\_ask\_evaluation(Agent, venture\_capitalist), s)$

**Fig. 3.** Partial Mapping of the $i^*$ Modelling to ConGolog Code

(Sub-)Tasks which are not decomposed any further are turned into primitive actions such as "decide". The transformation of goal elements and their fulfilling tasks is rather similar to the one of complex tasks (see procedure for "ask evaluation" in Fig. 3), but the sub-elements are combined by the nondeterministic choice operator *ndet* to reflect the fact that one of these alternatives has to be chosen at runtime. Resources and softgoals are represented by fluents. Precondition/effect elements are mapped to *poss* and *successor state* axioms, respectively. Figure 3 also shows the *poss* axiom of the primitive task "decide". This action is executable if the preceding task "ask evaluation" has been executed (captured by the generic fluent "executed(ACTION)").

## 2.3    SNet – A Modelling and Simulation Environment

The current SNet environment [10] supports the modelling of generic relationships within inter-organizational networks. The user can establish a concrete scenario by specifying agents that play the generic roles. This instantiation includes information such as the agent-specific durations of primitive tasks and (numerical) contributions to softgoals. Other details concern initial trust values the agents exhibit to each other, experiences, gain, and general characteristics concerning risk attitude and trust orientation. All the information is compiled as described above to ConGolog code that can be executed within the simulation environment. While the above mapping describes how these model-specific parts are generated from $i^*$ models, our modelling and simulation environment SNet provides some additional basic agent facilities. For example, we have equipped the agents with a decision-theoretic deliberative planning component and communication facilities to cope with delegations and nondeterminism on their own. This enables simulations where an agent exhibits situation dependent behaviour that reflects rational real world actor's decisions. The simulation user can influence the overall situation by the initial parameter settings as described above. An individual run is additionally determined by the triggering of proactivities of agents. This information can also be incorporated in a batch mode to run simulations without user intervention.

## 3   Modelling Actor Evolution

While the $i^*$ framework covers the dependencies as well as the internal rationales of actors, it (and several derivates, see for example [3, 8]) has a purely static view with regard to the distribution of roles across agents. It allows to model/instantiate varying scenarios and thus to evaluate their advantages and disadvantages, but transitions between them cannot be considered. Means to describe how an actor evolves, i. e. how roles are related in regard to the ordering they are played by agents or to capture that an actor evolves across several roles are missing. Building on the first author's master thesis [22], we describe an extension of the $i^*$ framework to overcome this deficiency.

### 3.1   Evolution Links

An *evolution link* between two role elements captures that if an agent is playing the role at the source of the link there is the possibility that at a later point in time she might also play the destination role. This depends on whether the concrete agent playing the source role is able to fulfil the annotated condition at some point in time within the simulations. Since positions only combine several roles, they are omitted for the sake of simplicity. Furthermore, evolution links from or to agent elements are not allowed since an agent represents a concrete individual instance that has an identity. In contrast to its capabilities (roles and positions) the latter is exactly not intended to change over time.

To alleviate modelling for a frequently occuring special case, we distinguish two kinds of evolution links. The first kind, denoted by $\Rightarrow$, enforces to lose the source role when acquiring the destination role and is thereby suited to capture mutually exclusive stages of actor evolution, while the other, denoted by $\rightarrow$,

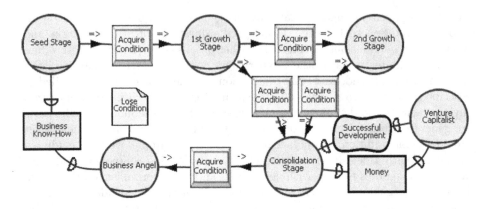

**Fig. 4.** Stages of an Entrepreneur (including some dependency relationships)

allows an agent to extend its capabilities by acquiring the destination role in addition to the roles currently played (including the source role).

Figure 4 shows a more detailed model of an entrepreneur. As research has shown [20], several stages can be distinguished that correlate with financing rounds. Their different characteristics (tasks, goals, dependencies, etc.) are captured with usual $i^*$ means such as roles and dependencies (only few added here to keep the example simple). For example, financial support is typically provided by business angels and venture capitalists. In general the former were successful entrepreneurs in the past with domain-specific knowledge who prevailingly invest in the so called "seed stage" of an enterprise. In this stage, market studies have to take place and business plans have to be elaborated. Venture capitalists are often banks with the financial power to support successful entrepreneurs in their money consuming later phases, for example, to bring the enterprise to the stock exchange. Evolution links allow to explicitly indicate the path of evolution an entrepreneur is to follow along "seed stage", "1st growth stage", "2nd growth stage", until finally reaching the "consolidation stage" or even becoming a "business angel" on its own. Figure 4 also shows that there can be several ways of acquiring a single role. For example, the entrepreneur may arrive at the "consolidation stage" either – normally – from the "2nd growth stage" or – if she is very successful – already from the "1st growth stage".

## 3.2   Acquire and Lose Conditions

In addition to the pure capturing of evolution relationships between roles, we enable to annotate also the circumstances of the modelled transitions by specifying an *acquire condition* as well as a *lose condition*. The former is associated with the evolution link while the latter is attributed directly to a role element (see "business angel" in Fig. 4). These conditions necessarily refer to information that is dynamically collected at simulation run-time for each agent. Thus,

**Table 2.** Properties of the Modelling Elements to Be Referenced in Conditions

| Model Element | Collected Information | Reference |
|---|---|---|
| agent | risk attitude, trust weight, confidence, and gain | $risk\_attitude,\ trust\_weight,$ $confidence,\ gain$ |
| role | currently played by, played in the past by, how often played, played for how long (last time, over all instantiations) | $ROLE.played\_currently,$ $ROLE.was\_played,$ $ROLE.how\_often,$ $ROLE.duration.\{last|all\}$ |
| task, goal | number of offerings, number of cooperations, number of successfully completed cooperations, duration (average, min, max), trust and distrust relationships (each for the last time the corresponding role was instantiated or overall) | $ROLE.\{TASK|GOAL\}$ $.\{no\_offers|no\_coops$ $|no\_successful|trust$ $|distrust\}.\{last|all\},$ $ROLE.\{TASK|GOAL\}$ $.duration.\{last|all\}$ $.\{avg|min|max\}$ |
| softgoal | average, minimum, maximum value (again either for the last time the corresponding role was instantiated or overall) | $ROLE.SOFTGOAL$ $.\{last|all\}.\{avg|min|max\}$ |

we have to explicitly state the pieces of information that are available within our simulations. Therefore, Table 2 lists the properties of the $i^*$ model elements that can be referenced.

From the above references, suitable relational expressions can be created. We omit the implicit agent parameter for each of them (that is added during the transformation to ConGolog, see Sect. 4). The "." notation known from object oriented programming is used to uniquely refer to a specific information item of a modelling element within a role. For example, to refer to the average of the softgoal "report quality" achieved during the last instantiation of "venture capitalist" the term $venture\_capitalist.report\_quality.last.avg$ can be used. Such terms can then be combined to relational expressions using common operators $=$, $<$, and $>$ as well as arithmetic computations. This allows, for example, to specify thresholds for historical achievements. Several of such relational expressions can finally be combined using $\wedge$, $\vee$, and $\neg$ and quantifiers as required. Thus, the expressive power of full first-order logic is available.

In our entrepreneurship example (see Fig. 4), the stages of an entrepreneur are mainly sequentially connected and mutually exclusive. Performing well in a particular stage and being in that stage sufficiently long, triggers the evolution to the next stage. For example, we could assume two softgoals "development" and "progress" to characterize the success during the "seed stage" (part of the SR model for "seed stage" that is not shown here). Due to the fact that in our simulations we emphasize that roles are executed several times, we usually refer to the average of the achieved softgoal contributions (mapped to a utility value between 0 and 1). Furthermore, let us assume a usual duration of one year (12 months) of this stage. Consequently, the resulting condition for acquiring the role "1st growth stage" could look as follows:

$$(seed\_stage.development.last.avg > 0.6 \lor seed\_stage.progress.last.avg > 0.8)$$
$$\land seed\_stage.duration.last > 12$$

Besides the model-specific information listed above, some general simulation information can be referenced in the conditions as well. To allow the definition of evolution simply according to some time scale, i.e. the evolution shall take place at a particular point in time, the *current simulation time* (*time*) can be referenced. Furthermore, as a unique feature of our particular simulation environment, SNet, *trust* (and *distrust*) relationships between agents associated with dependencies can be referenced as well. This example emphasizes also nicely that the identity of an evolving agent remains the same. In the entrepreneurship network example, a "business angel" does not need to build up a new trust relationship only because its entrepreneur partner has evolved from "seed stage" to the "1st growth stage". Instead, we expect the trust relationship to build on the trust relationship for the "seed stage".

The lose condition can refer to the same features and characteristics of involved roles as the acquire condition. Since in our example, the different stages of being an entrepreneur are mutually exclusive [20], this is already captured by using the $\Rightarrow$ type of evolution link.

### 3.3   Role Instantiation at Simulation Time

Since a role description is generic (see [11]), its $i^*$ model needs to be enriched with *instantiation functions* to compute the instantiation of a newly acquired role at simulation time. For roles that are played from the beginning, the user specifies contributions towards softgoals and durations of primitive tasks, i.e. tasks that are not decomposed any further (see Sect. 2.3). Similarly to conditions, we expect the instantiation functions to refer to features, characteristics, and experiences of direct predecessor as well as potentially earlier former roles. For example, the details of carrying out a business idea in the "1st growth stage", obviously depend on the characteristics of "suggest business idea" in the "seed stage" as well as the agent's performance in that stage. Thus, a simple instantiation function for the duration of "work" in the "1st growth stage" could average the execution times of the "suggest business idea" and multiply it with a factor, i.e. *duration(1st_growth_stage, work)* = *seed_stage.suggest_business_idea.duration.all.avg* ·1.5. This way the modeller can individually decide for her particular problem how complicated these functions have to be.

### 3.4   Tool Support for Modelling

We have extended the modelling tool, OME3, [17] to enable the specification of actor evolution. To reduce the complexity of the model, we allow for a separate definition of the evolution by importing roles from an SR diagram. The part models are easily integrated via ConceptBase [13], a deductive, object-oriented database system. This ensures scalability and additionally enables support for entering instantiation functions, acquire and lose conditions. For details see [22].

# 4  Mapping Evolution to ConGolog

Concerning the mapping to ConGolog, after enabling the dynamic assignment of roles to agents we will show how evolution links, acquire and lose conditions as well as instantiation functions are mapped.

## 4.1  Enabling Dynamic Assignment of Roles

To enable actor evolution in ConGolog, the assignment of roles to agents is now captured by a relational fluent, $ROLE.played\_currently(Agent, s)$.[1] Accordingly, two primitive actions, $acquire(Agent, Role)$ and $lose(Agent, Role)$, have been introduced that affect the above fluent by either adding or removing a role. The corresponding successor state axiom looks as follows:

$$ROLE.played\_currently(Agent, do(a, s)) \equiv (a = acquire(Agent, ROLE)$$
$$\lor (a \neq lose(Agent, ROLE) \land ROLE.played\_currently(Agent, s))$$

To check whether an agent is allowed to execute procedures that result from the mapping of task and goal elements of a particular role, all *poss* axioms of the corresponding generated primitive actions include a test of the corresponding relational fluent, $ROLE.played\_currently(Agent, s)$. For example,

$$poss(pre\_do\_evaluation(Agent, faculty\_member), s) \equiv$$
$$faculty\_member.played\_currently(Agent, s) \land [...]$$

This extension establishes at the same time the check for the suitability of a proactivity initiated by a user, since the same test is used within the *poss* axiom of the corresponding exogenous action. Thus, the initiation of "earn money" for an agent can only succeed if the specified agent is currently playing the role "venture capitalist".

Similarly, the current alternatives for delegation partners can also be derived from this check as shown below. The body of the delegation procedure formerly based on a set of nested *ndet* constructs that explicitly enumerates all (static) alternatives. This is now replaced by the following code making use of the non-deterministic choice operator *pi*:

$$proc(do\_evaluation\_delegated(faculty\_member),$$
$$pi(DelegateeAgent, do\_evaluation(DelegateeAgent, faculty\_member)))$$

We can omit an explicit test $faculty\_member.played\_currently(DelegateeAgent)$? since exactly this test is included in the *poss* axiom of the first primitive action that has to be executed within this delegated task as shown above. Thus, as

---

[1] Similarly to [21], we expect each agent to play at least one role, a default role if necessary, to avoid agents that cannot reenter a simulation any more.

soon as an agent is playing the role, the corresponding procedure constitutes an executable delegation alternative that will be investigated by the delegator's planning component on its search for an optimal plan.

## 4.2  Mapping Evolution Links, Acquire and Lose Conditions

Evolution links are simply mapped to extensions of the specified acquire and lose conditions. Consequently, for the evolution link from "seed stage" to "1st growth stage" in Fig. 4 the resulting condition looks as follows:

$$seed\_stage.played\_currently \land (seed\_stage.development.last.avg > 0.6$$
$$\lor seed\_stage.progress.last.avg > 0.8) \land seed\_stage.duration.last > 12$$

The conditions themselves are extended by the suppressed *Agent* parameter. Furthermore, the simplified reference notation (including the "." notation) must be mapped to the corresponding fluents storing the relevant information. We omit these details here, since the mapping is tedious but straightforward. Without loss of generality, we can assume that each requested piece of historical information is available in the current situation since we only have to introduce a fluent to record it.

Since the resulting conditions are both necessary and sufficient the most straightforward mapping uses the trigger construct *interrupt*. Three cases have to be distinguished.

| normal evolution link ($\rightarrow$) from role $s$ to $d$ | $interrupt(Agent, (s.played\_currently(Agent) \land [acquire condition]), acquire(Agent, d))$ |
|---|---|
| lose condition for role $r$ | $interrupt(Agent, (r.played\_currently(Agent) \land [lose condition]), lose(Agent, r))$ |
| change evolution link ($\Rightarrow$) combination | $interrupt(Agent, (s.played\_currently(Agent) \land [acquire condition]), [lose(Agent, s), acquire(Agent, d)]))$ |

All the individual triggers for all evolution links and lose conditions as described above finally only need to be combined into a single procedure using the concurrency construct *conc*. This procedure is then called from the simulation main loop. Afterwards, whenever a condition becomes true for some arbitrary agent, the corresponding acquire and/or lose action will be executed and immediately, the trigger is again ready for its next activation. In fact on the implementational level, a more complex mapping has been chosen that takes more advantage of the specified evolution links in order to reduce the set of parallel tests that need to be evaluated and thereby speeds up the simulations. Since this is only an optimisation and conceptually irrelevant, details have been omitted. For details see [22].

It might be important to mention that we have taken thereby a very simple, decentralized approach to potential interferences of various evolution conditions. We assume this to be valid since the modelling of the evolution links (and their automatic consideration within the conditions) enables a local investigation of interferences and thus should make it easy for the modeller to specify non-conflicting conditions. More complex strategies that, for example, could give precedence to the losing of roles over the acquiring of roles are conceivable and can be considered if future applications require them. Additional formal analysis means can be provided by relying on the integration with Formal Tropos as proposed in [24]. Note, that we do not consider the organizational perspective here. As with many other approaches [1, 6, 15], this is captured on a level of its own (see [25]).

### 4.3   Instantiating a Role at Runtime

The dynamic assignment of roles enforces that also the *role instantiation information*, i. e. softgoal contributions and durations, are now stored in suitable fluents. Otherwise these values could not be affected by the instantiation functions at simulation time. Furthermore, this enables that an agent that plays a role a second time can have varying instantiation characteristics realistically reflecting the experiences she has gained inbetween. Similarly to the renewed definition of *poss* axioms (see Sect. 4.1), the *successor state* axioms for softgoal contributions now reference the fluents instead of the concrete pre-specified value, i. e. for the contribution of "do evaluation" to the "report quality" within the role "faculty member" (see Fig. 2) the following *successor state* axiom is generated.

$$report\_quality(do(a,s)) = rq \equiv$$
$$(a = post\_do\_evaluation(Agent, faculty\_member) \wedge rq = report\_quality(s)$$
$$+ report\_quality\_contribution(Agent, faculty\_member, do\_evaluation, s))$$
$$\vee (a \neq post\_do\_evaluation(Agent, faculty\_member) \wedge rq = report\_quality(s))$$

Consequently, another effect of the *acquire(Agent, role)* action is the computation of the required fluent value from the specified instantiation function. Thus, *successor state* axioms of the following form need to be generated:

$$report\_quality\_contribution(Agent, faculty\_member, do\_evaluation, do(a,s))$$
$$= c \equiv (a = acquire(Agent, faculty\_member) \wedge c = [instantiation\ function])$$
$$\vee (a \neq acquire(Agent, faculty\_member) \wedge$$
$$c = report\_quality\_contribution(Agent, faculty\_member, do\_evaluation, s))$$

The same solution idea can be applied to the specification of durations of primitive tasks. Additionally, concerning the delegations the newly acquired role is involved in, the initial values of the corresponding trust and distrust relationships need to be established as well. While it is, of course, possible to ask the user similarly to define a suitable instantiation function, some simple generic means are conceivable as well. For example, for each pair of agents that play the roles involved in a new delegation, it can be checked whether there has already been a trust relationship regarding this or another delegation between the two. From this observation, some sensible initial value can be computed (e. g. simply averaging over the achieved trust values). If no trust relationship has existed before, a suitable default starting value possibly depending on the risk attitude of the agent can be chosen resulting in a rather low, medium, or rather high initial trust value.

### 4.4    Losing Active Roles

Since actor evolution and thus especially losing a role can occur at any time within the simulation as soon as the corresponding condition is fulfilled, it might be possible that the agent has already planned and scheduled some future tasks regarding this role or is even currently executing a task of this role. Since losing the role immediately disables any further activities (via the failing *poss* axiom of primitive actions), it has to be decided for the specific domain, whether this behaviour is appropriate. Other strategies can be implemented by specifying appropriate preconditions and/or effects of/to the *lose* action or even expanding the body of the triggers defined above. For example, we prefer a strategy that allows an agent to complete a currently executed task, but to simply cancel tasks scheduled for the future, potentially informing the delegator as well as the chosen sub-contractors via messages. This could easily be achieved by including a check in the precondition axiom that blocks the *lose* action as long as the current task (fluent *current_job*) concerns the role to be lost and by mapping the effect on the schedule, i. e. the elimination of planned tasks, as well as the sending of messages to effects of the *lose* action.

## 5    Deliberation about Alternative Evolutionary Paths

A disadvantage of the approach to evolution as it has been presented so far is its restriction to a purely reactive consideration of evolutionary steps. Our example in Fig. 4 has already shown a situation where one particular role can be reached via two possible evolutionary paths. An entrepreneur can arrive at its "consolidation stage" either via the normal evolutionary path along "1st growth stage" and "2nd growth stage" or she can leave out the "2nd growth stage". Which of these two alternatives is taken by a particular agent in a given situation depends in our current reactive implementation only on the specified acquire conditions. But the fulfilment of these conditions refers implicitly to the agent's performance throughout its lifetime, since the conditions are composed of the characteristics listed in Table 2. This in turn means that any or at least some choices an agent has made so far in her lifetime influences the possibilities for evolution now and in the future. It is only that the agents (or their deliberative components, respectively) are currently not aware of this.

To remedy the agent's unawareness about the influence of local decisions within a role on evolutionary aspects and to consequently give her more explicit deliberative control about her own strategic evolution, it seems natural to extend the already existing decision-theoretic deliberative component (see Sect. 2.3). While the set of actions (or alternatives, respectively) is not affected, the utility computation must be extended to cover next to trust, gain, and task-specific issues also strategic evolutionary considerations.

First of all, the modeller must be able to specify criteria according to which an agent can decide which evolutionary path to prefer. By introducing suitable, domain dependent softgoals and according contributions the existing models can be enriched by the advantages and disadvantages of the various roles. Figure 5

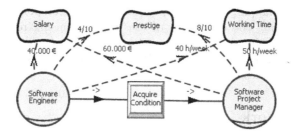

**Fig. 5.** Softgoals and Contribution of Roles in a Software Career Setting

shows an example within a software career setting. Interesting features of a potentially new job concern among others "salary", "working time", and "prestige". While "salary" and "prestige" for a "software project manager" are much higher than for a "software engineer", the same unfortunately holds also true for "working time". Utility functions (associated with the softgoals, see [10]) map these contributions suitably to a utility value between $[0,1]$. Eventually, this generic modelling needs to be augmented with instantiated weights for a particular agent in order to capture individual strategic preferences among the modelled criteria. This realization is thus conceptually identical to the existing approach (see [10]).

The evolutionary chances of an agent in a concrete situation are then given by the roles that are currently played (and can be lost), abbreviated as the set $CR$, as well as the roles that could be played in the future, $FR$, i.e. that are connected to the current roles via evolution links.[2] The following formula shows a first attempt of a utility computation concerning evolution:

$$u_{evolve} = w_{salary} u_{salary} \big( \underbrace{\sum_{r \in CR} c_r}_{\text{current}} + \underbrace{\sum_{q \in FR} p_q c_q}_{\text{acquire new}} + \underbrace{\sum_{p \in CR} p_r(-c_r)}_{\text{lose current}} \big) + w_{prestige} \cdots$$

$w_x \in [0,1]$ denotes a weight, $u_x$ a specific utility function, and $c_x$ a contribution. In addition, for prospective role changes (acquire or lose) the partial fulfilment $p_x \in [0,1]$ of the corresponding acquire and lose conditions need to be taken into account. Referring to the acquire condition example from Sect. 3.2, that the average utility value for the softgoal "progress" exceeds some specified threshold might take several iterations. Thus, even if a choice in the current iteration will not make the condition true, it can make a (more or less positive) contribution. Approaches to map partial fulfilment to some numerical value exist already in the field of heuristic planning, see, for example, [23]. Their adaptation to our setting seems possible and has to be investigated in future work.

No more adaptations at the ConGolog side, for example, concerning the mapping of evolution steps to the *conc* and *interrupt* structure (see Sect. 4.2) are

---

[2] The definition of a horizon for the consideration of transitive evolution links is conceivable. For the sake of simplicity, we restrict ourselves here to a horizon of 1.

needed. Via the mapping to utilities, the deliberative component takes care of heading for fulfilling the conditions of the most promising role changes. The evolution itself can then be triggered as described in Sect. 4.2 as soon as a condition is fulfilled. Altogether it should be rather straightforward to provide an implementation of these ideas.

## 6   Related Work

When considering dynamic adaptation of agent behaviour, most researchers do not prespecify the path of evolution but instead allow for and prefer arbitrary development and an emerging distribution of capabilities across an agent community. AALADIN [7] provides an organizational meta-model centered around the concept of a group consisting of several agents that play roles within this group. By entering a new group or leaving a group an agent acquires or loses the related roles. The assignment is determined by a centralized group manager. RoleEP [27] does not define an agent as an entity of the system at all, until an object needs a role to implement a task and assumes that role in its environment. But while agents are allowed to travel to different hosts to search for a function, they do not consider delegation. Instead all required functions are integrated until finally the agent is able to execute the task. Magique [18] initially equips agents only with the skill to learn a new skill and a communication skill. This enables the agent to search for a particular skill (communication) and learn it. But here, the evolution is limited by a pre-determined skill hierarchy. General learning techniques are applied by Stone [26] in the field of robotic soccer to, for example, adapt (restrict) the behaviour of a team to a specific opponent.

Odell et al. [21] use UML models to capture a generalization hierarchy and describe the associations between roles in the context of agent programming. This is intended to increase understandability and reuse in complex, dynamic settings. For example, the model describes that the assignment of a role to an agent must be qualified in a group context to avoid conflicts of interest for the agent. Accordingly such constraints limit the possible paths of evolution to prevent an agent from gaining inappropriate benefits for roles she plays. Others have also considered preconditions for acquiring (or losing, respectively) roles. Within the context of workflow modelling, Yu and Schmid [29] provide a detailed conceptualization of the requirements an agent needs to fulfil to acquire a new role by introducing qualification attributes referring to organizational policies and the agent's capabilities. But these qualifications are captured only informally via text and furthermore they do not consider conditions that make an agent lose a role. BRAIN [2] also knows starting requirements that represent the skill/experience level an agent must have to start using a specific role. But again, conditions for losing a role are not considered. An agent simply releases a role when it is no longer needed. There is no intention to model actor evolution, instead the goal is to provide means to ease maintenance (replacement) of role implementations.

In [12, 15] a framework for formal modelling and analysis of organizations and organizational change is described. Similar to us, a graphical representation as well as a sound formal foundation is given (in Temporal Trace Language (TTL) that is comparable to the situation calculus). While they emphasize the applicability of their approach to both real world as well as artificial organizations, they focus an organizational view and complex, mechanistic types of organizations in particular. Organizational change is intended to be centralized. In contrast to this, we take an agent perspective since in modern flat forms of organizations, such as networks, network rules cannot be imposed on the network members but must be adopted and adapted by them as constraints that might or might not be adhered to [9]. The latter aspect is partly addressed in $Moise^{Inst}$ [1] by conceptually enabling deliberation about the organizational model itself. Furthermore building on ideas from [6], it is possible to define a-priori transitions between contexts (encompassing groups and roles that are interacting) to define varying behaviour constraints for different situations. In SNet, such (minor) role behaviour adaptation is captured via task decompositions, goal alternatives, as well as a dedicated speech act perspective (see [9] for details) that is evaluated by the agent according to its current situation. We consider this to be different from actor evolution, for example, an entrepreneur becoming a business angel. Eventually, the structural dimension of $Moise^{Inst}$ allows the definition of role compatibilities and cardinalities constraints that cover parts of our acquire/lose conditions. Finally, DeLoach et al. [5] describe an organization model for adaptive computational systems (OMACS) that enables multi-agent systems to adapt their own organization at runtime. Thus, they do not aim at reflecting real world behaviour of (human) actors and again have a shared organizational perspective. Nonetheless, some technical means to adapt resemble ours. The assignment of roles to agents can be constrained by (application-specific) assignment policies, by behavioural policies taking the relationships of agents into account (not yet fully defined) as well as reorganization policies. But the latter is not binding and might be ignored if it does not help achieving the overall goal.

## 7    Conclusions

In this paper we have presented an extension of $i*$ that allows to capture actor evolution by specifying evolution links between roles. These evolution links can be enriched with acquire conditions. Similarly lose conditions can be associated with role elements. If the modelling of a role is finally extended by functions that are able to compute the instantiation information for a role, the altogether modelled information allows to consider actor evolution in agent-based simulations. This has been exemplified with an example from the entrepreneurship domain in our modelling and simulation environment SNet. A more advanced approach incorporating deliberation about evolution has been preliminarily investigated in the context of a software career setting.

There are two main contributions by this work. Firstly, means to specify the evolution of actors were up to now missing in $i*$. But it is well known in requirements engineering that a new system to be developed potentially also alters the behaviour of its users. Our extension allows to provide an integrated consideration of the various evolving settings and takes the transitions between them into account. This positions $i^*$ as a suitable formalism to support continuous requirements engineering. Secondly, when mapping the actor evolution information to simulations, we achieve an intermediary approach to the dynamic adaptation of behaviour. Instead of not considering evolution at all or providing very flexible means to adapt behaviour like free distribution of capabilities across a set of agents or learning, we allow the modeller to encode her domain-specific knowledge about evolution as part of the model. This alleviates the correct reflection of real world evolution within social simulations. More flexibility can be gained by allowing an agent to deliberate about alternative paths of evolution. Softgoals can serve as the relevant criteria here as well. Nonetheless, the key point remains that the modeller is able to pre-specify the core evolutionary direction.

One could argue that extensions of $i^*$ like the Formal Tropos framework [8] or our own extension by precondition/effect elements and sequence links [10] enable already evolutionary aspects. For example, a role "entrepreneur" could encompass all the different stages and connect the top level tasks via appropriate precondition/effect elements (capturing the acquire condition). While this approach is technically feasible, it blurs conceptual differences. For example, the different stages cannot be iterated independently and all dependencies exist over the whole lifetime of the actor although this does not correspond to the reality.

Within this work we focussed on the mapping of actor evolution in $i^*$ to simulations. For future work we need to investigate further how agent-oriented requirements engineering can profit from this extension. Furthermore, several case studies have to be carried out in order to validate the modelling means. We have already applied our approach to two other application domains, an e-democracy setting and a software process modelling setting. They suggest additional strategies regarding actor evolution (e. g. as soon as a voter is punished for a crime she loses the voter role disregarding the completion of current activities) as well as further extensions of the information that can be referenced (e. g. including an evaluation by a third agent or the explicit decision of a project manager to allow one of its software developers to evolve). Eventually, the ideas on deliberation about alternative evolutionary paths need to be implemented.

**Acknowledgment.** This work was partially supported by the Deutsche Forschungsgemeinschaft (Priority Program 1077 and Graduate School 643).

# References

1. Boissier, O., Gâteau, B.: Normative multi-agent organizations: Modeling, support and control, draft version. In: Normative Multi-agent Systems, Dagstuhl, Germany, March 18-23. Dagstuhl Seminar Proceedings, vol. 07122 (2007)
2. Cabri, G., Ferrari, L., Leonardi, L.: Rethinking agent roles: extending the role definition in the BRAIN framework. In: Conf. on Systems, Man & Cybernetics (SMC), The Hague, Netherlands, October 10-13, pp. 5455–5460. IEEE, Los Alamitos (2004)

3. Castro, J., Kolp, M., Mylopoulos, J.: Towards requirements-driven information systems engineering: The Tropos project. Information Systems 27(6), 365–389 (2002)
4. de Giacomo, G., Lespérance, Y., Levesque, H.J.: ConGolog, a concurrent programming language based on the situation calculus: language and implementation. Artificial Intelligence 121(1-2), 109–169 (2000)
5. DeLoach, S.A., Oyenan, W.H., Matson, E.T.: A capabilities-based model for adaptive organizations. Autonomous Agents and Multi-Agent Systems 16(1), 13–56 (2008)
6. Esteva, M., de la Cruz, D., Sierra, C.: ISLANDER: an electronic institutions editor. In: Conf. on Autonomous Agents and Multi-Agent Systems (AAMAS), Bologna, Italy, July 15-19, pp. 1045–1052 (2002)
7. Ferber, J., Gutknecht, O.: A meta-model for the analysis and design of organizations in multi-agent systems. In: Conf. on Multiagent Systems (ICMAS), Paris, France, July 3-7, pp. 128–135. IEEE, Los Alamitos (1998)
8. Fuxman, A., Liu, L., Pistore, M., Roveri, M., Mylopoulos, J.: Specifying and analyzing early requirements in Tropos. Req. Eng. Journal 9(2), 132–150 (2004)
9. Gans, G., Jarke, M., Kethers, S., Lakemeyer, G.: Continuous requirements management for organization networks: A (dis)trust-based approach. Requirements Engineering Journal 8(1), 4–22 (2003)
10. Gans, G., Jarke, M., Lakemeyer, G., Schmitz, D.: Deliberation in a metadata-based modeling and simulation environment for inter-organizational networks. Information Systems 30(7), 587–607 (2005)
11. Gans, G., Schmitz, D., Arzdorf, T., Jarke, M., Lakemeyer, G.: SNet reloaded: Roles, monitoring and agent evolution. In: Bresciani, P., Giorgini, P., Henderson-Sellers, B., Low, G., Winikoff, M. (eds.) AOIS 2004. LNCS, vol. 3508, pp. 68–84. Springer, Heidelberg (2005)
12. Hoogendoorn, M., Jonker, C.M., Schut, M.C., Treur, J.: Modeling centralized organization of organizational change. Comput. Math. Organ. Theory 13(2), 147–184 (2007)
13. Jarke, M., Eherer, S., Gallersdörfer, R., Jeusfeld, M.A., Staudt, M.: ConceptBase - a deductive object base for meta data management. Journal of Intelligent Information Systems 4(2), 167–192 (1995)
14. Jarke, M., Klamma, R., Marock, J.: Zu den Wirkungen des regionalen Kontexts auf Unternehmensgründungen, chapter Gründerausbildung und Gründernetze im Umfeld technischer Hochschulen: ein wirtschaftsinformatischer Versuch, pp. 115–154. EUL-Verlag (2003)
15. Jonker, C.M., Sharpanskykh, A., Treur, J., Yolum, P.: A framework for formal modeling and analysis of organizations. Appl. Intell. 27(1), 49–66 (2007)
16. Klügl, F.: Multiagentensimulation - Konzepte, Werkzeuge, Anwendung. Addison-Wesley, Reading (2001)
17. Liu, L., Yu, E.: Organization Modeling Environment (OME) [Accessed July 17, 2008], http://www.cs.toronto.edu/km/ome
18. Mathieu, P., Routier, J.-C., Secq, Y.: Dynamic skills learning: a support to agent evolution. In: Symposium on Adaptive Agents and Multi-Agent Systems (AISB), pp. 25–32 (2001)
19. McCarthy, J.: Situations, actions and causal laws. Technical report, Stanford, 1963. In: Minsky, M. (ed.) Reprinted 1968. Semantic Information Processing. MIT Press, Cambridge (1968)
20. Nathusius, K.: Grundlagen der Gründungsfinanzierung. Instrumente - Prozesse - Beispiele. Gabler, Wiesbaden (2001)

21. Odell, J.J., Van Dyke Parunak, H., Brueckner, S.A., Sauter, J.: Temporal aspects of dynamic role assignment. In: Giorgini, P., Müller, J.P., Odell, J.J. (eds.) AOSE 2003. LNCS, vol. 2935, pp. 201–213. Springer, Heidelberg (2004)

22. Roesli, A.: Agent evolution in a modeling and simulation environment for inter-organizational networks. Master's thesis, RWTH Aachen University (2006)

23. Schiffel, S., Thielscher, M.: Fluxplayer: A successful general game player. In: 22nd AAAI Conference on Artificial Intelligence, Vancouver, British Columbia, Canada, July 22-26, pp. 1191–1196 (2007)

24. Schmitz, D., Lakemeyer, G., Jarke, M.: Comparing three formal analysis approaches of the TROPOS family. In: Kolp, M., Henderson-Sellers, B., Mouratidis, H., Garcia, A., Ghose, A.K., Bresciani, P. (eds.) AOIS 2006. LNCS, vol. 4898, pp. 164–182. Springer, Heidelberg (2008)

25. Schmitz, D., Lakemeyer, G., Jarke, M., Karanfil, H.: How to model inter-organisational networks to enable dynamic analyses via simulations. In: Agent-Oriented Information Systems Workshop, Trondheim, pp. 697–711 (June 2007)

26. Stone, P.: Learning and multiagent reasoning for autonomous agents. In: IJCAI 2007, Hyderabad, India, January 6-12, pp. 12–30 (2007)

27. Ubayashi, N., Tamai, T.: RoleEP: Role based evolutionary programming for cooperative mobile agent applications. In: Symposium on Principles of Software Evolution (ISPSE), Kanazawa, Japan, November 1-2, pp. 243–251 (2000)

28. Yu, E.: Modelling Strategic Relationships for Process Reengineering. PhD thesis, University of Toronto (1995)

29. Yu, L., Schmid, B.F.: A conceptual framework for agent-oriented and role-based workflow modeling. In: Agent-Oriented Information Systems Workshop, Heidelberg, Germany, June 14-15 (1999)

# Author Index